CHRONICLES OF STRATHEARN

LECTOR HOUSE PUBLIC DOMAIN WORKS

CHRONICLES OF STRATHEARN

VARIOUS,
JOHN HUNTER

ISBN: 978-93-5614-067-7

Published: 1896

CHRONICLES OF STRATHEARN

**WITH ILLUSTRATIONS BY
W.B. MACDOUGALL**

**COVER DESIGNED BY
A. L. RANKIN**

1896

PREFACE

This book has been written in connection with a Bazaar held in Crieff in the month of August, 1896, for the better endowment of the Parishes of Ardoch, Crieff West, Glendevon, and Monzie. The Editorial Committee venture to hope that the contents will be of some interest to the dwellers in Strathearn, especially those within the bounds of the Presbytery of Auchterarder. The warm thanks of the promoters of the Bazaar are due to the ladies and gentlemen who composed the various Committees. To them, as representing many hearty sympathisers and willing workers, the "Chronicles of Strathearn" is respectfully dedicated.

In name of the Editorial Committee,

JOHN HUNTER, M.A., Crieff.
HUGH M. JAMIESON, Monzie.

CONTENTS

CONTENTS

LIST OF ILLUSTRATIONS

INTRODUCTION

THE OPENING UP OF STRATHEARN

BY REV. JOHN HUNTER, M.A., CRIEFF

Quite recently it was said to me by a man who had been holiday-making in Switzerland, that he greatly missed the Alps in every home landscape. The remark was made on the Knock of Crieff, one beautiful afternoon in the late autumn, when the sun was setting and the after-glow lay like a purple semi-transparent mist all along Glenartney from Ben Ledi to Comrie. I felt rich enough in the enjoyment of the surpassing loveliness of our own Strath to say "Laich in"—(I would not hurt any person's feelings for the world)—"Plague take your Alps, with their sky-scraping ridges and peaks and winding sheets of snow,—we don't want them here; they would simply spoil a scene like that before us." I don't know, and may never know, the meaning my companion read into my silence. Having shortly before made the frank confession that I had never seen the Alps, he may have intended to excite envious feelings within me, and imagined he had succeeded. But I can deny the fact with a good conscience, and until some benevolent person shall give me the opportunity of making a comparison between home and foreign landscapes, I shall continue to assert—happy in my ignorance, it may be, but still happy—that there is no fairer prospect upon earth than the Strath of Earn from the Knock of Crieff. "Where ignorance is bliss, 'tis folly to be wise."

Let me adventure to describe it. Right opposite to the south-west is Turleum—rising to the height of 1300 feet—the highest hill in Scotland wooded to the top, as our local boast was—shorn of its beauty somewhat in recent years, but, although bare, still picturesque enough with its comb of sturdy fir-trees, survivors from the destructive gale of November, 1893. To the right of it, and running due west, is the pass into the misty hill country by Comrie and St Fillans—the glen of Bonnie Kilmeny and Dunira. Midway between us and the mouth of the pass is a miniature Turleum—Tomachastel to wit, the site of the old Castle of the Earn, famous in the days when the Celtic Earls of Strathearn were a power in the land. Lovers of the old ways were these proud and wily Earls—fiercely impatient of the incoming Saxon customs which found favour at the Court of Malcolm Canmore and his sons—genuinely pious men, too, in some instances—(did not Earl Gilbert found or endow Inchaffray, so that masses might be said for his soul?)—of a keen courage as with Earl Malise, who at the Battle of the Standard dared his mail-clad fellows—the barons of King David—to show themselves a single foot in advance of his naked breast. Right worthy and most noble men they were in their noblest—they were not all so—cherishers of the national spirit in the dreary times that followed upon the death of Alexander III. at Kinghorn, like the one who gave a fair daughter of the house and land in tocher to the son of Sir Andrew Moray, patriot and friend of Wallace, in whom the Morays of Abercairny find their origin. Such were the men; and over there on Tomachastel was their home—a place famous then, and very noticeable still, with its gleaming memorial obelisk to "oor Davie" of Ferntower, the hardy soldier who overcame the fierce Tippoo Sahib at Seringapatam. Beyond lie the Aberuchill Hills, with the flat pyramidal face of Ben Voirlich filling up a gap, and sending its roots, on one side, down into "lone Glenartney's hazel shade," and, on the other, into Loch Earn—sixteen miles away. Further off, and only to be seen on rare days, when the sun's rays are dancing to be dry after rain, are sturdy, broad-shouldered Benmore, and slender, graceful Binnein, the twin guardians of the enchanted region beyond, where Beauty lies in the lap of Terror, and the Atlantic surf sings lullaby. There are the Monzievaird hills to the right, rising in Benchonzie to the height of 3048 feet, and to something under this figure in the Cairngorm or Blue Craig, upon which you see the stone-heap of Cainnechin—memorial, as it is said, of a battle fought within what are now the policies of Ochtertyre, and as the result of which Malcolm II. came to the throne of Scotia, having defeated and slain his rival Kenneth Duff or Don—Kenneth, the swarthy—"at a place where two valleys meet." Many battles have been fought out in the Strath, for it must always have been a rich prize; but this one has a special historical interest, inasmuch as it connects us with one of the great tragedies in our annals, in which the genius of Shakespeare found material for one of his masterly delineations of the strange workings of human passion. It is said that Fraoch, wife of Macbeth Maormor of Moray, had a good claim to the throne as the grand-daughter of this Kenneth Duff, and, prompted by ambition and revenge, instigated her husband to the murder of his Sovereign and guest—the gracious Duncan, grandson of Malcolm II., at Bothgowan, near Elgin. Loch Turret lies in the gorge that separates Benchonrie from the Blue Craig. It is likely enough that the descendants of the wild fowl that Robert Burns scared on the occasion of his visit to Ochtertyre still nest and pair in the solitude.

To the left of Turleum is a wider expanse, that carries the eye to the Moor of Orchill, which overlooks the plain of Ardoch—the Lindum of the Romans—traditional scene of the battle of Mons Grampus. Some miles away Stirling finds shelter under its rock,—not visible to us, however, where we stand, and only audible across the intervening twenty-two miles when birthday and other honours are paid to Royalty.

The Ochil range—memorial of fierce volcanic action when the lower old red sandstone was being deposited in the inland lake which stretched from east to west across the Lowlands of Scotland, and away southward without a break to the southern uplands, close to the border of England;—this Ochil range, which means high ground, as Glenogle means high glen, bounds our view to the south-east. It has no towering peaks, but Bencleuch and its neighbour, King Seat, command magnificent panoramic views to north and south from an elevation of 2000 feet. The gap before us is Gleneagles,—Glen-eccles—Kirk glen—one of the passes into the Lowlands of Fife and Kinross, by which, it may be, Agricola found his way into Strathearn after the conquest of Fife. In the very heart of the Ochils its name changes from Gleneagles to Glendevon. Here again we are upon classic ground—in the vale of the clear winding Devon, which more than any other stream recalls Yarrow with its hills green to the top and its pastoral melancholy. And let me note the fact that here, too, is the tiniest and daintiest parish church in Scotland—the outpost of the Presbytery of Auchterarder in this direction.

Between us and the gap, but much nearer the gap, is a bit of rising ground, running eastward almost parallel with the Ochils, with a downward slope from west to east, upon which may be seen, if the atmosphere is clear, smoking chimneys and a faint ruddy hue, as if with the memory of tiles now discarded for the prosaic if more permanent roofing slate. That is the "lang toon" of Auchterarder, climbing up the slope somewhat after the fashion of the Canongate and High Street of Edinburgh, not so conspicuously or hurriedly, however, as if aware that there was no Castle Rock from which to view the fertile Strath below. An ancient place, truly, pedigreed, but by no means penniless, the Presbytery seat, famous in ecclesiastical annals for its creed, crotchets, and conflicts; resonant, too, in profane history for its fifty drawbridges—the gift of the imagination and pawky Scotch humour of George Buchanan, Latinist, publicist, and tutor to that high and mighty Prince, the British Solomon, James I. of England and VI. of Scotland. The drawbridges are no more, for the "lang toon" is a burgh now, with a douce Provost of its own, and Bailies, and such like novel things and persons. But this we cannot tell from our present standpoint, and we might easily persuade ourselves this afternoon that Auchterarder has suffered no sea change, were it not that every now and again the columns of our local newspaper foam under the rage of its municipal contendings.

In the far east, the Strath seems to be shut off by the Moncrieffe Hill—wooded still, as in the days when it was first named. But the Earn slips between this seeming obstacle and the spurs of the Ochils, making such haste as it can through carse-like land to join the lordly Tay hard by Abernethy—the ancient capital of the Southern Picts—the centre of missionary enterprise, when darkness was thick upon the land after Ninian had died at Whithorn, on the Solway, and before Columba had set foot upon Iona. The valley at our feet, the limits of which I have attempted to mark off, is Strathearn—a right noble expanse of fertile soil, richly wooded, abundantly watered, dotted over with villages and guardian Parish Churches, like that of Muthill; bright with Castles that have left their names in history, and with mansion-houses of hardly less fame, that gleam from among their ancestral trees—a Strath that may be fitly characterised as the Scottish Esdraelon, in which many things have happened, and many men have been well worthy of being held in remembrance.

I had intended in this paper to give an account of some early inroads into Strathearn, but the exigencies of space have determined for me that I can deal with only one—the earliest of all—the Roman invasion. I should have liked to have told the story of the invasion by Egfrid of Northumbria, which ended so disastrously for him at Nechtansmere—most likely Dunnichen, in Forfarshire, in the year 685 A.D., and of which it may well be that we have a solitary trace in the name Abercairny—plainly identical with Abercornig—Abercorn in the Lothians—where the Angles founded a monastery under Abbot Trumuini, who, being engaged in Strathearn advocating the adoption of the Roman in opposition to the prevalent Columban cult, had to beat a hasty retreat beyond the Forth when disaster came to Egfrid. The larger subject would have included also the invasion by Siward, Earl of Northumberland, in support of the claims of Prince Malcolm, afterwards Malcolm Canmore, in opposition to Macbeth, the usurper, as he is commonly, perhaps unfairly, called. The first stage of the inroad ended with an encounter at Tula Amon—at the junction of the Tay and the Almond, near Perth. The result was not decisive, for it would seem that for a little while Macbeth kept possession of the country north of the Forth, being especially strong in Fife, where he had powerful family connections and friends in the Culdee brotherhood at Lochleven, while Malcolm reigned in the Lothians. And a little later, in connection with the complications into which Malcolm was forced through his fortunate marriage with Margaret, sister of the Atheling, we have traces—somewhat indistinct, truly, but still historical—of an inroad by the grim conqueror of England—William, and of a meeting between him and Malcolm at Forteviot. All this might have proved instructive in detailed exposition, but I must content myself with this condensed reference. My subject is, therefore, the earliest historical inroad into Strathearn—the Roman inroad, which I have called, in the heading of this paper, the Opening Up of Strathearn.

Everybody knows that Julius Caesar set foot in Britain and conducted a campaign against the native tribes in 55-54 B.C. He made no permanent impression. But successive expeditions were sent out, and the tide of conquest flowed further and further east and west and north till it reached the Solway. The details of the conflict do not concern us here. But it would be unpardonable to omit mentioning Boadicea, Queen of the Iceni, in the East, and of Caractacus, leader of the Silures, in the West, both of whom offered strenuous opposition to the Roman advance. The powerful tribe of the Brigantes, who possessed the country between the Humber and the Solway, made a stout defence in the North, but by the year 70 A.D. the Roman province was coterminous with the present southern boundary of Scotland. It was now that the Romans heard the name of a new tribe—the Caledonian Britons, who, according to report, lived upon fish and milk, clearly indicating a less advanced stage of civilisation than that of the tribes they had encountered hitherto. The unexplored territory in which they dwelt was vaguely called Thule. Tacitus, the historian, and son-in-law of Julius Agricola—the discoverer of Strathearn—imagined it to be an island formed by the meeting of the Firths of Forth and Clyde. But the time was now come when more accurate information was to be obtained concerning Caledonia and its inhabitants. Some external characteristics had been noted. The Caledonians were described as Caerulei, from the green colour with which they stained their bodies. It was also said that they fought with chariots like the Britons of the interior, whom Caesar heard of 125 years before.

Julius Agricola was the man who first brought the Caledonians within the ken of distinct history. He came to Britain in 78 A.D. His first campaign was on the Welsh border, his second in the territory of some outlying Brigantian tribes along the northern shores of the Solway. These were the Selgovae, who occupied what is now the county of Dumfries, and the Novantes further to the west in the modern counties of Kirkcudbright and Wigton. To the north of these lay the great nation of the Damnonii—of the same stock as those who occupied Devonshire in the south of England. They held extensive territories in the centre of Scotland, including the counties of Ayr, Lanark, Renfrew, south of the Firths of Forth and Clyde, and, north of these estuaries, the counties of Dumbarton and Stirling and the districts of Menteith, Stratherne, and Forthreve, or the western half of the peninsula of Fife. They were the "novae gentes," or new nations, whose territories Agricola ravaged as far as the "Tavaus," or Tay, in his third campaign. They were somewhat civilised, having towns, of which we know the names of six—three lying south of and three north of the Firths. The chief of the southern towns was Coria—Carstairs, near Lanark, on the Clyde. North of the Forth there were Alauna, where the Allan joins the Forth; Lindum—that is Ardoch, at our own doors; and Victoria, in Fife, situated on a small lake. The lake has disappeared, but the name Lochore remains, and is otherwise famous than as a town of the Damnonii. The natural division line between the Selgovae, Novantes, and Damnonii was the hilly country which separates the waters that flow north from those that find their way into the Solway—the Ituna Aestuarium, as its name then was. Crossing this mountain barrier, Agricola struck into the valley of the Clyde, passed with his legions through Lanarkshire and Stirlingshire, then by the fords of the Forth and the Vale of the Allan into Strathearn, thence onward to the Tay. There was an alternative route. A fleet accompanied his movements. He might have crossed the Firth of Forth—the Bodotria Aestuarium—and penetrated through Fife to the Tay. But Tacitus usually mentions the crossing of estuaries, and he omits it in this case. Besides, he states that the natives on the north shore of the Forth were new to him in the fifth campaign.

It was, therefore, in the year 80 A.D., during his third campaign, that Agricola entered Strathearn by way of Alauna. He did not effect a permanent conquest. His operations rather resembled a reconnaisance in force. But he meant serious business. He planted forts in commanding situations, choosing so wisely, from a strategic point of view, that not one of them was ever taken or surrendered. They were placed so as to command the principal passes into the Highlands. They form a ring-fence round the territory hastily overrun by Agricola in this third campaign. Beginning in the west with Bochastle, at the Pass of Leny, near Callander, we come successively to Dalginross, at Comrie; Fendoch, at the mouth of the Sma' Glen; the camp at the junction of the Almond and the Tay; and, Ardargie, in the parish of Forgandenny, on the River May, commanding an extensive prospect of the Ochils, and along the course of the road from the Tay to the great camp at Ardoch. Here was evidently the base of operations, with accommodation, if need arose, for the entire Roman army in Scotland.

Having thus viewed the land and pegged out his claim by means of forts, Agricola returned to winter quarters. In the following summer—the summer of 81 A.D., he made no forward movement. But he was meditating a great enterprise—no less an enterprise than to penetrate beyond the Tay and break the power of the

Caledonians in their remote fastnesses. It behoved him to be cautious, so he constructed the chain of forts which afterwards became the Wall of Antonine—from Borrowstonness, on the Forth, to Old Kilpatrick, on the Clyde. Meantime he was laying his plans with admirable foresight. He entrusted the forts in Strathearn to the courage of their slender garrisons, and the issue proved that he could do so safely. But there was unexplored territory westward and eastward. Nobody knew what dangers might be lurking there, ready to assail him in rear the moment he left the security of his fortified place. So we find him in the summer of 82 A.D., in Argyll and Kintyre, with a small force, not fighting so much, as simply exploring, at one point feasting his Roman eyes, greedy for conquest, upon the coast of Ireland, seen dimly in the distance, and perhaps scheming in his heart and head to add it also at a fitting time to the Roman domains.

Returning from the west country, Agricola entered upon the campaign of three years' duration, which issued in the Battle of Mons Grampus, the crowning glory of his arms in Scotland, and the immediate occasion of his recall. He chose the alternative route this time. From his chain of forts he could see the broad expanse of the Firth of Forth, the coast of Fife, the central Lomonds, and the distant hill-country, whose acquaintance he had already made. That distant point was the goal of his endeavour, and the shortest way to it was across the Firth of Forth, through the western division of Fife, and on by one of the Ochil passes—Glendevon, or some other further east into Strathearn. There was no time to lose. For, while he was engaged in the subjugation of Fife, the fleet, after exploring the harbours, had doubled the East Neuk, passed safely through St Andrews Bay, and entered the Firth of Tay. Its unexpected appearance caused the greatest consternation among the Caledonians. The immediate result was to greatly increase the peril in which the devoted garrisons in Strathearn stood. So great was their danger, and so well was it known, that there were those with Agricola who advised a retreat to the chain of forts between the Firths. But Agricola was not to be shaken in his resolve, which was to finally break the power of the tribes who dwelt to the north and east of the Grampians, and who, so long as they remained free and unchastised, were a standing menace to the Strath of the Earn and to the garrisons who held it at the hazard of their lives. He formed a camp to winter in at a place called Grassy Walls, on the east side of the Tay, near to Perth. But there was still time, before the winter set in, for a little exploration and a brush with the enemy to revive the courage of his soldiers, which had begun to droop a little. Advancing northward on the left bank of the river, Agricola reached the Isla, and not caring to cross it so late in the year, in the face of the enemy who were massed upon the Hill and Muir of Blair beyond, he diverged to the right, following the course of the Isla until he came to the place where Coupar Angus stands now. Here he paused. He had marched from Perth in three divisions to prevent surprise, and in this neighbourhood there are three positions marked by Roman remains that correspond with these divisions. The main force was stationed at Coupar Angus; the Ninth Legion at Lintrose, two miles south-east; a third small body at a place two miles south-west, overlooking the Tay, and guarding the passage. These details are important, as helping to determine the true site of the Battle of Mons Grampus. It may be taken for granted that the Roman General made good use of his opportunity to survey the ground upon which the decisive battle was fought. Before retiring to winter quarters at Grassy Walls, the Roman soldiers had a chance given them of testing the strength and valour of the Caledonians. The Ninth Legion was stationed at Lintrose, and here the enemy delivered their attack under cover of night. They had penetrated into the camp ere they were discovered, and it might have gone hard with the Legion if help had not been at hand. But the alarm quickly spread to where Agricola was stationed with the main body. On his arrival the Caledonians took to flight. With the first touch of winter the march southward was begun, and when the summer came the legionaries and the auxiliaries clamoured impatiently to be led northward to the final encounter.

The theory maintained in this paper regarding the last campaign of Agricola, and the site of the Battle of Mons Grampus was first broached in the Statistical Account of the parish of Bendochy, published in 1797. It has been since adopted by Skene in his classical work on Celtic Scotland, to which I desire in this place to acknowledge my great indebtedness. Other sites have been fixed upon, but there are none that can fairly be put in comparison with the neck of land at the junction of the Isla with the Tay. What may be called the traditional view of the site of the battle locates it at Ardoch, in the vicinity of the great camp. No doubt, good authorities can be quoted in favour of the correctness of the traditional view. But there are several reasons which render it highly improbable that the great battle was fought at Ardoch. The very name Mons Grampus implies the existence of some conspicuous eminence in the near neighbourhood. There is no such eminence near Ardoch. Further, we know that Agricola's scheme of operation embraced joint action on the part of the fleet and land forces. There could have been no such co-operation if the movement of the legions had been west of the Tay. And it is a fatal objection to the Ardoch site that there are not three stations corresponding to those which we have seen the three divisions of Agricola's force occupied on the night of the surprise. General Roy, indeed, has tried to turn the edge of this objection by placing the Ninth Legion at Dalginross, the main body under Agricola at Ardoch, and the other division at Strageath, overlooking and guarding the Earn. But it has been retorted upon him that Agricola could have made no worse disposition of his forces, from a strategic point of view, than to have stationed his weakest division at Comrie, nine miles distant from the main body, in the very heart of the enemy's country, close to the hills, from which they could rush down upon any favourable opportunity, and to which they could retreat in the event of a repulse.

Besides, help came from the main body in the course of a few hours—between night and morning. It would be a difficult task even now for a body of men to cover the ground between Ardoch and Comrie in the dead of night; and we must remember that in the time of Agricola the country was a pathless wild, rough with woods in the higher parts, and covered with treacherous morasses in the valleys. The Damnonii—within whose territories Ardoch, Comrie, and Strageath lay— were more highly civilised than the Caledonians beyond the Tay and the Grampian range. They had towns, as we have seen; they probably engaged to some extent in agriculture; their food did not altogether consist of fish, milk, and the produce of the chase. But their towns were few and far between, and the means of communication very imperfect. The native tribes were not road-makers, and the Romans had not been long enough in possession, nor had leisure been granted them to form the solid and straight lines of communication upon which, everywhere, their power was based. We have Roman roads in Strathearn, and I daresay a careful student of the district could walk every foot of the way from Ardoch to Perth along these roads—street-roads, they are called locally, as I discovered one night to my surprise on making inquiries as to the shortest route between the manses of Gask and Trinity-Gask. But these roads were not in existence when the Battle of Mons Grampus was fought. Much rough pioneering work had to be gone through ere it was possible to lay them down. Meantime, the respective positions of the Romans and Caledonians had changed somewhat. The tide of conquest did not remain at the high-water mark of Agricola's advance. The Roman garrisons were withdrawn from Strathearn and from Ardoch. The Wall of Hadrian, between the Solway and the Tyne, was substituted for the frontier chain of forts between the Forth and Clyde, and, in consequence, the native tribes kept pressing ever southward. Hadrian's Wall checked their progress, but their presence in ever-increasing numbers was a danger to the province. They had now come to be known as the Caledonii and the Meatae—the men of the hills and the men of the plains. At length the spirit of Rome revived in the Emperor Severus, who determined to revisit the scene of Agricola's early conquests. He came to Britain in 208 A.D., fully one hundred and twenty years after the Battle of Mons Grampus had been fought and won. He moved slowly, but did his work effectively. It was a costly process both in treasure and human life; but, from the point of view of permanent conquest, it was well done. Roads were formed, bridges built, and the habits of civilisation introduced into the wilds of Strathearn, and far away in the North. For, marching by way of Forfar, Kincardine, and Aberdeen, Severus reached the Moray Firth, and got from the Caledonians a cession of land to the north of the Tay. It has been conjectured that he returned south by way of Fortingall and Fendoch and Ardoch, where are Roman remains of a peculiar kind, of which no more satisfactory explanation can be given than that they mark the sites of his stations. Severus was borne on a litter in his northward march, frail and aged. He accomplished his purpose, but the undertaking was greater than his strength had warranted. He died at York in 211 A.D.

But to return to Agricola—to whom the honour belongs of opening up Strathearn. He had gone into winter quarters near Perth, after his autumn expedition to the Isla. All hesitation had vanished from the minds of his soldiers. They were impatient to try conclusions with the barbarian Caledonians; and so soon as the season permitted, the camp was broken up. They retraced their steps to the Isla, and found the enemy occupying the old position on the lower slopes of the Hill of Blair—battle-hill; probably so called in memory of the big fight now impending. It was a well-chosen position, showing no little military skill on the part of Galgacus, the Caledonian chief. From the foot of the hill a plain extended southward to the junction of the rivers. The Isla bounded the plain on the east, while a series of morasses, moors, and small lochs stretched to the west, in the direction of the Grampian range. Upon their defeat, the Caledonians made their escape this way. The Roman army boldly crossed the Isla this time, and began to throw up entrenchments. Traces of a rampart are to be seen extending from Meikleour on the Tay across country to the Isla. In connection with this a fort was constructed and a triangular bit of ground enclosed, capable of containing the whole force. The local name of the rampart is Cleaven Dykes, and all the while the Caledonians were gathering from all parts—from the distant Highlands and from the siege of the Strathearn forts. The Buzzard Dykes, on the lower slopes of the Hill of Blair, marks their position. At length they thought themselves strong enough to begin the attack. A defensive policy would have been wiser. But the concentrated power of a trained army—the very regularity of its motions always draws the attack of a less highly disciplined force. Probably the Caledonians deceived themselves into thinking that fear was the cause of the inaction of their opponents. It was not so. Agricola had come so far in order to fight, and his soldiers were impatient to be led against the enemy. They had gained confidence from the experience of the year before—they were hungry as wolves for the honour of victory. They knew that upon their valour depended the lives of their fellow-soldiers, who had been fighting for well nigh four years against tremendous odds away west in Strathearn. And when the Caledonians came on, Agricola promptly advanced to meet them, having 8000 auxiliaries in his first line, protected on the wings by 3000 cavalry. The legionaries were stationed behind these—veteran Roman soldiers, upon whose steadiness he could rely if there should come repulse and panic. The rampart at Meikleour was in the rear of the reserve force—to serve as a last defence if the worst happened. Agricola himself went to the front with the colours. As usual, the battle began with a discharge of missiles from a distance. The darts and stones flew thick, and all the while the Caledonians were edging away to right and left in the hope of surrounding the Romans. Agricola strained his thin line almost to breaking point, but his opponents had the advantage of numbers, and still pressed him. The danger of a gaping centre grew imminent. The crisis of the conflict came. Three Batavian and two Tungrian cohorts charged sword in hand. The issue was not long in doubt. The small shields and long swords of the Caledonians were ill-fitted to encounter the straight home-thrust of the finely-tempered blade, 19 inches in length, with which the Roman soldiers were armed. They wavered, and then the end came quickly. The whole line of the auxiliaries charged uphill and carried everything before them, and although the war chariots, armed with scythe-blades, were brought into action, they did more harm than good. The ground was rough, and unsuitable for the effective use of these murderous weapons of warfare. Their own men, now in hopeless confusion, were the chief sufferers from them. And although the Caledonian reserve succeeded in getting behind the Roman first line, they were promptly checked by a cavalry attack. It was never necessary to bring the Roman reserves of legionary soldiers into action. The fight was over, and the Caledonians sought safety in headlong flight among the morasses which stretched westward in the direction of the Grampian range.

Agricola did not push his advantage further. He was content with the victory he had gained, He could now hope that there would be peace in Strathearn, bringing with it the opportunity of extending the boundary of the Roman province to the Tay. His eager Roman spirit was planning other enterprises. He had seen the coast of Ireland from Kintyre, and doubtless courted the distinction of annexing it to the Empire. One can't help thinking what a pity it was that the opportunity of doing so was not given him. Had the distressful country got the benefit of the firm and civilising Roman rule, a happier history might have been hers. From his winter quarters behind the Firths of Forth and Clyde, Agricola sent his fleet to explore the distant northern parts. His sailors visited and took possession of the Orkney Islands—sighted a distant peak, which became the "Ultima Thule" of history; noted the peculiar feature of the West Coast of Scotland—the sea-lochs now so well known to the tourists of every land; circumnavigated the island till they reached the Trutulensian harbour—Dover, as we call it now; and then returned to their station in the Firth of Forth. It was not permitted to Agricola to turn the information thus acquired to practical use. His brilliant success in Scotland had excited the jealousy of the Emperor Domitian, and he was recalled under the pretence of appointing him to a higher command. The traces of him in Strathearn and elsewhere were speedily obliterated. The Roman province shrank to the wall of Hadrian between Tyne and Sol-way; civilisation was beaten back, and kept back for four generations.

CELTIC SAINTS
AND ANCIENT CHURCHES
OF STRATHEARN

S. FILLAN, DUNDURN

S. RONAN, STROWAN

S. BEAN, KINKELL AND FOULIS

S. SERF, DUNNING AND MONZIEVAIRD

S. KESSOG, COMRIE AND AUCHTERARDER

S. PATRICK, STROGEATH

S. FERGUS, MUTHILL

S. CATTAN, ABERUTHVEN

S. BRIDE, ABERNETHY

CELTIC SAINTS AND ANCIENT CHURCHES OF STRATHEARN

BY REV. JAMES RANKIN, D.D., MUTHILL

The vale or strath of the Earn may best and simplest be said to extend from the head of Loch Earn along the course of the River Earn to its junction with the Tay, two and a quarter miles above Newburgh. The distance from top to bottom as the crow flies is about thirty-six miles, and the direction is very nearly due west and east. The valley may be sub-divided into four portions. The uppermost is Loch Earn itself, which is six and a half miles long and 306 feet above sea-level, so that the descent of the river in its thirty miles of course is not much. The surface of Loch Earn, James' Square in Crieff, and the Manse of Muthill, across the valley, are as nearly as possible on the same level. The Earn may be sectioned as follows:—From Loch Earn to the Bridge of Comrie; thence to the Bridge of Crieff; thence to the Bridge of Kinkell; thence to Bridge of Earn; thence to junction of Earn with Tay. For our present purpose we may stop near Forteviot, at the Earn boundary of the Presbytery of Auchterarder.

Before we can rightly appreciate the more or most ancient Christian history of the Strath, we require to lay aside, and partly reverse, certain modern associations as to lines of travel. We think of Strathearn as running westward from Auchterarder, which lies on both the turnpike and railway route from Stirling to Perth. But in the days of our early Christianity it was mainly the sea on each coast that joined north and south of Scotland; whereas the more frequented routes were across country from west to east, because the west was then the seat of government and source of culture. Our early Christianity came from Ireland, and the route was by the Firth of Clyde, where Kintyre, Arran, Cumbrae, Bute, Kilmun, Dumbarton, Luss, and Balquhidder were all already provided with places of worship. The Vale of Leven and Loch Lomond were the natural approaches from the west to the upper end of Loch Earn and Strathearn. Another route connecting Perthshire with Iona was by Loch Etive, Dalmally, Tyndrum, and Glendochart. But the Leven and Loch Lomond route, judging by the saints to whom the oldest churches were dedicated, was the actual one usually traversed in reaching the valley of the Earn.

The oldest settlement is that of S. Fillan, at Dundurn. His day in the Kalendar is June 22, and he died about 520 A.D. Dundurn=Dun d'Earn. In the martyrology of Donegal (for he was a pure Irish Celt) he is called of Rath Erann—*i.e.*, the fort on the Earn. Besides the old chapel and burial-ground, a memorial of the Saint is in Dunfillan, where are his chair and well. A fine eye for the picturesque the good man must have had to select a hill of so striking aspect and commanding so charming a landscape as Dunfillan. A little later Dunfillan became a king's seat or fort. S. Fillan is called *an lobar*, leper, or perhaps stammerer, to distinguish him from S. Fillan the abbot, connected with Strathfillan and Killin, whose day is January 9, and who died about 703, nearly 200 years after his namesake the leper. He of Dundurn was of the race of AEngus, King of Munster, and was trained under S. Ailbe of Emly. Dr. Marshall, in his "Historic Scenes in Perthshire," in company with several other writers, mixes up the two S. Fillans. Bishop Forbes, in his "Kalendars of Scottish Saints," gives a clear account of each, mentioning that Aberdour, in Fife, is dedicated to him of Dundurn, as was also Cill or Kil-Faelin, in Leinster.

The Tower, Muthill.

Tullichettle and Comrie may be taken together, the distance between them being only one mile; the former meaning "The Vale of Sleep," now known mainly by its little kirkyard, having once been the more important of the two. The proof of this is seen in an extract from the Register of Ministers and Readers in the Miscellany of the Wodrow Society. In 1574, where our Presbytery has now sixteen parishes, there were only four ministers and sixteen readers, thus grouped:—Auchterarder—Stipend, £100, and kirk-lands—had readers at Auchterardour, Kinkell, Abirruthven, and Dunnyng. Strogeith—£60, and kirk-lands—had readers at Strogeith, Muthill, and Strowane. Foulis—£80, and kirklands—had readers at Foulis, Madertie, Trinite-Gask, and Findo-Gask. Tullichettil—£100, and kirk-lands—had readers at Tullichettil, Cumrie, Monivaird, Monzie, and Crieff. The system of readers was a beggarly makeshift for the Christian ministry, and shows the sore straits to which the Reformed Church was reduced after what was supposed to be the grand victory of 1560. Then Tullichettle was more than Comrie, as Strageath was more than Muthill. The dedication of Tullichettle does not appear in any record that I have seen, but that of Comrie is evident from its fair, which bears the name of S. Kessog. There is also a Tom-na-chessaig, just behind the old Free Church, now a public hall. The old name has a modern recognition in a local Freemasons' Lodge of S. Kessack. What is known of the Saint is given further on under Auchterarder.

Downwards on Earn the next ancient riverside church is Strowan, which, being a small parish, was united to Monzievaird before 1662. The site is one of remarkable beauty and quiet, almost ideal as a place of worship and burial. Ronan or Rowan was a bishop and confessor under King Maldwin, Feb. 7, 737, according to Adam King's Kalendar. He was of Kilmaronen or Kilmaronoc, in Lennox. Other dedications to him are Kilroaronag, in Muckairn; Teampull Ronan of Ness, in Lewis; Port Ronan, in Iona. At his death in 737 A.D., S. Ronan was abbot of Kingarth, in Bute. Connected with the church of Strowan is a Ronan pool on the Earn, and a bell remains from the old days. An adjacent farm is called Carse of Trowan.

The old church of Monzievaird on the east avenue to Ochtertyre, and now the private burial-place of the Murrays, is dedicated to S. Serf. But his legend may be reserved till we reach Dunning, at the end of our narrative.

The next in order of the old Celtic Churches on the Earn is that at Strogeit, or usually Strageath. This church and churchyard are close on the Earn, at a very picturesque spot, where are two very old mills—one on each side of the river—and a mill-dam between, and serving for both. The church is dedicated to S. Patrick, of Ireland, and was planted by an Irish missionary called S. Fergus.

Patricius was bishop and confessor—his day of death and commemoration, March 17, 493. He was the son of Calphurnius, a Roman decurio or magistrate at Dumbarton, his mother being Conkessa, sister or niece of the great S. Martin of Tours. He was born at Kilpatrick, on the Clyde, and called Succat=Succoth, the name of a neighbouring estate. At sixteen, Patrick was carried off to Ireland by pirates, and sold to a chief, Michul of Antrim, where he served six years, when he escaped to Scotland. He then went to S. Germanus of Auxerre for forty (more probably four) years' study. After becoming monk with his uncle S. Martin, he visited Rome, and was sent to Ireland, where he laboured sixty years, consecrating 365 churches and bishops, and ordaining 300—some say 3000—presbyters. Writings of S. Patrick are his "Confessions"—"Hymn before Tara," called "Breast-plate," in eleven verses, and "Letter to Caroticus, Caradoc, or Ceretic Guledig," from whom the kings of Alcluith, Patrick's birthland, were descended. (See Christian Classics—The Writings of Patrick, the Apostle of Ireland. Religious Tract Society, London.) S. Patrick's churches in Scotland are sixteen, of which three are in Muthill—viz., Strogeit, on the Earn; S. Patrick's, at Blairinroar; and S. Patrick's, at Struthill; each of the two latter having a S. Patrick's Well, anciently used in baptism. At Blairinroar, five miles west from Muthill, two or three cot-houses still bear the name S. Patrick's, but I don't know that the site of the original chapel is identifiable. At Struthill, two miles south of Muthill, both chapel walls and ancient burial-ground remained till about 50 years ago, when they were shamefully turned—the one into dyke material, and the consecrated soil and remains into top-dressing for corn land. The sacred well was also run off into a drain, and the site marked by a modern cattle trough. The burial-ground at Strageath is still in use, but the corner stones of the old church have been brutally abstracted for use in neighbouring buildings. These desecrations ill agree with what is truly stated by my predecessor in the New Statistical Account, that "the inhabitants of Muthill, until very lately (*i.e.*, about 1835), held S. Patrick's name in so high veneration that on his day (March 17) neither the clap of the mill was heard nor the plough seen to move in the furrow." Across the Earn from Strageath is a farm called Dalpatrick, and a ford known as Dalpatrick Ford.

This well-deserved honour to the patron saint of Ireland is traceable here to the presence of one of his disciples and countrymen, S. Fergus, whose work, however, must have been about 150 years after S. Patrick's death. After his work of chapel building in Muthill, S. Fergus quitted his hermitage at Strageath and went northward to Caithness and Buchan, on the same gospel errand, where, after good work again, he moved southwards to Glamis, the scene of his death and burial. The churches dedicated to him are six—viz., Wick, Halkirk, S. Fergus or Lungley, Inverugy, S. Fergus, at Banff; Dyce. Glamis has S. Fergus' cave and well. There was a S. Fergus chapel in the church of Inchbrayock, at Montrose, and a chapel and well at Usan, three miles south-east of Montrose. His head was preserved at Scone in a silver casket, his arm in a silver casket at Aberdeen, and his staff, baculus or bachul, at S. Fergus, in Buchan. In 721, *Fergustus Epis. Scotiae Pictus* signed at Rome canons as to irregular marriages. He belonged to the party that conformed to Rome as distinguished from the strict adherents of the old Celtic ritual.

About one mile below Strageath is the old Collegiate Church of Innerpeffray, dedicated to S. Mary, mentioned in 1342, and made collegiate in 1508 by the first Lord Drummond. But as this belongs to a later ecclesiastical system (1200-1560) it may be passed over for the present.

About two miles lower than Innerpeffray is Kinkell Church, dedicated to S. Bean. Here we come on a group of three, the next being Aberythven, three miles east of Kinkell, dedicated to S. Cathan; and Auchterarder, one mile south of Aberuthven, dedicated to S. Makessock. These three churches, along with Strageath and Madderty, have this in common at a later date—viz., 1200 A.D., that they were granted by Earl Gilbert of Strathearn and his Countess Matildis, as endowment to the newly-founded Abbey of Inchaffray. A few years later the Church of S. Bean of Foulis and the Church of the Holy Trinity of Gasc were added to the same endowment. Although now desolate, and appearing as a pendicle to an adjacent farm-steading, the old Kirk of Kinkell occupies a beautiful site in the valley, on a knoll, close by the river, and the kirkyard is still occasionally used. S. Bean, who was bishop and confessor, died about 920, and his day in the Kalendar is 26th October. He was uncle of S. Cadroe, who was taught at Armagh, and whose mission in Scotland marks the origin of the Culdees, strictly so-called, as is traced in Skene's Celtic Scotland, II., 346, in connection with Kinkell and Abernethy.

Particularly interesting is the Church of Aberuthven, now in the parish of Auchterarder. The eastern end of the building is evidently of extreme antiquity, with two narrow windows, between which would stand the altar, probably of stone. The dedication was to S. Cathan or Cattanus, bishop, May 17, 710. Cathan was uncle of S. Blain, of Bute, whom he ordained and consecrated bishop. Cathan is most closely associated with Bute, his original chapel having been on the south side of Kilchattan Bay. Cattan, the Pict, planted a church in Gigha, then went to Colonsay, which has another S. Cattan's, and to Iona, and settled at Scarinche, in Lewis, where his remains were preserved, and where, after Bannockburn (1314), a church was built and dedicated to S. Cattan, and affiliated to Inchaffray. There was also a Clan Chattan. (See Hewison's Bute, I., 136-8.)

Kessog, Kessogus, or Makessock, was born at Cashel, the capital of Munster, of the line of the Kings of Ireland, and miracles are attributed to his early years. He is depicted with bow and arrow as patron of the warriors of Leven and patron saint of Cumbrae. He lived as hermit in the island of Inch-ta-vanach, in Loch Lomond, and was martyred at Luss, where a cairn, Cam Machaisog, remained till 1796. (Anderson's Early Christian Times, I., 212). His day is 10th March, and the date of martyrdom, 520. Coming between the times of S. Patrick and S. Columba, S. Kessog and several saintly contemporaries are the fruits of the fervour of the former and the pioneers of the latter. The doctrines and rites of these earlier missionaries are described in Hewison's Bute, I., 118-131. S. Kessog's bell was preserved and honoured in Lennox in the 17th century. Besides Auchterarder, the Churches of Comrie, Callander, Luss, and Cumbrae were dedicated to S. Kessog. Callander has a fair on the 21st March=10th March (old style), called Fel-ma-chessaig, and the site of the old kirk, on a conical hill, is called Tom-na-chessaig. Cumbrae has a Kessog's Fair on the third Wednesday in March. Kessog Ferry, at Inverness, is another memorial of the Saint; so is the Strathearn name of M'Isaac, Makisaig, and Kessack. The old Kirk of S. Makessok lies in a hollow to the north of modern Auchterarder, whose church dates only from about 1660, and was enlarged in 1811. Makessock's Well still exists on the farm of East Kirkton, beside the old glebe and manse, which are now part of that farm, having been "excambed" about 1800.

There is a dedication to S. Mungo connected with Auchterarder, but as it seems not to have been a distinct building, we may consider it to have been only an altar, or side chapel, in the Church of S. Makessog. (The evidence for the S. Mungo dedication is "Historians of Scotland, Vol. V., p. xc."; also New Statistical Account,

Perth, 290.) Craigrossy paid dues to S. Mungo's altar in Glasgow. (Historians of Scotland, V., 357, and Orig. Par., I., 2.) The name Mungo has a marked currency in Strathearn. I have known six examples.

Before passing to Dunning, allusion may be made to Gask and Trinity-Gask, both of which are bounded by the Earn, the latter especially to a great extent. Gask was anciently known as Findo-Gask, the dedication being to S. Findoka, Fincana, or S. Fink, one of the nine daughters of S. Donevald or Donaldus, who led a religious life in the Glen of Ogilvie, in Forfarshire. S. Donevald's day is 12th July, and he died in 712. The Churches of Bendochy and Innishail (in Glenorchy) were also dedicated to S. Fink; while Finhaven, Strathmartin, and Touch were dedicated to S. Donevaldus. Trinity-Gask is mentioned under this name in a charter of Inchaffray shortly after 1200. To the Holy Trinity was a favourite dedication of the Culdees, who held firmly by the Apostles' Creed. The Cathedral of Brechin was dedicated by King Kenneth (971-995) to the Holy Trinity, and Culdee abbots continued in Brechin till 1219, although the See was founded in 1150 by David I., and re-dedicated to the Trinity. Thus the very name carries back the Church of Trinity-Gask to the times of the Culdees, if not to the Celtic Church directly.

The patron saint of Dunning is S. Servanus or Serf, who appears in the Kalendar as bishop and confessor, his day being July 1. He is said to be the son of Alma, daughter of a Pictish King; was ordained by Palladius, and dwelt at Culross in a monastery, where his most famous scholar was Kentigern, of Glasgow. Palladius died in 432, and Kentigern in 603, so that the same man in an ordinary life-time could not be *ordained* by Palladius and teach Kentigern. To escape this difficulty, the Aberdeen Breviary makes two S. Serfs. The legend runs—"In a place called Dunnyne the inhabitants were harassed by a dreadful dragon, which devoured both men and cattle and kept the district in continual terror. S. Serf, armed with a breastplate of faith, attacked the monster in his lair, and slew him by a blow of his pastoral staff." In proof of this legend, and in memory of this event, the scene to this day is called the Dragon's Den. The oldest part of the Church of Dunning, which dates between 1200 and 1219, would be the successor of the humbler Celtic building of the original dedication. If there were two S. Serfs, he of Dunning is the later, and is the same who is associated with Airthrey, Tillicoultry, Alva, Culross, and especially Pitmook, or Portmoak, and S. Serf's Isle, in Loch Leven. Other dedications are Monzievaird, Creich, Dysart, Redgorton. A S. Serf—probably the earlier, if there were two—was associated with Orkney. In the west of France, near St. Malo, is a town of St. Servan. The neatest of all the S. Serf legends, probably invented to suit some prehistoric soiree at the foot of the Ochils, tells of a robber who had stolen and eaten a pet lamb of the Saint, and who, having cleared himself by an oath taken over the Saint's staff, was immediately contradicted from within by a ba, ba, in response to the Saint's voice and the false oath. In Glasgow on the Thursday of the Fair week is a horse market known as Scairs, Skeers, or Sair's Thursday, Sair being one of the forms of Serf. There is a S. Sares Fair in Aberdeenshire, at Monkedge or Keith Hall, which has been removed to Culsalmond.

Although lying beyond our Presbytery limits, allusion may be made to the very ancient religious house at Abernethy, one mile south of the Earn, and near its junction with the Tay. The dedication of Abernethy is to S. Brigid or Bride. About 590, when Abernethy was the seat of the Pictish rule, Columban monks were planted here under King Lartnaidh. In 717 they were expelled by Nectan III. for non-conformity to Rome; but in 865 the old order was re-established by Abbot Kellach, of Iona. This continued to 908, when the See was transferred to St. Andrews. Culdees appear at Abernethy in the reign of Edgar (1097-1107), and they still held the old nunnery associated with S. Brigid in 1189-1198; and in 1272 the Culdees were changed into a priory of Augustinian monks. The famous Round Tower is assigned by Dr Petrie to 712-727, under Nectan III.; by Dr Skene to 865, the year of Kellach's visit; Dr Muir makes it later than Brechin, *i.e.*, 950; while Mr Anderson makes it one or two decades later still. For our purpose here the most important fact relative to Abernethy is the original dedication to S. Brigid. She was Abbess of Kildare, and died Feb. 11, 523 (Feb. 1 in Irish Kalendars). She received the veil from S. Mel, nephew of S. Patrick; wore a leathern belt over a white kirtle, and had a veil over her shoulders. Her cell was under a large oak, Kildara = cell of the oak, and she founded communities of women; died at the age of 70. Many miracles are ascribed to her, one of which reveals a very ancient ecclesiastical usage, parallel to the buns and ale associated with Scottish communions of three generations ago, as described in "The Holy Fair." From one barrel, S. Bride supplied beer to eighteen churches, the beer lasting from noonday, Thursday, in Holy Week, till after Easter.

Reviewing these primitive local churches and churchmen, we see that the general Christianisation of our Strath began about 500 A.D., and has continued and grown ever since. The three earliest dates above, given are S. Fillan, +520; S. Kessog, +520; and S. Brigid, +523. The three latest are S. Cattan, +710; S. Rowan, +737; and S. Bean, +920; all these being dates of death. This Celtic form of church began earlier in Scotland, and especially in Ireland, but in this district we see it in considerable strength from 500 onwards, and we know that it continued in vigour till about the year 1200, when it was superseded by a better organised and more developed form of Christianity, with direct recognition of Rome as the seat of authority.

The difference between the Roman and the Celtic or Culdee Church consisted in such matters as these:—The Celtic Church, while acknowledging many of the saints common to Christendom—especially those of the East—had in addition a very extensive local calendar, deeply venerated, which outnumbered the Roman element. It had also peculiarities in a frontal instead of a coronal tonsure for monks; in a shorter Lenten fast, which made up the forty days by including Sundays, and began on Monday instead of Wednesday; in a different time for Easter, dependent on a more ancient method of reckoning; in the absence of special or obligatory Easter communion; in the regular celebration of the Holy Supper with what were by Romanists called "barbarous rites."

The most marked features of the Celtic Church were its government and orders, where monasteries took the place of dioceses, where abbots were above bishops, where bishops were without dioceses, where ordination was conferred occasionally, if not habitually, by one single bishop instead of three, where bishops were too numerous to be diocesan, and where (latterly at least) abbots were frequently married, making church lands hereditary in their families.

A further characteristic of the Celtic Church was the rudeness and smallness of its buildings, which were of three styles—wattle and daub, timber beams, and unhewn stones. No examples of the two former survive, but the third and more solid style is still visible in Teampull Bennachad, in Lewis; Tempull Ronan, in North Rona; and the Beehive Cells, in Eilan na Naoimh (Nun's Island.) These old Strathearn churches would seldom be larger than 12 feet wide by 20 long, built of undressed land stones (like a field dyke), and thatched with heather, bracken, or sedge. The great storehouse of reliable material with minimum of controversy relative to the early Christianity of Scotland is Warren's Liturgy and Ritual of the Celtic Church. (Clarendon Press, 1881.)

The view given by Mr Hewison in "Bute in the Olden Time" (Vol. I., p. 119) of the doctrine and ritual of the Celtic Church in Ireland in the days of S. Patrick may safely be accepted as generally applicable to the Celtic Church in Scotland from 500 to 1000 A.D.:—

"We are dependent upon the 'Tripartite Life of S. Patrick' for definite information regarding the teaching and modes of worship in the Church in his day. It is clear the early teachers faithfully maintained the Holy Scriptures as the rule of faith, and used the version of the Bible prepared by S. Jerome. There are substantial reasons for believing that they also possessed a vernacular version, if not of all, of some of the books of the Bible, the Greek portions of which were studied by the more famous evangelists, like S. Brendan. A liturgy was also used, and, from surviving fragments, it appears to have been related to the 'Ephesine,' rather than to the 'Petrine' family of liturgies—that is to say, it was different from the Roman, and if not identical with the Gallican liturgy, was similar to it. Of the co-equality of the Trinity they had no doubt. In the 'Tripartite Life,' Baptism and Eucharist are mentioned as sacraments, but penance, marriage, holy orders, and extreme unction are not referred to as sacraments; while confirmation, if not accepted as of divine institution, was esteemed to have an imperative importance. There is only a slight trace of the honours paid to the Virgin Mary in the same work. According to the editor, 'The Blessed Virgin Mary is never mentioned either by Patrick, or Secundinus, Muirchu, or Tirechán.' Communion was partaken of in both kinds, the wine being mixed with water in the chalice, and sucked through a fistula. Prayers and fasting on behalf of the dead were indulged in, and much virtue was attached to severe fastings and ascetic mortifications of body and soul. Every day was consecrated to unremitting labours in the Gospel. Sunday was, indeed, a day of worship, divided into eight watches, like the other days of the week, and was fully observed in the saying of mass, the chanting of the 150 psalms, and preaching to the people. The clergy—deacons, presbyters, and bishops—were married. A notable feature of consecration of bishops was the practice of consecration by a single bishop, sometimes at a leap, without the candidate having received orders as a deacon or priest. Priests and virgins had a 'roving commission' to 'sing and say' over the land. It is interesting to find that the catacombs in Rome have preserved the monuments of 'virgines peregrinae,' like those of the Celtic Church. The size, importance, and influence of a complete ecclesiastical establishment (*muintir*), such as that presided over by S. Patrick, may be inferred from the functions of the 24 persons who were in office along with him— viz., bishop, priest, judge, bishop-champion (polemic), psalmist, chamberlain, bell-ringer, cook, brewer, two waiters, charioteer, fire-wood man, cow-herd, three smiths, three artizans, and

II.—RELATION OF AUCHTERARDER PRESBYTERY TO THE DIOCESE OF DUNBLANE.

Of the thirteen dioceses in Scotland, that of Dunblane was the smallest. In its Parochiale, or list of parishes, were 43 entries; but 3 of these were not parishes at all, but prebends, representing respectively the Abbots of Cambuskenneth, Arbroath, and Inchaffray. Of the churches and parishes proper that constituted the diocese, no fewer than 18 are now included in the Presbytery of Auchterarder; while 12 constitute the Presbytery of Dunblane, and 6 are in the Presbytery of Perth. Thus quite one half of the old diocese finds its corporate representative in Auchterarder, while the other half is subdivided between Perth and Dunblane.

Dunblane was formed into a bishopric by David I. out of the old Pictish Bishopric of Abernethy, which in the division was allotted as a parish to Dunblane. The date of erection was previous to 1150—some say 1140. Dunblane was already a Columban, and (notwithstanding Dr. Skene's argument to the contrary[1]) also a Culdee settlement. The church dates back to the seventh century, and was an offshoot of the Church of Kingarth, in Bute, for its founder was St. Blane. He was of the race of the Irish Picts, and nephew of that Bishop Cathan who founded Kingarth; he was himself bishop of that church, and his mother was a daughter of King Aidan of Dalriada. Dunblane and its church were burnt under Kenneth MacAlpin (844-860) by the Britons of Strathclyde, and in 912 were ravaged by Danish pirates, headed by Rognwald.

"At Dunblane," says Goodall,[2] "the Culdees continued near a hundred years longer than at Dunkeld. Cormac Malpol, their prior, with Michael, parson of Mothil, and Macbeath, his chaplain, are witnesses to a confirmation by William, bishop of Dunblane (1210 — —), of a gift of the Church of Kincardine to the monks of Cambuskenneth, to be seen in their chartulary, fol. 80; and Malpol, the prior, and Michael and Malcolm, Culdees, are witnesses to a charter by Simon, bishop of Dunblane (1170 — —), one of William's predecessors.[3]

[1] II. 403.
[2] Preliminary Dissertation in Keith's "Bishops," iv.
[3] See Crawford's "Officers of State," vi.

"At last, in the year 1240, the election of the bishop of that See was devolved upon canons-regular, by a mandate of Pope Gregóry IX., which was obtained in this manner: Clement, bishop of Dunblane, went to Rome, and represented to that Pope, how of old time his bishopric had been vacant upwards of a hundred years, during which period almost all the revenues were seized by the seculars; and although in process of time there had been several bishops instituted, yet, by their simplicity or negligence, the former dilapidations were not recovered, but, on the contrary, the remainder was almost quite alienated; so that, for near ten years, a proper person could not be found to accept of the charge; that the case having been laid before the Pope, he had committed the trust of supplying that vacancy to the bishops of St. Andrews, Dunkeld, and Brechin, who made choice of this Clement; but he found his church so desolate that he had not where to lay his head in his cathedral: there was no college there, only a rural chaplain performed divine service in the church that had its roof uncovered; and the revenues of the See were so small that they could hardly afford him maintenance for one half of the year.

"To remedy these evils, the Pope appointed William and Geoffry, the bishops of Glasgow and Dunkeld, to visit the Church of Dunblane; and if they should find these things to be as represented, he authorised them to cause the fourth part of the tithes of all the parish churches within that diocy to be assigned to the bishop thereof; who, after reserving out of these tithes so much as should be proper for his own sustenance, was, by the advice of these two bishops and other expert persons, to assign the rest to a dean and canons, whom the Pope enjoined to be settled there, if these matters could be brought about without great offence; or, if otherwise, he ordered that the fourth of the tithes of all such churches of the diocy as were in the hands of seculars should be assigned to the bishop, and that the bishop's seat should be translated to St. John's monastery of canons-regular (*i.e.*, Inchaffray) within that diocy, and appointed that these canons should have the election of the bishop when a vacancy should happen thereafter."

As the bishop's seat was not transferred from Dunblane to Inchaffray, we may infer that the *former* part of the alternative was carried out—viz., that dean and canons were found for Dunblane, and the bishop also provided for out of the fourth of the tithes of all churches in the diocese. The decay of clerics at Dunblane in Bishop Clement's time (1233-1258) may as well have applied to *Keledei* declining there, and does not imply that they never were there, but existed only at Muthill (13 miles to the north), and that the Culdees of Muthill, being in the diocese of Dunblane, were called Culdees of Dunblane. "We find," says Skene,[4] "the *Keledei* with their prior at Muthill from 1178 to 1214,[5] when they disappear from the records, and Muthill becomes the seat of the dean of Dunblane, who had already taken precedence of the prior of the *Keledei*. It is probable that, under the growing importance of Dunblane as a cathedral establishment, the possessions of the *Keledei* had fallen into secular hands." This would be the more easy, as the monastery of the Culdees was a distinct institution about a mile south of the church and village of Muthill.

---

[4] II. 404.
[5] Reeves' "British Culdees," Evidences, S., 141.

The foundation of the present cathedral is attributed to Bishop Clement, originally a monk, who received the tonsure from St. Dominic himself. The cathedral which he has left has since his day been extended both to east and westward; and what he built he joined on to the more ancient square and perpendicular tower. The cathedral consists of an aisled, eight-bayed nave (130 by 58 feet, and 50 feet high), an aisleless choir (80 by 30 feet), with a chapter-house, sacristy, or lady chapel, to the north. The nave is almost entirely pure first-pointed. In the clerestory the windows are of two lights, with a foiled circle set over them, plainly treated outside, but elaborated by a range of shafted arches running continuously in front of the windows within, so much apart from them as to leave a narrow passage round the building in the thickness of the wall. The east window is a peculiar triplicate, with the centre light much taller and wider than the others. The west front has over the doorway and its blind arch on either side three very long and narrow two-light windows of equal height, with a cinquefoil in the head of the central window and a quatrefoil in the head of the side windows; whilst above is a vesica, set within a bevelled fringe of bay-leaves, arranged zigzag-wise, with their points in contact—the last the subject of a well-known rhapsody by Ruskin. The root of the cathedral history in this case lies in the tower. It stands awkwardly a little out of line in the south aisle of the nave, an evident remnant of an older church, exactly like the similar tower in Muthill, of the eleventh century, retained in a church built c. 1430. A tower, almost exactly similar, but more ornate, probably twenty or thirty years later in date, exists at Dunning, in the same diocese, and also a Celtic Church settlement associated with St. Serf. The old Culdee Church of Markinch has a tower of the same peculiar style, originally with a square, upright, saddle-backed roof, and crow-stepped gables. Some vestiges remain of the bishop's palace, overlooking the Allan on the south-west of the cathedral; and the triangular space in front of the south side of the cathedral, and forming the end of the High Street, has some old houses which are believed to have been canons' manses.

The chapter consisted of—Dean (Muthill), praecentor, chancellor, treasurer, archdeacon; *Prebendaries*—Abbot of Cambuskenneth in 1298, Abbot of Arbroath for Abernethy from 1240; Crieff *primo* (probably parish of), Crieff *secundo* (probably St. Thomas at Milnab), Logie, Fordishall, Kinkell, Kippen, Monzie, Comrie. Eighteen finely carved oak stalls of the dignitaries and canons belonging to the sixteenth century still survive. Other carved work was destroyed in 1559 by the Prior of St. Andrews and the Earl of Argyll. The line of bishops ended with three of the neighbouring family of Chisholm of Cromlix. Bishop James Chisholm was eldest son of Edmund Chisholm, and was a good administrator. Bishop William Chisholm, his half-brother, was an ecclesiastic of the worst possible type for fornication, church robbery, and persecution of so-called heretics. Bishop William Chisholm, nephew of the robber-bishop, became, after the Reformation, a Carthusian monk at Lyons. He is supposed to have taken with him the writs of the See, which have been lost. Marshall[6] gives an account of this branch of Chisholms. The same writer says[7]: "Among the sepulchral monuments in the cathedral is that of Malise, eighth Earl of Strathearn, and his countess. It is in the vestry of

---

[6] "Hist. Scenes in Perthshire," 346.
[7] Ibid., 343.

the choir, and is a flat block of gritstone, having on it full-sized figures of the Earl and Countess. When discovered in the choir, the block was above a coffin of lead with date 1271. In the centre of the choir is the dust of Lady Margaret Drummond, mistress (but probably privately married) of James IV., and her sisters the Ladies Euphemia and Sybilla, daughters of Lord Drummond, who were poisoned (apparently to clear the way for the King's marriage to the Princess Mary of England in 1503). Their remains were deposited here by permission of their uncle, Sir William Drummond, then Dean of Dunblane. Three blue slabs covered and marked their resting-place. The recumbent figure attired in pontifical vestments and mitre, and which is in a niche of the wall under a window of the choir, on the right of the pulpit, is supposed to represent Bishop Finlay Dermock, and to be his sepulchral monument. The other recumbent figure under one of the windows of the nave represents Bishop Michael Ochiltree, who greatly added to the rich adornments of the cathedral."

BISHOPS OF DUNBLANE.

Laurence, attests a charter of Malcolm IV., 1160.

Simon, 1170.

Jonathan, archdeacon, buried at Inchaffray. Great endowment of the See by Gilbert, earl of Stratherne, c. 1195-1210.

William de Bosco, chancellor, 1210.

Abraham, 1220 to c. 1223.

Osbert, abbot of Cambuskenneth, +1231.

Clement, a Dominican friar, consecrated by Bishop William of St. Andrews at the Stow Church of Wedale; founded cathedral; made exaggerated wail of poverty to the Pope, who in 1238 appointed a commission of inquiry, 1233-1258.

Robert de Prebenda, dean, ambassador in 1277 to Edward I.: in 1265 was Conservator of Council at Perth, 1258-1283.

William, one of the arbiters between John Baliol and Bruce, 1290 to c. 1292.

Nicholas de Balmyle, monk of Arbroath, parson of Calder, lord chancellor, 1307-1320.

Maurice, abbot of Inchaffray, Bruce's chaplain at Bannockburn with crosier of St. Fillan; a brave patriot priest, with the old piety that reverenced relics, yet was true and fervent, 1320-1347.

William, 1347-1361.

Walter de Cambuslang or Conentre, 1362-1370.

Andrew, seals Act for succession of crown at Scone, 1st April, 1373.

Dougal, c. 1380-1399.

Finlay Dermoch, built bridge over Allan Water, tomb in cathedral on north side of nave, 1400-1419.

William Stephen, divinity-reader in 1411 at St. Andrews, Conservator of Council at Perth, 1420, 1420-1429.

Michael Ochiltree, dean in 1425, built Knaik Bridge at Ardoch, Bishop's Bridge at Culdees, rebuilt Culdee Church at Muthill; crowned James II. in 1437 at Holyrood, 1429-1447.

Robert Lauder, sent on several embassies, founder of several prebends, 1448-1458.

Thomas, 1459.

John Hepburn, a lord of session, 1467 to c. 1479.

James Chisholm, son of Edward Chisholm of Cromlix, chaplain to James III., 1534; a careful administrator and good bishop, 1489-1527.

William Chisholm, half-brother of the preceding, who resigned in his favour; a shameless wretch, who wasted the See by fraudulent tacks to his three bastards and his nephew, and who burned men for heresy, 1527-1564.

William Chisholm, nephew of the robber bishop, appointed by Papal brief of 2nd June, 1561, and nominated by Queen Mary in 1564; was in exile Bishop of Vaison in France, became a Carthusian of Grenoble, and died at Rome, 1564-1593.

PAROCHIALE DUNBLANENSE

Dunblane, St. Blain. Chapelry of Kilbride at Kilbride Castle.

Aberfoyle in Menteith. Dependent on *Inchmahome*. Has five lakes.

Abernethy, St. Brigid. *Arbroath*. Prebend, 1240. In See of Dunkeld in 1446. For four vicars. Probable date of round tower, 854. At first had Dron, Dunbulg, and Erole as chapels.

Auchterarder, St. Mungo. *Inchaffray*. Old church in a valley, one mile westward. Mackessock in charter of Innerpeffray.

Aberuthven, St. Cathan. *Inchaffray*, 1200. Later to Arbroath. Now joined to Auchterarder. Very ancient church survives.

Tullibardine. A collegiate church. Now in parish of Blackford.

Bondington or Boddington. *Arbroath*. In 1369 the lands of Boddington belonged to Peter de Innerpeffry. Bonnyton, near Montrose. (Jervise, 93.)

Blackford, St. Patrick. Original church was Strogeith, now in Muthill.

Dundurn, or St. Fillans. St. Fillan the Leper. Church here since c. 550. Associated with a fortress on Dunfillan. Now in Comrie.

Comrie, St. Kessog, R.[8] *Paisley Abbey*. Prebend. Chapel at Tullikettle. Had St. Kessog's Fair, third Wednesday of March.

Dron. Once chapel under Abernethy. Now includes Pottie, at the mouth of Glenfarg (see deanery of Gowrie, St Andrews), and Ecclesia Macgirdle ("Exmagirdle") at Glenearn.

Dunning, St. Serf, c. 1200.

Dupplin. Family chapel of castle. In 1618 joined to Aberdalgie.

Foulis, St. Methven and St. Bean (Foulis-Wester.) *Inchaffray*. Chapel of St. Methven at Buchanty Bridge. Also chapel at Gorthy, 1266. Renewed in 1454 by agreement between Abbot of Inchaffray and Tristam of Gorthy.

Fordishall or Ferdshaw. Prebend. Again under Dunkeld.

Gask, Holy Trinity (Trinity-Gask). *Inchaffray*.

Innerpeffray, St Mary. Mentioned 1342. Collegiate, 1508, by first Lord Drummond. In Monzie, *quoad sacra* to Muthill. Had Lady Fair on 25th March.

Kilmadoc, St. Madocus or Aidus (Doune.) *Inchmahome* Priory.

Kincardine, St. Latan or Lolan. Mentioned c. 1190 (Kincardine in Menteith). *Cambuskenneth*. Old parish of Lany in Kincardine, and chapelry of Balquhapple.

Kinkell, St. Bean. Prebend. *Inchaffray*. Now in Trinity-Gask. Minister of Kinkell hanged at Crieff, 1682.

Logie, St. Woloc (Logie, Stirling). Prebend.

Kippen, St. Davius or Movean. In Menteith. Prebend.

Lecroft or Leckraw, St Moroc or Maworrock (Lecropt, Bridge of Allan). *Cambuskenneth*.

Monzie in Stratherne. Prebend. St. Laurence Fair, 22d August. Included Logiealmond. Chapel at Tomenbowie, and Stuck Chapel with burial-grounds.

Monedie. Included Logiealmond, detached from Monzie.

Monyvaird, St. Serf, with Strowan (St. Rowan or Ronan). United before 1662.

Madertie, St. Ethernan (Maderty). An old abthane. Has Abbey of *Inchaffray*.

Capeth Moothill (Muthill). The Dean. Chapels and wells of St Patrick at Struthill and at Blairinroar; also, Dalpatrick across the Earn, from St. Patrick's of Strageath; Easter and Wester Feddal and Bennie (now in Ardoch), belonged to *Lindores Abbey* from 1198.

---

[8] R=Rectory.

Port [of Monteith]. Included old parish of Lany or Leny.

St. Madocus or Aidus (St. Madoes, Perth), R. Also Samadoss.

Tullicultrie, St. Serf. *Cambuskenneth*. Colvilles of Tillicoultry, 1483-1634.

Crieff, St. Michael, R. Prebend. Religious house—St. Thomas at Milnab (= Abbot's Mill), belonging to Inchaffray. Besides Crieff *primo* and Crieff *secundo* in Strathearn, there was also a Crieff *tertio* in Perthshire, probably the outlying portion of the parish in Glenalmond round Corrymuckloch.

Logie-Airthray, St. Serf (Airthrey, Bridge of Allan). *Nuns of North Berwick.*

Strogeyt or Strageith, St Patrick. Once church of Blackford, now in parish of Muthill. *Inchaffray*. Planted by St. Fergus c. 700.

Callender, St. Kessaig. Chapel of Kilmahog or St. Chug.

Fyndogask, St. Findoca (Gask). *Inchaffray*.

Tuelliallan (Tulliallan), R. Seat of the Blackaders, who gave an archbishop to Glasgow.

Glendovan (Glendevon), R. Old church in Gleneagles (= Glen Eglise). *Cambuskenneth*.

Fossowy (Fossoway). *Cupar Angus*, c. 1310. Included Tullibole, *Culross Abbey*. United in 1614.

Buffuder, St. Angus (Balquhidder). Has Strathyre and Glenogle.

Prebendary, 1298, Abbot of Cambuskenneth *ex officio*.

Prebendary, 1240, for parish of Abernethy, Abbot of Arbroath *ex officio*.

Preceptor or Provost of Dunblane, Abbot of Inchaffray *ex officio*.

NEAR THE PICTISH CAPITAL

BY REV. P. THOMSON, B.D., DUNNING

The title is retained as it was given. But it would be more correct to say, "Near a Pictish Capital," for, as is well known, of such capitals there were more than one. Nobody, however, who keeps in mind the origin and range of the present volume will need to be told that "The Pictish Capital" here meant is Forteviot—or, as it is often otherwise spelt in legends, and chronicles, and charters—*Fertebeith, Ferteuioth, Fertenyoth, Ferthevioth, Fetherthauethn, Fethirthant, Fothuirtabaicht, Fortewyot, Fetherteviot.*

When Forteviot attained the dignity of being a royal abode cannot be definitely ascertained. Dr Stuart gives it as his opinion that the royal residence is to be identified with the "Dun Fothir" mentioned in the Irish annals, which is recorded to have been twice besieged—in 681 and 694 A.D.; and it has been suggested by the same authority that probably the name means "the dun of the district, or of the men, or of the King of Fortren," which term latterly meant the kingdom of the Southern Picts.

Whatever probability there may be in the above suggestion, when we refer to the Legend of S. Andrew, we find what appears to be corroborative evidence that Forteviot was the residence of Pictish kings from a very early period. According to this legend, it was to Forteviot, in the hope of seeing the King there, that S. Regulus and certain of his followers made their way with the relics of the most holy Apostle Andrew, after their landing at Muckros or Kylrimont (now Saint Andrews). It so happened that the King (Hungus, or Ungus, or Angus, who died A.D. 761) was not at home, having gone on an expedition into Argyle (Argathelia). But they found his three sons[9] residing at Forteviot, and these princes gave the tenth part of the town[10] to God and S. Andrew, the holy men blessing the place and the royal family who abode there. They then went in further search of the King himself, and having met him at Kindrochet, in Braemar, and subsequently at Monichi (Monikie), they returned in company with him to Forteviot, where he built a church ("basilica"[11]) to God and S. Andrew.

---

[9] *Hwonam et Nechtan et Phinguineghert.*—(See Skene's *Chronicles of the Picts and Scots,* p. 185).

[10] *Decimam partem de urbe Fortevieth.*—(See Skene's *Chronicles of the Picts and Scots,* p. 185).

[11] This word, originally, was the name applied by the Romans to their public halls, either of justice or of exchange. Inasmuch as the early Christian Churches generally followed the ground plan of these buildings, such churches long retained the same appellation.

But these are not the only references that we have. According to one of the Pictish chronicles, it was at Fothuir-tabaicht that Drust (Filius Ferat), the last King of the Picts, was killed.[12] It was here—"in palacio suo de Fothuir-tabaicht"—where Kenneth MacAlpin, the first of the Scotic dynasty (formed by the union of the lines of the Picts and the Dalriadic Scots), died in 860. It was here, in Fothuir-tabaicht, where Donald I., Kenneth's brother and successor, established with his council the mode of succession to the throne, confirming "the rights and laws of the kingdom of Aodh, son of Eocha."

According to Skene, Forteviot continued to be a royal residence until the reign of Donald II., the son of Constantine, when the capital was transferred to Scone. But it would appear that the ancient "palace" at Forteviot was subsequently restored by Malcolm Canmore, and that his successors at least occasionally came to live in it. Malcolm the Maiden (1153-1165) is found to have granted at Fetherteviot a charter conveying certain lands—the names of Ada, the King's mother, and of William, his brother, appearing as witnesses. And even so late as 1306, during the English invasion, there is mention of a letter, dated from Forteviot by Edward, Prince of Wales.

The traditional site of the "palace," which would, no doubt, correspond also with the site of the early church dedicated to S. Andrew, as before mentioned, is still pointed out a little to the west of the village, and is known as the Halyhill or Holyhill. Whether this first church was built of stone is not known. But that there was a stone church at Forteviot at an early date is made comparatively certain by the discovery, in 1830 or thereby, of a large semi-circular and arched stone lying in the bed of the River May, and directly under the Halyhill. How long this most interesting arch had been hid away no one can tell; but it was a fortunate "spate" that washed it bare and exposed it to the light of day. It is now in the Antiquarian Museum in Edinburgh, where the writer recently made an inspection of it. An excellent engraving of it is contained in J. Romilly Allen's *Christian Symbolism in Great Britain and Ireland*, and with the kind permission of that gentleman it is here reproduced.[13]

The arch is 4 feet in span and 21 inches high. Carved in relief in the centre of the stone is a cross, on one side of which is an animal—very probably intended for the Agnus Dei; while, on the same side, a little below the Agnus Dei, there are three figures with helmets on their heads and swords in their right hands. On the other side of the cross there is a robed figure in a sitting posture, with a sword across his knees, and with one foot resting on the back of a horned animal.

It has been erroneously supposed by some that this arch must have formed part of the principal doorway of the "palace," but from the fact of its bearing such symbols as the Cross and the Agnus Dei, there is no doubt that it belonged to an early church.[14] Bearing in mind the legend of the founding of a church to S.

---

[12] Other chronicles give the place as Scone.—(See Skene's *Chronicles of the Picts and Scots*, p. 174).

[13] Both palace and church would be within the King's Rath or circular fortification.

[14] "The custom of placing a cross over the doorway of a Christian building may be traced back to the sixth century in Palestine, where the Chi-Rho monogram occurs on

Andrew in the time of Hungus, perhaps the suggestion of Dr Joseph Anderson has great probability—viz., that the four figures are "not contemporary, but early representations of King Hungus and his three sons."[15]

All lovers of antiquarian lore will be interested in knowing that, a few years ago, there was brought to light at Forteviot, and through the kindness of the parish minister, Dr Anderson, exhibited to the Society of Antiquaries a fine specimen of a bronze bell of Celtic type (the fifth of the kind known in Scotland), whose date is believed to belong to about the middle of the 10th century.

NEAR THE PICTISH CAPITAL would be found, as a matter of course, the royal hunting-grounds. Very probably these were on both sides of the Earn—stretching westward into the neighbouring parish of Dunning, the northmost part of which is still called Dalreoch or Dailrigh, a word which, in Gaelic, means the King's haugh or field.

To DUNNING, or rather to some of the objects in it, that are of the greatest archaeological or antiquarian interest, the remainder of this chapter will be devoted.

In many ways that we can readily conceive, traces of the proximity of Dunning to a royal residence must have existed from an early period. The existence of hill forts, as at Rossie-Law, and the discovery, from time to time, of arms and stone coffins, indicate that the parish must have been often the theatre of strife and bloodshed. Duncrub,[16] or, as it is called in a Pictish chronicle, "Dorsum Crup," is said to have been the scene of a battle, which is thus referred to by Robertson in his *Early Kings*—"The reign of Duff, the eldest son of Malcolm the First, and representative of the senior branch of the Royal family, appears to have been passed in a continued struggle against the pretensions raised by the now rival line of Aodh in the person of Indulf's son Colin, and, though at first successful, defeating Colin at the Battle of Duncrub (A.D. 965), in which the Mormaor[17] of Atholl and the Abbot of Dunkeld, partizans apparently of the defeated prince, were numbered amongst the slain, he was subsequently less fortunate, and was driven by his rival from the

---

the lintels of the doorways of the houses. The meaning of the symbolism is explained by the blood of the lamb, which was struck upon the lintels of the doors of the houses of the Israelites in Egypt at the Passover (Gen. xii., 21-23), and our Lord's words—'I am the door, by me if any man enter in, he shall be saved,' (John x., 9)."—(J. Romilly Allen's *Christian Symbolism*, p. 238).

A good example of such a cross is on the lintel of the doorway of a 7th century church at Fore, Co. West Meath; and another, equally good, is on the doorway of one of the oldest churches in Ireland, on High Island, off the coast of Connemara. In connection with the Round Towers at Antrim and at Brechin there are similar crosses.

[15] See *Proceedings of the Society of Antiquaries of Scotland* (Vol. xxvi., p. 438.) Dr Wilson, in his *Dunning: its Parochial History*, states that the large figure with the sword "is said to be a representation of Alexander the First, who died in the year 1124" (p. 3.)

[16] Sir Herbert Maxwell, in his *Scottish Land-Names: their Origin and Meaning*, gives as the derivation of Duncrub, the old Gaelic dún craeb=hill of the trees.

[17] Otherwise spelt *Mormaer*. Except that the constituent elements are inverted, it is the same word as *Maormor* (Gael. *maer, maor*, a steward, and *mor*, great), and was the ancient name for a royal steward of high dignity, placed by a Scottish king over a province, and acting as a royal deputy.

throne, losing his life on a later occasion at Forres ... where his body is said to have been hidden under the bridge of Kinloss, tradition adding that the sun refused to shine until the dishonoured remains of the murdered monarch received the burial of a king."[18] Part of the ground which is believed to have been the site of the Battle of Duncrub now forms the village tennis-ground and the village bowling-green, and yearly are witnessed on it fightings still—though of a very different kind. The traditional spot where the Abbot (by name Doncha) was slain is marked by the "Standing-Stone," on "the acres," a little to the east of the tennis-ground, while a similar "standing-stone," on the farm of "The Knowes," is said to mark the place where the Mormaor met his doom.

The spelling of the name Dunning, at various times, and in various records and charters, is rather interesting—*Donyng, Dunnyne, Dunyne, Dinnin, Dunin,* or (as *e.g.,* in the inscription on the Communion cups presently in use, of date 1702) *Duning.* The word is generally thought to be derived from the Gaelic term dún (already referred to), which means a hill, or a hill with a fort.[19]

On first appearing on the page of tolerably trustworthy history, Dunning formed part of the Stewartry or Earldom of Strathearn, which dates back to a remote period. Among the ancient Earls of Strathearn there were some very notable figures. Particularly so was Malise, the Earl of Strathearn, who figured prominently in the Battle of the Standard. But, more particularly notable still, was his grandson, Gilbert, who held the Earldom in the reign of David I. Like his King—proverbially known as the "sair sanct for the crown"—Gilbert was most lordly in gifts to the Church, which was then fast rising into power. Dr Wilson[20] quotes an old writer to the effect that, at this time, the Earldom of Strathearn included "the haill lands lying betwixt the Cross of MacDuff, at Newburgh, and the west end of Balquhidder, in length, and the Ochil Hills and the hills called Montes Grampii, or the Grampians, in breadth." Even though we make some reduction as to all this, and regard as somewhat legendary what Fordun tells us—viz., that Gilbert divided all his huge territory into three equal parts, giving two to the Church, and keeping only one to himself, still there cannot be a doubt but that he was one of the most liberal and extensive church-endowers on record. It was by him that the Bishopric of Dunblane was founded; it was by him that the Abbey of Canons-regular, at Inchaffray, was richly endowed through his attaching to it the tithes of many of the neighbouring parishes. The foundation charter of the Abbey, dated 1200 A.D., in the thirty-fifth year of the reign of William, records the giving and making over to the Abbey of the Church of S. Kattan, at Aberuthven; the Church of S. Ethirnin, at Madderty; the Church of S. Patrick, at Strageath; the Church of S. Mockhessoc, at Auchterarder; and the Church of S. Bean, at Kynkell. It will be seen that Dunning is not in this list. But it appears along with some other parishes in a second charter

[18] Robertson's *Early Kings* (Vol. I., p. 77).

[19] Sir Herbert Maxwell states that dún in its original and restricted sense means "Enclosure or fortress, being closely related to A.S. tûn, Eng. town.... The diminutive, or noun plural, yields innumerable names, like *Dinnans* and *Dinnance,* in Ayrshire and Galloway; *Duning* and *Dinnings* in Dumfriesshire; and *Downan,* near Ballantrae." Ought not Sir Herbert to have added *Dunnin* or *Dunning,* in Perthshire?

[20] See *Dunning: its Parochial History,* p. 4.

granted by the same Gilbert in 1217, which charter confirmed the grant of previously gifted parishes, and adds "the Church of S. Serf at Monzievaird, S. Bean at Foulis, S. Bridget at Kilbryde, the Holy Trinity at Gask, Tullichettel at Comrie, and S. Serf at Dunnyne."

It is highly probable that between 1200 and 1219—say, about 1210—the Church of S. Serf at Dunning was built. And that we have a considerable portion of the original building still remaining is rendered almost certain from what is known of the style of architecture of the period referred to—viz., the Norman in transition—the Norman entering on a First Pointed. The grey Tower, with its quaintly-mullioned windows and saddle-back roof; the wall adjoining the Tower on the north, and containing a fine Norman doorway and an interesting line of corbels; the handsome arch rising from massive pillars, and showing beautifully scolloped mouldings, all afford corroborative proof of the date above assigned.[21]

If Dunning Church was built about the time we have mentioned, it would, no doubt, be about the same time when the lands around it were erected into a parish. We have one or two very early references. In a charter of date 1247, Malise, Earl of Strathearn, granted 20 merks annually "de Thanagio de Dunnyne et Pitcairn." In 1283 we find that there was made to the Church of S. Serf a grant of "20 merks from our fermé[22] at Dunin, to be paid half-yeirlie, at the Feast of Pentecost and the Feast of S. Martin; and 10 merks of silver from our holding of Pitcairn, to be paid in the same manner." And in 1358 there is ratified a grant, previously made, of "42 merks yearly from the Thanage of Dunnyne"; also "the tithe of all the rents, cane, corn, cheese, flesh, fish, fowl, and game, and of all the food used in the Earl's Court, and 20 merks from our fermé at Dunnyne."

It may interest lovers of archaeological studies to know that when the Church of S. Serf at Dunning—originated and endowed as above described—was being re-floored some thirty-five years ago, there was dug up, from among earth and bones in the nave, a good specimen of a Celtic cross, which is now erected in a fitting place underneath the Tower. Mr A. Hutchison, F.S.A., Scot., Dundee (a reliable authority), has examined it, and has pronounced it "of the true Celtic type." He adds the opinion that "the fact that no mention is made in contemporary documents of an earlier church (*i.e.*, earlier than 1210) does not prove that such a church did not exist.... It is a fair inference from the existence of this early cross that an earlier ecclesiastical settlement existed at Dunning, and that the present church superseded a pre-Norman, or Celtic Church, in all probability on the same site."

---

[21] The marks of a gable of a former nave with a very highly-pitched roof are still distinctly seen on the Tower.

[22] The word here used, occasionally spelt *ferm*, sometimes means not so much a piece of land turned to agricultural use and cultivated by owner or tenant, as *an account, a reckoning*: It is akin to *farm* from the A.S. fearm or feorm=food, a meal. A trustworthy authority says that the meaning of farm "arose from the original practice of letting lands, on condition that the tenant should supply his lord's household with so many nights' entertainment." Hence "Reddet firmam trium noctium." (He will supply three nights' entertainment).— *Doomsday Book.*

St Serfs, Dunning (Dunning Tower).

At the risk of its being regarded as an unpardonably wide digression, reference may here be made, not to another cross, but to a monumental stone of another kind and of a much later date (although no date is inscribed upon it.) It is what is known as the "Ebenezer" stone of the parish. Though at one time lying flat and covered with crop-bearing soil, it now stands erect, and on what is believed to have been its first site. It is placed on a field on the farm of Easter Gatherleys, and about three-quarters of a mile west of the farm-house. Its origin is said to have been this:—The farmer of Gatherleys of the time—who was also "laird" of the place—had for long been in doubt and spiritual darkness—to all appearance hopelessly perplexed. Sitting down, here, one day, he found comfort, peace, and light. Showing a most laudable example, he not selfishly received the blessing, but most gratefully acknowledged it, raising on the spot his "Ebenezer" of indebtedness to Him from whom our blessings flow. On the surface of the stone facing the east are inscribed in English the words of Is. l., 10; while on that facing the west we have the following:—

EBENEZER

========

Hic
EX TENEBRIS
LUX LUXIT
ERGO
PATER, FILIUS, ET
SPIRITUS SANCTUS
MEUS DEUS,
ET NOMEN
HUJUS LOCI
LUX[23]

Both as to size and shape the stone is similar to the quaint early 17th century "head-stones" in the older portion of the graveyard around Dunning Church.

Something must be written of the bells which have been connected, at one time or another, with the Church of Dunning. One bell, no longer in the Tower, came to sudden grief when discharging its duty on a certain happy occasion. The Master of Rollo of the time, who was living at Masterfield, having been blessed with four daughters, but no son and heir, was met one evening by a messenger bringing the welcome news that a son had just been born to him. "Go," he said, "and make the bell ring till it crack." The order was literally obeyed—a broken bell being the result. Its fragments having been taken to Duncrub, were, many years after, re-cast into a bell, now used in connection with the private chapel there. The inscription on the cracked bell, for a copy of which the writer is indebted to the present Lord Rollo, was of a very interesting and suggestive nature. Round the top were the words—"Soli Deo Gloria. Joannes Oaderogge me fecit. Roterodami, 1681"; and on the body of the bell, the following words placed thus:—

"HAEC AD EVANGELIUM
HOC AD CHRISTUM
HIC AD CAELUM
VOCAT PBCCATORES."[24]

---

[23] Here, out of darkness Light shone. Therefore the Father, Son, and Holy Ghost [shall be] my God, and the name of this place Light.

[24] This [bell] calls sinners to the Gospel, it to Christ, He to Heaven.

Arch in Tower, Dunning.

His Lordship adds—"The bell, I believe, was in a vessel that was captured in the American War, and it was brought here by my predecessor, Andrew, fifth Lord Rollo.... It was broken in April, 1773, and I had it re-cast by Mears in 1860, with the original inscription replaced."

Of much interest, also, are the two bells still in the Tower of Dunning Church. The older and smaller bears the Dutch inscription:—"IC BEN GHEGOTEN INE

IAER ONS HEEREN MCCCCCXXVI."[25] But in addition to this, the bell shows a two-fold representation that seems to give it a value quite unique. What we have is—(1) a scallop-shell,[26] on which are three figures—a central-seated figure, and two smaller figures kneeling alongside. The central figure seems to hold something, which may be a book, in the left hand close to the breast. The right hand is extended, and seems to hold a staff and a garland. The figure has a *nimbus*, and a curious triangular head-dress. (2) On the side opposite the shell and figures is what appears to be a representation of the Virgin and Child, alongside of which is a figure of the Crucifixion.[27] This old bell is used to announce the half-hour as measured on the Steeple Clock,[28] as also to tell the living that the mortal remains of some brother or sister are about to be laid beneath the turf.

The large bell—used to announce the services of the church, and, through the kindness of Lady Rollo, to ring at "matins" and at "even-song"—is of very full tone. It was a gift to the church by a highly-respected heritor of the parish, and bears this inscription:—

"T. Mears of London fecit.

"This Bell was presented to the Parish Church of Dunning by Mark Howard Drummond, Esq. of Kelty, Major of the 72nd Regiment of Albany Highlanders, in token of his attachment to his native parish, and of his zeal to promote religious, industrious, and early habits among the parishioners.—August 3d, 1825."

Mention has already been made of the fact that the patron Saint of Dunning was S. SERF. The same Saint had churches dedicated to him at Monivaird (Monzievaird), at Creich, and at Dysart. But, inasmuch as he seems to have lived for some considerable time at Dunning, and also to have died there, perhaps this is the most fitting place for a page or two as to his history.

That he was a real historic personage does not admit of doubt; but the exact time at which he acted his part on the world's stage is involved in great obscurity. The legends of him are very conflicting, so much so, that it has been supposed by some that there were two S. Serfs. It is the legends, however, that are two-fold, and not the Saint. According to the Aberdeen Breviary, and writers who follow its guidance, S. Servanus, or S. Serf, or S. Serb, or (in Aberdeenshire) S. Sair, belonged to the 5th century, and was the disciple of S. Palladius; others putting him a little further on, and making him out to have been the instructor of S. Kentigern at Culross. But most people who carefully read the pages of Skene[29] will be satisfied that S. Servanus belongs to a later period still. It so happens that there is preserved

---

[25] I was born in the year of our Lord, 1526.

[26] In heraldry a scallop-shell is the badge of a pilgrim. It is the symbol of S. James the Greater, who is generally represented in pilgrim's garb. In this sense it is sometimes written *Escallop*.

[27] The writer is indebted to Dr Joseph Anderson for kindly examining two casts of these figures, carefully prepared by Mr James Henderson, F.S.A., Scot., Dunning.

[28] Erected by public subscription, and inaugurated 3rd November, 1890. (For architectural correctness, its four dials are omitted in Mr Ross's drawing of the Tower).

[29] See his *Celtic Scotland*, p. 31, ff.

in the Marsh M.S., Dublin, and printed in Skene's *Chronicles of the Picts and Scots* (p. 412, ff.), a Life of the Saint, which, notwithstanding some excessively wild and incredible-looking stories mixed up with it, is the only life of his that is consistent with itself and with otherwise-ascertained contemporary facts. This life makes the Saint contemporary with Adamnan, Abbot of Iona, who belonged to the 7th century, and with Brude, son of Dargart, King of the Picts. According to Skene,[30] this Brude, son of Dargart, may be identified with Brude, son of Derile, who reigned from 697 to 706, and preceded that Nectan, son of Derile, who expelled the Columban monks from his kingdom. And confirmatory proof of this identification being correct is furnished by Gray's *Scalacronica*, which has under this Brude that we have been referring to—"En quel temps veint Servanus en Fine."[31] Moreover, in the Chartulary of S. Andrews there is reference to an early charter of the Celtic period, by which "Brude, son of Dergard, gives the Isle of Lochlevine to the Omnipotent God, and to Saint Servanus, and to the Keledei hermits dwelling there, who are serving, and shall serve God in that island."

According, then, to the life in the Marsh Library M.S.—the life which, its many wild accounts notwithstanding, seems most free from anachronisms—the Saint is the son of Obeth, King of Canaan, and Alpia, daughter of the King of Arabia. His father dying, he gives up his right to the throne in favour of his twin brother Generatius, takes orders, and is appointed Bishop of the Cananeans. After twenty years as Bishop in that region, admonished by an angel, he comes to Jerusalem, where he is Patriarch for seven years. He then goes to Constantinople, and thence to Rome, where, for seven years, he reigns as Pope. Quitting Rome, and accompanied by a band of pilgrims, he makes his way into regions remote and crosses the Mare Icteum (Straits of Dover) dryshod, and, after travelling from place to place, arrives at the Forth. Adamnan, who, at the time, was an abbot in Scotland, receives him with great honours on the island of Inchkeith, and afterwards gave him, as his field of labour, Fife, and from the Mons Britannicus to the Mons Okhel (from the mount of the Britons to the Ochils.) He is next found at Kinel, then at Culenros, where he met King Brude and founded a church; then at an island, in Loch Leven, where he meets Adamnan and has the island presented to him. After constructing churches throughout the whole region of Fife, and labouring for years in the province assigned to him, and at many other places, he died at Dunning, and was buried at Culross. The deeds ascribed to S. Serf are certainly astounding, and the stories associated with him extraordinarily "wild"; still, as the scenes of not a few of them are laid at places in the Ochils district, and, accordingly, "Near the Pictish Capital," it may not be inappropriate if a few of them are rehearsed here.[32]

At Tuligbotuan (Tullybody) the Devil, having entered into a poor man, filled him with an insatiable appetite. He ate and ate, and still the wolf within craved for more. Though he consumed a cow and a calf, a sheep and a lamb, all was of no avail. At length, when the family were eaten "out of house and hall," his relatives

---

[30] See *Celtic Scotland*, p. 259.

[31] See *Chronicles of the Picts and Scots*, p. 201.

[32] In telling one or two of these stories, we have tried to combine with the Marsh M.S. version the somewhat fuller details of the Aberdeen Breviary.

take him to S. Serf, who clapped his thumb[33] into the man's mouth, which immediately satisfied him—the Devil flying out of him with a howl.

At Alveth (Alvah) Servanus and his company lodged, on one occasion, at the house of a very poor man, who had nothing to put before them but his one pig. It was forthwith cut up and eaten, the bones, however, being carefully preserved from being broken. Next morning, to the great delight and surprise of the poor man, the pig came grunting to the door, restored to flesh, and life by the Saint.

At Atheren (Airthrey) a robber, one night, broke into S. Serf's cell, and, finding a sheep roasted in his larder, comfortably sat down and entirely consumed it. Next day Servanus met the fellow and charged him with the robbery. The man swore innocence, but it was of no use; he was instantly convicted, for the wether bleated in his bowels.

At Dunning, S. Serf is said to have healed three blind, three lame, and three deaf men. But his great feat here was killing the dragon. (Had no princes or knights come to Forteviot as yet, that such work was left to the priest?) The story, as given in the Marsh M.S., is as follows:—"At that time the Saint was in his cell at Dunning (*in cella Dunenensi*), and news was brought to him that a dragon, great and terrible, and very loathsome (*deterrimus*), was coming into his township (*civitatem suam*), whose aspect no mortal could suffer. Saint Servanus, however, coming out to meet it, and taking his staff in his right hand, fought with the dragon in a certain valley, and killed it. From that day, moreover, that valley was called the Valley of the Dragon."[34]

The circumstances connected with the Saint's death and burial are touchingly described. The holy man, after many miracles, after divers works, after founding many churches in Christ, when his peace had been given to his brethren in his cell at Dunning, gave up and commended his spirit to the most High Creator on the first day of the Kalends of July. After his death his disciples and the people of nearly the whole province carried his body to Culenross (Culross), and there, with psalms and hymns (ymnis) and chantings (canticis), honourably buried him, where flourish his merits, and the virtues of his merits unto this day—to the glory and honour of the Omnipotent God, who in the Perfect Trinity liveth and reigneth through endless ages of ages.

Only the limits of space forbid allusion to additional features of considerable importance near the Pictish Capital, and connected with the parish of Dunning. Room, however, must be found for stating that, as is to be expected, Dunning, like other places in Strathearn, is not without interesting traces of the "Rising" of 1715. In the Session records, under date 18th September, 1715, there is the following entry:—"There was no sermon this day, and for several Sabbaths following, on account of the commotions that were in the county by reason of Mar's unnatural rebellion." When Mar quitted the field of Sheriffmuir, he, on the 12th November, 1715, withdrew his army into Angus, and in order to hinder the progress of the

[33] Baring Gould (*Lives of the Saints.* London, 1874), using probably a version of the legend reading *pulicem*, instead of *pollicem suum*, has *clapped a flea into the man's mouth*.

[34] The Dragon is the name still given to that part of the parish in which is situated the Village of Newtown of Pitcairns.

Royalist forces, he burned down all the villages on the line of march as far as Perth. The villagers of Dunning, actuated by the same feelings as led the citizens of London to erect the "Monument" after the great fire of 1666, planted a thorn tree to commemorate the destruction of their village. This ancient tree, standing in the square opposite the east approach to the manse, is well protected, and is likely to be spared to tell its memorable story to generations to come.

THE HISTORIC PRESBYTERY
OF AUCHTERARDER

BY REV. G. D. MACNAUGHTAN, B.D., ARDOCH,
CLERK OF PRESBYTERY

The district embraced within the bounds of the Presbytery of Auchterarder belonged for the most part to the ancient Diocese of Dunblane. Within it lay the famous Abbey of Inchaffray, and the minister of Muthill was usually Dean of Dunblane. As originally erected, the Presbytery was, indeed, the Presbytery of Dunblane, but in 1593 the General Assembly ordained the Presbytery of Dunblane "to be transportit to Auchterardour, with liberty to the brethren of Dunblane appealing to resort either to Auchterardour or Striviling as they please." When at last it got into shape it consisted of the following fifteen parishes, viz.:—Auchterarder, Blackford, Comrie, Crieff, Dunning, Fossoway, Foulis-Wester, Gask, Glendevon, Madderty, Monzie, Monzievaird, Muckhart, Muthill, and Trinity-Gask. Beginning on the shores of Loch Earn, it followed on both banks the river of that name for more than twenty miles, stretching upwards on either side to the surrounding hills. Northwards it reached even the banks of the Almond, while southwards it found its way into the uplands of Strathallan, and, breaking by the pass of Gleneagles into the Ochils, it went right through them to the level ground beyond, following the windings of the Devon. As a background, rose the mighty peaks of the Grampians; in the foreground lay the gentler, greener, rounded heights of the Ochil range. The seat of the Presbytery was Auchterarder, a long, straggling village, built along the crest of a rising ground; a mile or two distant from the south bank of the Earn, and at the same time not far from the top of Strathallan. Towards the close of the sixteenth century we have to think of the various parishes above named as being duly supplied with Protestant pastors, who met regularly in Auchterardour for the "weekly exercise," and to dispose of any church business that came before them. Most of these first members of the Presbytery seem to have been cadets of the leading families of the district, and, amongst them, Drummond, Graeme, Murray or Moray were common names. The Presbytery of Auchterarder first begins to take a prominent part in public affairs during the religious troubles of Charles I. The Jenny Geddes riot in St Giles has just taken place, and petitions are pouring in from all quarters against the ill-fated service-book. The Privy Council is at its wits' end as between a king resolved on innovations and a nation that will have none of them. It sends up to London specimens of the petitions received—one from the nobility, one from the gentry, one from the burghs, and a fourth from the clergy. The clerical petition thus honoured was that from the "Presbytrie of Auchtererdoch." The petition of this Presbytery was probably selected not on account of the zealous character of the opposition of its members, but on account of their known loyalty. The impression to be produced on the King's mind was that, if even Auchterarder opposed his designs, his projects were hopeless. The Covenant was sworn, but Auchterarder was not zealous for the Covenant. In the divisions of opinion, which led eventually to the rising of Montrose, Auchterarder sympathised with the minority. A Warning and Declaration with reference to these divisions was ordered by the General Assembly to be read from every pulpit, and "the brethren of Auchtererdoch" took it upon them to disobey. It was the first illustration of that independence of judgment for which they have more than once been famous. It was resolved to make an example of this disobedient Presbytery, and they were cited before the Assembly of 1643. "The Presbytery of Auchtererdoch was under the rod," writes Baillie, "to be made an example to all who would be turbulent." "After long examination of their business," he continues, "at last they were laureat. Some two or three of that Presbytery (when many of the gentry who were not elders were permitted to sit among them and reason against the Warning and Declaration, and when Ardoch presented reasons in write against these pieces, yet they were proven to have been forward for the present reading) were commended. Others who, notwithstanding of the Presbytery's conclusion of not reading, yet did read, were, for voicing the continuation, gently rebuked. Others who at last caused read parts of them, and Mr James Rowe, who caused read them before himself came in, were sharply rebuked, and their names delete from among the members of this Assembly. Ardoch, ane old reverend gentleman, for his former known zeal was spared, only, was urged upon oath to reveal the persons from whom he had the reasons contrary to the Warning." This is a curious picture of the internal condition of the Presbytery, and exhibits in strong relief the friendly relations existing betwixt its members and the gentry of the district. The James Rowe referred to was minister of Muthill, and was married to Margaret Stirling, a daughter of the laird of Ardoch, the "old reverend gentleman" above named.

When, after the Restoration, Episcopacy was re-established, Auchterarder once again formed part of the Diocese of Dunblane, and was for a time under the mild sway of the Episcopate of Leighton. The Episcopacy was almost nominal. There was no liturgy; the service continued to be much what it had been before, though Leighton encouraged the brethren to make their preaching "plain and useful for all capacities, not entangled with useless questions and disputes, nor continued to a wearisome length"; "to read larger portiones of the Scriptures"; "to restore the Lord's Prayer to more frequent use, likewyse the Doxologie and the Creed." The Presbytery continued to meet as usual, and virtually elected its own Moderator. The chief difference was that at the Synod the Bishop as of right occupied the chair. At this period we have another interesting glimpse of the internal condition of the Presbytery. It was complained to one Synod that "some young men, ministers within the Presbytrie of Ochterarder, had behaved themselves somewhat irreverendlie and undeutifullie towards some of the brethren who were older than themselves both for age and work of the ministrie. The Bishop having taken the samyne to consideration, desired the Moderator of the Presbytrie of Ochterarder, that at their first Presbyterial meeting, to admonish such brethren, that in time coming they should absteine from such unbeseeming misbehaviour, otherwyse to shew them that he would advert to it hereafter." The young lions of Auchterarder had evidently begun to roar, catching something of the independent spirit of their seniors.

In this district there was but little of the Covenanting feeling that was rampant in the West. An Abdiel, however, was found among the faithless in the person of William Spence, minister of Glendevon. In 1678 he laid a paper on the table of Presbytery in which he testified against the errors of the times. He was dealt with with great leniency and patience, but in the end he proved incorrigible. After long delay he was at last, in the beginning of 1681, deposed and excommunicated by the Bishop and Synod. From that time onwards he became a political agent, and was mixed up in the plots which filled the closing years of the reign of Charles II. In 1684 he was arrested and questioned. Though made to undergo the torture of the boot, he refused to disclose anything. He was then handed over to the tender mercies of General Dalziel, the "Muscovy beast who would roast men," and was kept from sleeping for eight or nine days till his enemies themselves were weary. He had to be thumbscrewed, and told that they would screw every joint of his body, one after another, before his courage began to fail. "Yet such was the firmness and fidelity of this poor man," writes Bishop Burnet, "that even in that extremity he capitulated, that no new questions should be put to him, but those already agreed on; and that he should not be obliged to be a witness against any person, and that he himself should be pardoned." After the Revolution he came back to Glendevon; in 1691 was translated to Fossoway, and, having outlived all his troubles, died there in peace in 1715 at the age of eighty. The policy, with which he had associated himself as a minority of one, had triumphed.

The Revolution fell upon the Presbytery of Auchterarder like the very crack of doom. All its members, with two exceptions, were ousted. These were the Rev. James Roy, minister of Trinity-Gask, and the Rev. Robert Sharp, M.A., minister of Muckhart. Unfortunately, at this interesting period the Presbytery records are a blank. The last minute before the Revolution is that of September 7, 1687; the next is that of November 9, 1703. When the curtain thus rises again at the beginning of the eighteenth century the *personnel* of the Presbytery has completely changed. Elsewhere the transformation seems to have been accomplished with little difficulty; but it was different in the Episcopal stronghold of Muthill. That parish, we find, has not yet submitted to the authority of the Presbytery, and is still vacant. It was not till August 3rd, 1704, that Mr William Haly was ordained as minister of Muthill. On the day of his ordination there was a riot, "several in the parish keeping the doors of the kirk and kirkyard with swords and staves"; and not until the following year (March 20, 1705) were the keys of the church of Muthill finally laid upon the table of the Presbytery. The new members of the Presbytery were very different from the old. They were now strongly Presbyterian in feeling, and ultra-evangelical in theology. In 1711, when threatened with the Queen Anne Act restoring Patronage, we find them instructing their commissioners to the Assembly "to take all care that Patronages be not again restored," and in the following year "to give a testimony against the encroachments made on this church by the tolleration and patronages." They were earnest in prayer on behalf of the Protestant Succession of the House of Hanover. On account of the Jacobite rising of 1715 there was no meeting of Presbytery from August 30, 1715, till February 9, 1716. At this meeting reference is made to "the Popish and Jacobite rebells who had infested the bounds, threatening ministers not to pray against them and their pretended king, by reason whereof ministers were forced to flee; and spoiling the goods of the people, and robbing and burning their houses and corns; and now that they were driven out of their bounds by the good providence of God accompanying the king's forces with success against them."

The Presbytery of Auchterarder had now to deal with a matter, small in itself, which, nevertheless, created considerable stir in the Church Courts, and ultimately led to secession. On December 11, 1716, Mr William Craig, student of divinity, appeared before them for license. The Presbytery being deeply impressed with "the errors of the times," examined him strictly as to his soundness of faith. Further consideration of the matter having been delayed for about a month, Mr Craig was again (January 15, 1717) before the Presbytery; was asked by them to sign the answers formerly given by him, and though he "seemed to scruple a little at something of the wording" of some of them, he finally did so, and was licensed. His signature still stands at that date in the Presbytery's copy of the Confession of Faith. The most famous statement signed by him was to the following effect:—"And further, I believe that it is not sound and orthodox to teach that we must forsake sin in order to our coming to Christ and instating us in covenant with God" —language capable of bearing an Antinomian meaning, and soon to be known as the "Auchterarder Creed." At next meeting of Presbytery (February 12, 1717) Mr Craig came back, representing that he was troubled with scruples anent the paper he had subscribed, that he had done so hastily, and that he now wished to explain his explanation. The Presbytery, after hearing him, resolved to declare his license null and void, and in the end he had to appeal to the Assembly. The Assembly of 1717 was somewhat startled at the theological language of Auchterarder, ordered the Presbytery to restore Mr Craig's license, declared the chief article of the new creed to be "unsound and most detestable," and asked them to explain its meaning to a meeting of the Commission. The Presbytery was of course able to show that their meaning was both pious and orthodox, and that they had been only a little over-zealous for the purity of the faith. In the old Auchterarder fashion, they had been thinking for themselves, instead of taking ready-made opinions from other people. One good result of the commotion was that Presbyteries were henceforth prohibited from putting queries of their own, preliminary to license, but "those and no other" which had received the authority of the Church. Yet it had other results which were evil. The discussion over the "Auchterarder Creed" led to the re-publication of the "Marrow of Modern Divinity," and the "Marrow Controversy" led directly to the secession of the Erskines. The *origo mali* was in Auchterarder.

The "Rising" of 1745 did not interfere so much with the business of the Presbytery as that of 1715 had done. During that eventful year it continued to hold its meetings as usual. The only reference is that on May 1, 1746, a fortnight after

Culloden, the Presbytery appoints that if His Royal Highness the Duke of Cumberland shall come this way in his return from the North, certain members should wait upon him to congratulate him upon the victory obtained by him over the rebels.

On December 14, 1756, the celebrated tragedy of *Douglas*, written by John Home, minister of Athelstaneford, in East Lothian, was acted in Edinburgh. This atrocious fact caused much searching of heart in all ultra-evangelical circles. The awful news reached Auchterarder. Meeting in Glendevon Church on May 12, 1757, for the ordination of Mr David M'Gibbon, the Presbytery came to the following resolution:—"The Presbytery, taking into their serious consideration the general fame that a minister of this Church has composed the tragedy of *Douglas*, and has been at great pains to get it represented on the stage both at London and at Edinburgh, to the scandal of very many; and the Presbytery further considering how hurtful stage plays are to the interest of religion, and to the morals of the people, and always were held to be so in every well-regulated government, heathen as well as Christian, therefore did and hereby do instruct their representatives in the ensuing General Assembly humbly to insist with the venerable Assembly that they would be pleased to make effectual enquiry, without loss of time, into the ground of the above flame; and if it shall be found to be indeed true that ministers of the Gospel, members of this Church, have done and behaved as above alledged, that the General Assembly would be pleased to enquire if such adequate censure has been inflicted on these brethren as their crime deserves; and if it has not, that the venerable Assembly would order it to be done, and that they would be further pleased to give some publick testimony of their abhorrence of such practices, that the world may see the just resentment of this Church against so uncommon and unprecedented a behaviour in some of her undutiful sons, and that they would do this in such a manner as shall appear to the venerable Assembly to be most effectual for preventing the like in any of their members of whatever degree in time coming." The zeal of Auchterarder was burning with a holy fire.

In the course of the eighteenth century the best known members of the Presbytery were the dynasty of Moncrieffs at Blackford, and Dr. John Kemp, of Trinity-Gask. Of the former, three generations succeeded each other from 1697 to 1775, in which year Sir Henry Moncrieff left Blackford to become minister of the West Kirk, Edinburgh. Of Dr. Kemp, who left Trinity-Gask in 1776, to become minister of New Greyfriars, Edinburgh, a full account will be found in Kay's *Edinburgh Portraits*. He was three times married, his second and third wives being Earls' daughters.

The century was now drawing to a close. Since the Reformation there had been no church extension within the bounds of the Presbytery. At last, however, there was to be an awakening from this long sleep. The district of Ardoch formed the southern portion of the parish of Muthill. In the centre of it lay the famous Roman Camp, one of the most ancient historic spots in Scotland, whose earthen trenches had been thrown up by the soldiers of Agricola. It was the traditional site of the Battle of Mons Grampius, where Galgacus and his Caledonians fought for liberty, and, after all that has been written on the subject, is as probably the real site as any other. There, in 1780, a chapel of ease was built, and opened for worship on March 25, 1781. The bounds of the chapel also included a small portion of the parish of Blackford, and a larger portion of that of Dunblane, the Presbytery thus extending its jurisdiction down the banks of the Allan to within a few miles of the cathedral city. The Chapel at Ardoch was the Presbytery's first-born child. In later years, in connection with the Church Extension movement, promoted by Dr. Chalmers, the West Church was built in Crieff in 1838, and the Chapel of Blairingone, in the parish of Fossoway, in 1840. Thus equipped, the Presbytery of Auchterarder was to meet the storm of 1843.

In the earlier years of the nineteenth century there were even to observant eyes no signs of the coming blast. The Act of Queen Anne, restoring Patronage, though long protested against, had been sullenly acquiesced in by the Church. Moderates and Evangelicals, though contending together in the several Church Courts, kept themselves carefully within the limits of the Church's constitution. But a new era was about to dawn. The struggle for political liberty which found expression in the great Reform Act of 1832, had its counterpart also in the ecclesiastical world. Patronage was again felt to be an intolerable burden, and the rights of the Christian people to require vindication. In these changed circumstances it became a difficult and delicate matter to "redd the marches" between the Church and State. With level-headed common-sense upon both sides it might have been done. Unfortunately, in the struggle our most prominent national characteristics, instead of being combined, got opposed to one another. The proverbial "canniness" of the Scottish nation was all upon the one side; the equally proverbial *perfervidum ingenium* was all upon the other. Led by the latter feeling, the Church resolved to fall back on her own inherent rights and to get quit of Patronage by a side wind. In 1834 she passed the Veto Act, giving power to "the major part of the male heads of families, members of the vacant congregation," in any parish to get quit of an unpopular presentee. The Presbytery of Auchterarder was doomed to be the cockpit in which this great fight was to be fought out. In the autumn of 1834 the Rev. Robert Young was presented to the parish of Auchterarder by the Earl of Kinnoull. At the moderation of his call on 2nd December the Rev. John Clark, Blackford, preached from Mark xii., 10-11, a text somewhat interesting in the light of what afterwards took place—"And have ye not read this scripture: The stone which the builders rejected is become the head of the corner: This was the Lord's doing, and is marvellous in our eyes?" Mr Young's call was signed by three persons, for the Earl of Kinnoull as Patron, and by two members of the congregation. He was vetoed by 287 male heads of families, and the Presbytery had no option under the Act but to reject the call. This decision was confirmed on appeal to the Assembly, and Mr Young and the Earl of Kinnoull had to seek redress in the Civil Courts. The "Auchterarder Case" now attracted the attention of the whole country. It raised the question of the legality of the Veto Act. In November, 1837, it was heard before the whole Court of Session, and the Judges by a majority found that, Mr Young having been duly presented, the Presbytery was bound to take him upon trials. An appeal was ultimately taken to the House of Lords, and by it, in 1839, the decision of the Court of Session was re-affirmed. By the highest legal authority the Veto Act was found to be worthless. But the Church had gone too far to retrace her steps, and she now raised the banner of Spiritual Independence. Other questions had come to the front which heightened and intensified the feeling that prevailed. By the equally illegal Chapel Act, also passed in 1834, chapel districts were formed into parishes *quoad sacra*, and their ministers found entitled to seats in the Church Courts. The minister of Ardoch Chapel at once took his seat in the Presbytery, and was followed in due time by the ministers of the West Church, Crieff, and the Chapel at Blairingone. The Church had been led into an *impasse* from which there was no outlet but by secession. The secession came. In defence of their somewhat mysterious principles no fewer than 451 ministers, on the 18th day of May, 1843, left the Church. All the world wondered. It was said that in no country other than Scotland could such a spectacle have been seen. Yet one cannot help looking back with sorrow upon the blundering that made it possible. Like the Charge of the Light Brigade at Balaclava, it was "magnificent, but not war."

With the addition of the chapel ministers the membership of Auchterarder Presbytery had risen to eighteen. The parish of Auchterarder was still vacant. Of the remaining seventeen, eight were found to have seceded. Of these, five were legal members of Presbytery—viz., James Carment, Comrie; Peter Brydie, Fossoway; John Reid Omond, Monzie; John Ferguson, Monzievaird; and James Thomson, Muckhart. The three others were the chapel ministers—Samuel Grant, Ardoch; Finlay Macalister, West Church, Crieff; and Andrew Noble, Blairingone. The case of Mr Brydie, of Fossoway, was somewhat peculiar. On October 13, 1843, he petitioned the Presbytery asking it to annul its judgment with regard to him, and submitted a medical certificate to the effect that at the time of his secession he was "in a state of lunacy." The Presbytery, having consulted the Synod, reponed him, on the ground that at the time he separated himself from the Church he had been in a state of unsound mind.

The Presbytery now once more consisted of fifteen parishes and three chapels. The vacancies in the parishes were easily supplied. It was different with the chapels. A new minister was, indeed, ordained at Ardoch in December, 1844, but it was 1848 before the West Church, Crieff, and the Chapel of Blairingone were once more re-opened for worship in connection with the Church of Scotland. The decks had been cleared after the storm, the rigging re-fitted, and the sails spread once more to catch the favouring breeze. In a few years the Presbytery's organisation had become more efficient than ever. In 1854 certain portions of the parishes of Monzie and Foulis were disjoined from the Presbytery to form a part of the new parish of Logiealmond. In 1855, Ardoch was erected into a parish *quoad omnia*. In 1864, the West Church, Crieff, became a parish *quoad sacra*. The Chapel of Blairingone was also by and by to become a parish; yet, when it did so, it no longer formed a part of the Presbytery of Auchterarder. In 1856 the General Assembly determined to create a new Presbytery of Kinross, and for this purpose to disjoin the two parishes of Muckhart and Fossoway (the latter including Blairingone) from the Presbytery with which they had been associated for two hundred and fifty years. Auchterarder refused her consent, and protested, but in vain. She was bereaved of her children.

This change somewhat altered the centre of gravity of the Presbytery. Hitherto Auchterarder had been its natural centre, and its most convenient place of meeting. From this time onwards it began occasionally to meet at Crieff. In 1866 an Act of Assembly was passed ordaining it to meet alternately in Auchterarder and Crieff.

After the Secession of 1843 a subtle change began to creep over the opinions of the Presbytery. It was no longer the ultra-evangelical body which it had been for more than a century. It began to take broader views of culture and of human life. Were another minister of the Church of Scotland now to write a new tragedy of *Douglas* he would be likely to receive its congratulations rather than its denunciations. Its theology became sweeter, and it is in no danger of framing a new "Auchterarder Creed" upon the lines of the last. When the new movement began for the improvement of public worship there was, indeed, enough of the old leaven left to lead to a vigorous resistance. This struggle centred round "The Crieff Organ Case" in 1866-67. Ultimately, however, the new views prevailed, and at the present moment (1896) the once hated "kist of whistles" has found its way into no fewer than thirteen out of the sixteen parishes which at present compose the Presbytery. Since the days of that conflict, indeed, its spirit has broadened and broadened. The old independent tone, for which it had been conspicuous even in the seventeenth century, has become more and more marked. In recent years the Presbytery has never been willing tamely to follow the lead of Assembly leaders and Assembly Committees, but has insisted on expressing a vigorous opinion of its own upon all the questions of the day.

In the course of the present century several ministers, afterwards to become better known, have begun their respective careers within the bounds of the Presbytery. Dr. William Robertson, latterly minister of New Greyfriars, Edinburgh, was ordained as minister of Muckhart in 1831. Dr. Robert Home Stevenson, minister of St. George's, Edinburgh, Moderator of the General Assembly of 1871, was ordained in 1840 as assistant and successor in the parish of Crieff. Dr. John Cunningham, minister of Crieff from 1845 to 1887, was Moderator of the General Assembly of 1886, and was latterly Principal of St. Mary's College, St. Andrews. His successor in the Moderatorship of Assembly, Dr. George Hutchison, Banchory-Ternan, was ordained as minister of Monzie in 1845. Dr. Paton J. Gloag, then of Galashiels, Moderator of the Assembly of 1889, was ordained in 1848 as assistant and successor in the parish of Dunning. Dr. John Wilson, a genial man, much beloved by all his brethren, was minister of Dunning from 1861 to 1878, Clerk of Presbytery from 1864, and author of "Index to the Acts of Assembly." Dr. William Mair, minister of Ardoch from 1865 to 1868, is now of Earlston, and author of the well-known "Digest of Church Laws."

The loss of Muckhart and Fossoway, the addition of Ardoch and Crieff West left the Presbytery still with its original number of fifteen parishes. There was yet another to be added. In the extreme west of the parish of Comrie, at the point where the River Earn leaves its parent lake, was the district of Dundurn. Next to Ardoch, it was probably the oldest historic spot within the Presbytery. There, first of all places within the bounds, had the Gospel in the course of the sixth century been preached by the saintly Fillan. It was still haunted by sacred memories. It had been the site of a pre-Reformation chapel. It had long been a preaching-place for the minister of Comrie. Latterly there had sprung up by the shores of the beautiful lake a hamlet which called itself St. Fillans. It became a favourite place of summer resort. In 1879 a new chapel was built, and in 1895 the district of Dundurn was erected into a parish *quoad sacra*.

At the present moment (1896) the Presbytery thus consists of sixteen parishes, all fully equipped; 94 elders and 5023 church members form its effective strength as a part of the Church militant. It has faced many a serious crisis in the past; with a calm cheerfulness it faces the future.

MEMORIES OF GASK
BY REV. JAMES MARTIN, GASK

The parish of Gask is a comparatively small one both in population and in territorial extent. The earliest historical record we have of it goes back to the time of the invasion of Britain by the Romans. The road which passes along the ridge of high ground was originally made by the Romans, and was designed to form a line of communication between the camp at Ardoch and the camp at Bertha, near the junction of the Almond with the Tay. On the north side of it, in this parish, there are still to be distinctly seen two small camps or stations, and on the south side of it there is a larger one. The Romans have left traces of their presence here in the works they constructed, which the lapse of eighteen centuries has not entirely obliterated.

Coming down the stream of time, we find that Wallace, that noble and disinterested patriot, sought a hiding-place in time of danger amid its dense woods. During a visit to Perth in 1296, a plot was laid by the English to capture him, but, having received timely warning, he made his escape with his small band of followers to Gascon Ha'. This is generally supposed to have occupied a different site from the ruin near the River Earn which now bears that name, and which is celebrated by Lady Nairne in the song of "Bonnie Gascon Ha'." The Gascon Ha' to which Wallace repaired for safety from his treacherous and relentless enemies is said to have stood a mile and a half to the north-east of that ruin in the midst of the Gask woods. Here they prepared to pass the night, and having obtained two sheep from a neighbouring fold, they kindled a fire and made ready their evening repast. Greatly exhausted with their long and fatiguing march, Wallace proposed that his followers should rest while he would keep watch. During the course of the night he was startled by the "blowing of horns mingled with frightful yells, proceeding apparently from a rising ground in the immediate neighbourhood." Scouts were sent out from time to time, but all failing to return, the patriot was at last left alone. He wandered about till morning, killing two of the English whom he encountered, one of whom was Sir John Butler, and then hastened with all speed to Torwood, near Dunipace, where his uncle was parish priest.

At an early period the lands now comprehended in this parish belonged to the Earl of Strathearn, the great landowner in this district at that time. It is said that he possessed all the lands lying between the Cross of Macduff, near Newburgh, and the west end of Balquhidder in length, and between the Ochils and the Grampians in breadth. It was out of his lands of Nether Gask that he granted liberty to quarry stones for building the Abbey of Inchaffray, along with two acres of ground on which to erect workshops.

The Auld House of Gask.

The lands of Gask have now been in the possession of the Oliphant family for nearly six hundred years. The name was originally written Olifard, then Olyfaunt, and now Oliphant. Sir William Olyfaunt was the first of that name on whom these lands were bestowed by King Robert the Bruce. Sir William occupied a prominent position in the early history of our country. He was Governor of Stirling Castle, and when summoned in the name of Edward I. to surrender it, made the noble reply, "I have never sworn fealty to Edward, but I have sworn to keep the Castle, and must wait the order of my constituent." And when the Castle was besieged by Edward and his army he defended it for three months, and only capitulated from the scarcity of provisions. He was a member of the Parliament held at Aberbrothock in 1320, and subscribed along with some other Scottish Barons the famous letter to the Pope, which so nobly asserted the independence of Scotland. To that document were affixed the seals of Sir William Olyfaunt and Malise, Earl of Strathearn. He died in 1329, and was buried in the Church of Aberdalgie, where a monument of black marble was erected to his memory. When the present Church of Aberdalgie was built in 1773 the site was changed, and the monument to Sir William Olyfaunt was left in the open churchyard. In 1780, Mr Oliphant of Gask erected a stone covering over it to protect it from injury by the weather.

Sir William was succeeded by his son, Walter Olyfaunt, who married a daughter of King Robert the Bruce, and, "having resigned the lands of Gask into the hands of his brother-in-law, David II., obtained, in 1364, a new charter confirming them to the said Walter and his spouse Elizabeth, our beloved sister, on a peculiar tenure for the reddendum of a chaplet of white roses at the feast of the nativity of St. John the Baptist at the manor place of Gask." This incident has been happily expressed in a poem by Miss Ethel Blair Oliphant, now Mrs Maxtone Graham, who inherits much of the poetic genius of her great-grand-aunt, Lady Nairne.

THE TRIBUTE OF GASK

Now ken ye the gift Gask has brought to the King?
'Tis an off'ring sae royal, sae perfect, and fair,
Than jewels o' siller more dainty and rare,
A crown for a maid or a monarch to wear.
The courtier's tribute is but a poor thing,
For what can he offer and what can he bring,
Than the crown of White Roses from Gask to the King?

Now ken ye the service Gask does for the King?
All for his sake, in the bloom of the year,
In the gardens of Gask the white blossoms appear—
The Royal White Roses to Scotland sae dear.
Then far o'er Stralhearn let the praise of them ring,
Let them live once again in the song that we sing,
The crown of White Roses from Gask to the King.

Now ken ye what Gask will yet do for the King?
In the days that may come, when the roses are dead,
When the pledge is forgotten, the vows left unsaid;
What then shall lie found for an off'ring instead?
Oh! then at his feet his heart he will fling.
Truth, Honour, Devotion, as tribute will bring
For the crown of White Roses from Gask to the King!

This charter, which has always been highly prized by the Gask family, had a rather singular history during the last century. In 1746 the Duke of Cumberland sent out Sir Joseph York from Perth to search the House of Gask, when he took away a box containing the charter, and it was not till forty years after that it was traced to its hiding-place, restored to its rightful owners, and safely deposited in the Gask charter chest. The Oliphants obtained large estates in different parts of Scotland, and were raised to the Peerage by James II., in 1450, by the title of Lord Oliphant. The fifth Lord, styled in the Gask papers "ane base and unworthy man," squandered away the large estates he inherited not only in Perthshire, but also in Forfarshire, Kincardine, Caithness, and Haddington. One of the younger branches of the Oliphant family purchased from his spendthrift cousin the lands of Gask, which have ever since continued in the same family.

Laurence Oliphant was, in the year 1650, knighted by Charles II., when that monarch was at Scone. He for a capricious reason disinherited his eldest son, Patrick, and gave the lands of Gask to his second son and his heirs. About fifty years thereafter the estate of Gask, from the failure of heirs in the younger branch, came into the possession of James, the eldest son of the disinherited Patrick.

While James Oliphant resided at Williamston, before he succeeded to Gask, he devised and carried out a great practical improvement in that locality. He along with some others applied to the Scotch Parliament in 1690 for an Act to compel all the adjoining proprietors to contribute their share towards the expense of cutting a channel sufficiently deep and broad to carry off the water, which at that time must have frequently flooded the fields, and thus reclaimed much valuable land. About forty years ago a considerable sum was expended in still further deepening and broadening the Pow, and that stream never overflows its banks now unless in very rainy seasons. As the estate of Gask is bounded by the Pow on the north side, it shared in the benefits resulting from that improvement. Mr Oliphant succeeded to Gask in 1705, and would doubtless display the same practical sagacity in carrying out improvements on the estate which then came into his possession. He probably planted some of those noble trees which still surround the mansion-house, and which are undoubtedly of great age.

At the Revolution in 1688, when James II. was driven from the throne of Britain, the Oliphants still retained their steadfast allegiance and devoted loyalty to the exiled monarch, and regarded his successors as usurpers. Cherishing these sentiments, we can well imagine they would hail every enterprise that had for its object the restoration of their hereditary king. An opportunity soon occurred. In 1715, a "Rising" took place to accomplish this end. The laird of Gask, though strongly favouring the movement, yet with great prudence remained at home, and saved his estate from forfeiture. But he sent his two elder sons to join the standard which the Earl of Mar had reared for the restoration of the Chevalier St. George, the only son of James II. They both took part in the battle which was fought at Sheriffmuir, on the 13th November, between the Jacobite forces, led by the Earl of Mar, and the Government forces under the command of the Duke of Argyle. It was an indecisive battle, both sides claiming the victory. The Jacobites, retreating through Strathearn, burned many of the villages, inflicting great hardships on the peaceful inhabitants by rendering them houseless during the rigour of winter. The attempt to restore the Chevalier St. George soon collapsed, but it does not seem to have been followed by the thrilling scenes, the hairbreadth escapes, and the rigorous treatment which marked the close of the subsequent rebellion.

James Oliphant died in 1732, and was succeeded by his eldest son Laurence, who is styled the "Jacobite Laird, *par excellence.*" He had been in hiding for some time after the "Rising" of 1715. He, however, soon returned home, freed from all Suspicion of disloyalty. He married, in 1719, a daughter of the second Lord Nairne, "who was as staunch a Jacobite as himself." At Gask House there is a wooden cup, with a silver rim near the top and another near the bottom. The upper one has the inscription—"*Spumantem calicem paternum in regis legitimi hoeredetarii salutem redditumque felicem loete haurimus*"; and a free translation of this inscription is on the lower one—"Our grandsires' flowing cup we drink, and sing God save; restore our true-born lawful King. Amen. L.O.G. June 10th, 1740." This discloses the strong Jacobite tendency which he cherished, and the ardent longing which he felt for the happy return of his hereditary King. He had not long to wait till another opportunity occurred of making a second attempt to accomplish the object so dear to him. In 1745, Prince Charles landed in the Western Isles, when the Highland Clans rallied to his standard with many others favourable to his cause. The laird and his son—both Laurence—joined Prince Charles at Perth, and incurred the risk of loss of life and property. Gask was greatly annoyed that he could not induce his tenants to enlist in the cause of the Prince, and he had recourse to a very extreme measure to enforce compliance with his wishes. In connection with this we have a very interesting statement in "The Jacobite Lairds of Gask," being a quotation from Dr. Chambers' *History of the Rebellion.* Perhaps no one experienced so much difficulty in his levies as the good laird of Gask, though he was at the same time, perhaps, the person of all others the most anxious to provide men for the service of his beloved Prince. This enthusiastic Jacobite was, it seems, so extremely incensed at the resistance he received from some of his tenants that he actually laid an arrestment or inhibition upon their corn-fields, in order to see if their interest would not oblige them to comply with his request. The case was still at issue when Charles, in marching from Perth, observed the corn hanging dead ripe, and eagerly inquired the reason. He was informed that Gask had not only prohibited his tenants from cutting their grain, but would not permit their cattle to be fed upon it, so that these creatures were absolutely starving. Shocked at what he heard, he leaped from the saddle, exclaiming, "This will never do," and began to gather a quantity of the corn. Giving this to his horse, he said to those that were by that he had thus broken Gask's inhibition, and the farmers might now, upon his authority, proceed to put the produce of their fields to its proper use. It was on this occasion that the laird of Gask had the high honour of receiving and entertaining the Prince at his house. The table on which he breakfasted is still in the House of Gask, and in good preservation. It bears the inscription—"Charles, Prince of Wales, breakfasted at this table in the low drawing-room at Gask on the 11th September, 1745." The chair on which he then sat was not allowed to be occupied by any other for many years thereafter. There are still at Gask House several interesting relics of Prince Charles, which are carefully preserved—viz., his bonnet, the Royal brogues, crucifix, and ribbon of the Garter, his spurs, and a lock of his hair, &c. The high honour conferred on the Gask family by this visit from their Prince would tend to inspire them with greater zeal and ardour in advancing his cause. They continued faithful and devoted followers of the Prince in the romantic attempt he made to regain the throne of his ancestors, and they took part in many of the battles that were fought to secure that object. They were both present on the field of Culloden and fought with great bravery on the fatal day that proved so disastrous to the Prince's cause, and which must have all but extinguished the most sanguine hopes of the keenest Jacobite. After the Battle of Culloden the Oliphants endured great hardships for six months while hiding among the hills of Buchan, and had many narrow escapes, until at last they landed in Sweden on the 10th November, 1746.

But while they were involved in many troubles in those trying times, there arose one from an unexpected quarter, which caused them great annoyance. In 1740, Mr Oliphant, as almost sole heritor, intruded the Rev. John M'Leish into the parish, in opposition to the wishes of a large majority of the people. But he lived deeply to regret the step he then took, for, on the outbreak of the Rebellion in 1745, the minister became one of his most bitter enemies. Some of the colours taken at the Battle of Prestonpans "fell to Mr Oliphant, which he sent to his own house at Gask." Mr M'Leish, knowing this, searched for them to deliver them to the Duke of Cumberland, but Emily Dewar, a faithful servant at the house, hid them in the pump, so that the minister could not find them. He told the tenants not to pay their rents to a rebel landlord. When the Duke of Cumberland, at the request of Lady Gask, sent out a guard from Perth to protect that lady in those troublous times, the minister, on hearing this, was highly indignant, and said—"What right had they to protect a rebel lady?" He also said that he would go to Perth next day and speak to the Duke of Cumberland about this. He said and did so many things calculated to annoy and irritate the Gask family, that years after, when hiding on the Continent, Mr Oliphant wrote saying—"That ingrate man's actings have tried my patience more than all that has happened to me." The conduct of the minister to the laird during this trying period was surely most harsh and unkind, even though he entertained different political views. Mr M'Leish would probably regard, as a national calamity, the restoration of the Stuarts, knowing well the arbitrary and unconstitutional way they often acted when in power. He might also fear that there would be great danger to the Protestant cause were a Roman Catholic to occupy the throne of Britain. But while we sympathise with these sentiments, and think that Mr M'Leish was quite entitled to hold them, it was surely ungrateful and unkind to act in the way he often did, not only to Mr Oliphant, but also to his lady. The Oliphants were thoroughly conscientious in holding their principles, and they gave the strongest proof of this in risking their life and the loss of all their worldly substance in maintaining them. At the same time, we are of opinion that theirs was a mistaken loyalty, and it was well that they did not succeed in accomplishing their object. Had they done so, it is probable that the civil and religious history of our country would have been different, and Britain might not have attained to the high position she now occupies among the nations. But, while holding this opinion, we cannot fail to admire the inflexible steadfastness with which they adhered to their principles, and the noble sacrifices they made in support of them. It is supposed that, as Lady Nairne would often hear from her father of the doings of Mr M'Leish, she has a hit at him in one of her songs—

"M'Leish's ae daughter o' Claverse-ha' Lee,"

In his latter days, Mr M'Leish was in a very infirm state, and unable to discharge his ministerial duties. During the two last years of his life there was only public worship in Gask Church once a month. The days on which divine service was held, and the names of the ministers who officiated, are still to be seen in our Session records. During his long illness it is interesting to read of the tender sympathy which Mr Oliphant expressed for him, and the Christian spirit of forgiveness which he manifested towards him. He wrote from the Continent:—"I'm sorry to hear that Mr M'Leish has been so much distressed in his health. It will perhaps be agreeable to him, and let him know that I do heartyly forgive him all the injurys he has done me undeservidly.... I shall mention no other particulars of the way he has treated me, but as I have sincerly forgiven, I pray our commune Father to forgive him, which I hope he will be earnest to obtain." There is no record that Mr M'Leish ever felt or expressed regret at the unkind way in which he had treated his benefactor.

The Oliphants, after making their escape from this country to the Continent in 1746, continued to reside in different places there for seventeen years. And during that long period they sent home to their friends in this country a great many letters giving a detailed account of their movements, and of their meeting with other exiles suffering with them in the same cause and for maintaining the same principles of loyalty. And these papers and letters, preserved in the Gask charter-room, have been turned to excellent account by the present Mr Oliphant in the very interesting volume he compiled entitled *The Jacobite Lairds of Gask*.

As both father and son took part in the Rebellion, the estate of Gask was forfeited. But it was re-purchased from the Government in 1753 by Mr Oliphant of Condie, who was understood to be acting for the Gask family, at the sum of £17,800. The estate was, however, larger then than it is now, including both Cowgask and Williamston. The two latter were afterwards sold to pay part of the purchase money for Gask. It was at one time proposed to sell the Ross and Newmiln, but Mr Oliphant objected to this, as he considered these two farms the most improvable part of the estate. We are told in *The Jacobite Lairds of Gask* that few lost more than the Oliphants by the "Rising" of 1745. If we reckon the seven years in which the estate was withheld from them, and the large sum for which it was bought back from Government, these losses would come to about £60,000 of our money.

The Oliphants returned to Gask after an absence of seventeen years, in November, 1763. As Mr M'Leish died on the 24th March of the same year, the laird and the minister never met again.

After all the dangers to which they had been exposed on the field of battle, and all the hardships they had to encounter during the long period they were in hiding on the Continent, they were at last permitted to return in safety to their native land, to spend the evening of their days in their "Ain dear wee Auld House."

The elder Jacobite laird died in 1767, and was gathered to his fathers in the old Kirk of Gask. He was succeeded by his only son, the younger Jacobite laird. He continued to adhere with the most unshaken steadfastness to the cause of the Prince, for whom he had done and suffered so much, and brought up his family in the strictest principles of loyalty to the King over the water. When his family read the newspapers to him after his eyesight became impaired, if the names King or Queen occurred, they must only indicate this by employing the initials K. or Q., otherwise he sharply reproved them.

When Prince Charles died in 1788, leaving an only brother, Cardinal York, many of the Jacobites transferred their allegiance to George III., and most of the Scotch Episcopalian clergy began to pray for the reigning family, which they had not hitherto done. Among these was Mr Cruickshanks, Episcopal minister at Mut-hill, who occasionally officiated at Gask. When Mr Oliphant heard this, he at once wrote to Mr Cruickshanks that, as he had now disqualified himself for officiating at Gask, his services would be henceforth dispensed with. He sent to him his of-ficial robes, and returned some books, the reading of which he had got from Mr Cruickshanks. It is said that George III., hearing of Gask's unswerving constancy, sent, by the member of Parliament for Perthshire, his compliments—not the com-pliments of the King of England, but of the Elector of Hanover—to Mr Oliphant. He died in 1792, and was succeeded by his eldest son Laurence, the third of that name in succession. It was this laird who pulled down the "Auld House" in 1800, except a part of the front wall, which was allowed to stand, as an interesting ruin, and around which now centre so many tender and hallowed associations. He also built the present large and substantial mansion-house, which occupies a com-manding situation a few yards from the "Auld House." With the concurrence of the Presbytery, he removed the Parish Church and manse from the site on which they had stood for several centuries to another about a mile to the north. This must have been in many respects a very desirable change, both for the laird and the minister. There were only a few yards formerly between the mansion-house and the manse, and this proximity must have at times been rather uncomfortable for both. A more eligible site, however, could easily have been got on which to build the new church and manse, but it possesses the great advantage of being central for the whole parish.

About the period at which we have now arrived in our narrative there was emerging into fame a member of the Oliphant family, who was destined to throw as bright a lustre around that name as any who had ever borne it—who is styled "the brightest jewel in the Oliphant crown." I refer to Carolina Oliphant, who was the third daughter of the younger Jacobite laird, and who was named after the King over the water. She was born in the "Auld House"—which she afterwards celebrated in song—in the year 1766. She gave early indication of superior poetic genius and high musical accomplishments. Her great aim was to purify the na-tional songs, and to render them more suitable for the use of the people. And she was led to attempt this from an incident related in her memoirs. "Driving, during the annual fair, through a small hamlet in the neighbourhood, she remarked many persons holding in their hands a small book with a yellow cover. Desirous of as-certaining what a publication so popular might contain, she despatched her footman to purchase a copy. It proved to be a collection of songs and ballads, many of which were ill suited for the hands of youth." But she also composed a large number of original songs of great excellence, two of which are of exquisite beauty and tenderness—"The Land o' the Leal" and "The Auld House." In early life Miss C. Oliphant had an intimate friend and companion in Miss Erskine, daughter of the Episcopal minister at Muthill. Miss Erskine was afterwards married to Campbell Colquhoun of Killermont. Their first child died when scarcely a year old. This led Carolina Oliphant to write "The Land o' the Leal," which she sent with a letter of condolence to Mrs Colquhoun in her sad bereavement. But the strictest secrecy was enjoined as to the writer of it, and for many years thereafter only a very few knew that this beautiful and touching song was written by Carolina Oliphant. At one time it was supposed to have been written by Burns on his death-bed, and the first line then was—"I'm wearin' awa', Jean"; but it never appeared in any collection of his poems. The songs of Lady Nairne have now become so well known and so highly appreciated, that it is scarcely necessary to refer to them at fuller detail here. She was married to Major Nairne in 1806 in an upper room of Gask House. As Major Nairne then held an official appointment in Edinburgh, they took up their abode in that city, in a cottage built for them by the old Chief of Strowan, called Carolina Cottage. She there employed her pen in composing songs for the *Scotish Minstrel*, while she enjoyed the intellectual society into which she had been introduced, and in which she was so well fitted to shine. One of her songs, "The Attainted Scottish Nobles," had a great influence in restoring them to their former titles. When George IV. visited Edinburgh in 1822, Major Nairne and other attainted Scottish Peers were introduced to the King at Holyrood. And when it came to the knowledge of the King that Mrs Nairne had written that song it made him favourable to the introduction of a measure which passed through both Houses of Parliament, and received the Royal sanction in June, 1824, for the reversal of the attainders. Major Nairne was then restored to his rank in the Peerage as Lord Nairne, and Mrs Nairne became Baroness Nairne, by which she has ever since been known.

Lord Nairne died in 1830, and was succeeded in the title by his only son, William, sixth Lord. Lady Nairne felt deeply her bereavement, but was sustained under it by the comforts and consolations of religion. She henceforth devoted all her efforts to the mental culture and moral and religious training of her only child. She removed to different parts of the country for the benefit of his health. But with all her maternal care he sickened and died at Brussels in 1837. By the death of her son the ties which bound her to the world were in a great measure severed, and her thoughts and affections were raised to that higher and holier state on which those who were nearest and dearest to her had now entered. She returned to Gask in 1845, and spent the last two years of her life within a few yards of the spot where she was born. She had received early religious impressions when on a visit to Murthly Castle, and these were greatly deepened by the successive trials and bereavements wherewith she was visited. She still continued to take a great delight in doing good and in contributing to advance the cause of religion in the world. Having a sum of money at her disposal, she consulted Dr. Chalmers as to the most useful and charitable purposes to which it might be applied. And it was at this time that she contributed £300 to Dr. Chalmers' West Port Mission, on the condition that he should never reveal the name of the donor. She was as careful to conceal her good deeds as she had been to conceal the authorship of the beautiful songs she composed. She gradually became weaker and weaker, but as the "outward man decayed the inward man was renewed day by day." In her song of the "Auld House" she beautifully describes how, at the evening of the day,

> "The setting sun, the setting sun,
> How glorious it gae'd doon."

So in the evening of the day of her life her sun went gloriously down to rise and shine in a fairer land—"The Land o' the Leal." She was buried in Gask Chapel, which is erected on the site of the old Parish Church, and to the building of which she contributed. A few years ago a granite cross of beautiful design and workmanship was erected to her memory by Mr Oliphant in the grounds of Gask. It bears the appropriate inscription:—

CARMINA MORTE CARENT
CAROLINA OLIPHANT
BARONESS NAIRNE
BORN AT GASK, 1766
DIED AT GASK, 1845

If superior poetical genius, great moral worth, and high Christian character deserve to be held in remembrance, there are few more entitled to this honour than Lady Nairne. Nor could a more appropriate spot have been chosen by Mr Oliphant on which to rear this tribute of affectionate regard to the memory of his grand-aunt than in the midst of that beautiful scenery which she loved so well, and which she has immortalised in her songs. Lady Nairne, however, has reared for herself a monument far more durable than that of brass or granite, in her beautiful songs, which, as the inscription truly says, will never die.

I must here make a brief reference to a native of this parish, who, although born and brought up in humble life, yet attained to great eminence in his profession. I refer to Laurence Macdonald, who for some time wrought as a common mason, but who showed a strong genius for sculpture. The first piece of work of that kind that he did was the family coat-of-arms of Garvock House. Mrs Oliphant discerning his rising genius in this direction, took him to the Continent when the Gask family removed there in 1822, to afford him better opportunity for the cultivation of this art. He ultimately settled in Rome, and became one of the first British sculptors in that city. He was there known as Lorenzo de Gasco, from his native parish. In recognition of the kindness he had received from the Gask family, he afterwards sent as a gift to the laird one of his best works, which now occupies a prominent position in the House of Gask.

James Blair Oliphant died in 1847, and was buried in the Gask Chapel. "He was the eighteenth in unbroken male succession from the William Oliphant upon whom Robert Bruce bestowed the lands of Gask." After his death the estate was under trustees for nearly twenty years. And during this period a litigation was carried on as to the right of succession. Mr Oliphant of Condie was confident that he could establish his claim to be the nearest male heir. But there was a link wanting in the chain of evidence, and he failed to realise his sanguine expectations. The estate then came into the possession of the late laird's sister's family, when the eldest son, Mr Kington Oliphant, succeeded to it nearly thirty years ago.

We have briefly traced the history of the Oliphants during the long period they have been in possession of Gask estate, and while many of them have been distinguished in different walks of life, none of them ever occupied the high position which the present Mr Oliphant does for literary attainments and scholarly accomplishments. He has unfolded the history of his family with all that fulness of information by which he is characterised in *The Oliphants in Scotland* and The *Jacobite Lairds of Gask*. And I must express my great indebtedness to Mr Oliphant for the information I have derived from these volumes in writing this article. But I am persuaded that Mr Oliphant's literary fame will rest more on another work he produced some years ago, entitled *The Old and Middle English*, in one volume, and *The New English*, in two volumes, than on the other two, interesting as they are. In these volumes Mr Oliphant has traced the development of the English language during the last 600 years. The most competent scholars and critics have spoken of these volumes in the highest terms of commendation, and declared that Mr Oliphant has done, unaided, what would have required a company of philologists to achieve. Mr Oliphant, however, is not only devoted to literary pursuits, but he also takes a practical interest in the welfare of all in the parish; often visits them in their dwellings, and has a great pleasure in promoting their social enjoyments. In these respects he is cordially supported by Mrs Oliphant. And I only express the best wishes of all on the estate that they may be long spared together to dwell among their own people, and to maintain the same friendly relations with them in the future as they have done in the past.

AT THE HEAD OF STRATHEARN
BY REV. JOHN MACPHERSON, COMRIE

The head of Strathearn may be said to be the parish of Comrie, because it comprises some miles of the strath as well as the lake from which the strath derives its name. The name Comrie is taken from a Gaelic word *Comhruith*, signifying confluence or running together of streams, and is aptly applied in this case. This one can easily see by standing for a few moments upon the Bridge of Dalginross. Looking westward, he sees the River Ruchill joining the Earn behind the Parish Church; and, turning to the east, at a distance of a few hundred yards he sees the Lednock discharging its waters into the same river. Hence the name Comrie, probably in the first instance applied to the village built at the junction of the three rivers, was afterwards given to the parish. The parish of Comrie, as presently constituted, includes what was formerly called the parishes of Comrie and Tullichettle. Hence the minister of Comrie owns two glebes—the Tullichettle glebe in the vicinity of the manse, and the Comrie glebe situated on the south bank of the Earn. The date at which this union took place is not known, but in the year 1702 the Commission of Teinds, at the request of the General Assembly, made additions, *quoad sacra*, from the parishes of Monzievaird, Strowan, and Muthill, and annexed a portion of the parish of Comrie lying upon the north side of Loch Earn, also *quoad sacra* to the parish of Balquhidder. This arrangement holds good at the present day. The parish *quoad civilia* extends from the Bridge of Lednock to Lochearnhead, a distance of thirteen miles, and is about nine miles in breadth. It contains some of the grandest mountains of the Grampian range—Benchonzie, 3048 feet; and Ben Voirlich, 3224 feet above the level of the sea. The latter, it is said, can be seen from Perth, Edinburgh, and Ayrshire.

The beauties of Strathearn have often been pictured by writers of poetry and prose, but without reaching the head of Strathearn these beauties can be only partially seen. The drive from Crieff to Lochearnhead in a summer day is universally regarded as one of the finest in all Scotland. To within a mile or so of St. Fillans the road resembles one long avenue stretching along the base of the Grampians. The scenery is unequalled for its mixture of grandeur and beauty. There you have the rough, rugged hills of the Highlands combined with the cultivated plains of the Lowlands, and waving woods, affording an air of warmth and freshness to the landscape. The great storm of 1893 has, indeed, laid low many of our finest plantations and marred the beauty of our scenery. Turleum Wood, which used to wave its shaggy head so high, is now laid prostrate, and appears to the eye what its Celtic name implies—*tor lom*, a bare hill. And yet, as far as appearance and scenery are concerned, there are few places which can as well afford to part with some of its trees as the head of Strathearn. Comrie is best known to the public generally by its earthquakes, and as a quiet summer resort, with sequestered walks over hills and dales and along the banks of flowing streams. But to the botanist, the geologist, the antiquarian, and the lover of ancient legend and historic incident there is, besides all this, something to awaken interest and engage attention. The number and variety of plants is very considerable. Slate is the predominant rock, but there are also limestone, whin, the old red sandstone, and granite. At one time there were two slate quarries wrought on the Aberuchill Hills, but for the last twenty years they have been closed. A lime quarry on Lochearnside in former times supplied the whole district with material for lime, but carriage, labour, and fuel have become so expensive, that both builders and farmers find it more economical to get lime ready for use from the south. There is granite in Glenlednock, and as the railway has now been extended to the village from Crieff, it is possible that some day it may be a source of industry to the inhabitants. In several places in the district of which we write there are traces of what are supposed to be Druidical remains. One cannot help regretting that the old Druids should have confined the knowledge of their religion to their own order, and that they should have left so few traces of their mystical rites to posterity, except what may be gathered from rude stones scattered here and there throughout the country. On the plain of Tullybannocher, and near the east lodge of Dunira, there are several standing-stones, which antiquarians believe to be the remains of Druidical circles. On the plain of Dalginross, also, near the junction of the manse road with the public road, there are three large stones, supposed to be the remains of a Druidical temple. One of these, about 8 feet in length, stands, or rather leans, at an angle of 45 degrees; the others are lying flat upon the ground. One of them, a round, flat boulder, bears upon its surface cup-marks arranged in irregular concentric circles. Was this the sacrificial stone of an ancient Druid; or are these boulders relics of the glacial period, and were the marks alluded to caused by the action of the weather? When we come to deal with Roman remains we stand upon firmer ground. On the same plain of Dalginross, and a short distance to the north of these boulders we have referred to, is the site of the old Roman Camp, Victoria. About the end of last century the outlines of the fortifications seem to have been quite distinct, but since that time the plough has obliterated almost every trace of them. There seem to have been two camps at Dalginross—a larger and a smaller one, the former capable of holding 10,000 troops. Here, it has been held by some writers, the great Battle of Mons Grampius was fought between the Caledonians under Galgacus and the Romans under Agricola. This, however, is not probable. Seven cities of the ancient world laid claim to Homer's birth-place. About the same number of places are pointed to as the scene of the Battle of Mons Grampius. Gordon says it was at Dalginross, Chalmers says it was the Moor of Ardoch, some say it was in Fife, others at Urie, in Kincardineshire. Skene, in his *Celtic Scotland*, places it on or near the Muir of Blair, about the junction of the River Tay with the Isla. Mr Hill Burton abandons the task of determining the site as hopeless. If we accept the description given by Tacitus, in so far as it says the battle was fought *"in conspectu classis"* —that is, "in sight of the fleet," the place could not have been Dalginross, and for this one reason, that unless the Earn was very different in the days of Agricola from what it is in our day, the Roman fleet could not possibly have sailed to a point within sight of Dalginross. Judging, however, from some place-names in the neighbourhood, there is little doubt that Dalginross has been the scene of some bloody conflict or conflicts during the period of the Roman occupation of Britain. The name of the farm adjoining the old Roman Camp, for example, is Blardhearg, which in Celtic means "the red battle-field." To the west, and beyond the River Ruchill, is Dalrannaich, in Celtic, *Dailranaich*—"the field of mourning or lamentation"; and a little to the north is Dalchonzie, in Celtic, *Dailachaonaidh*—"the field of weeping." To the south of the plain of Dalginross, and upon the road to Ardoch, there are still traces of the Roman occupation of Strathearn. At Blairinroar there must have been a bloody conflict between the Romans and the Caledonians. The very name of the place implies it, for Blairinroar in Celtic is the "field of violent onset." There are still to be seen in this neighbourhood huge slabs of standing-stones, some of them 20 feet in height. Those upon the level ground probably mark the graves of distinguished Romans or Caledonians who fell upon the field of battle; but others, which run in a line extending north and south, were probably landmarks to guide messengers on their way from Lindum, the camp at Ardoch, to Victoria, the camp at Dalginross.

At the west side of the new cemetery, close to the public road, there is a curious round knoll, which at one time must have been used as a place for the burial of the dead. The attention of the writer of this was drawn to it about twenty years ago. There were three large slabs of stone lying upon the ground, which apparently had been at some former period placed erect by some loving hands to mark the last resting-place of some departed friend or hero. By the aid of some of the Comrie masons the stones were placed in a standing position. Curious to know what lay beneath the surface, we dug up the earth in front of the largest slab, and came upon a stone cist placed north and south, 7 inches long, 1 foot 8 inches broad, and 1 foot 3 inches deep. The only remains discovered was a thigh-bone, but whether it at one time formed a part of the leg of a Celt, a Roman, or a Saxon we could not tell. An old man who then lived in the village of Comrie told us that in his young days the same mound was dug up, when an urn filled with ashes was discovered. This, perhaps, would indicate that it formed a place of burial for Romans rather than for Caledonians. The spot is called Dunmoid, or "hill of judgment." Besides the parish churchyard, there are three old burying-grounds in the parish—Leckin, on Lochearnside; Dundurn, and Tullichettle. From an antiquarian point of view, the most interesting, perhaps, is Tullichettle. It is situated in a sequestered spot on a rising ground on the right bank of the River Ruchill, near the farm-house of Cultabraggan. The name, which is Celtic, *Tulachchadail*—"hill of sleep"—well describes the place, for a more solitary spot could hardly be selected for the repose of the dead. Judging from the inscriptions upon the tomb-stones it has been for long the burying-place of the Macnivens, the Macgreuthers, the Maccullochs, and other clans. There is a curious slab over the grave of the Riddochs. The following description of it, extracted from the proceedings of the Society of Antiquaries, has been kindly sent by the Secretary, Dr. Anderson:—

"It measures 5 feet 6 inches in length and 18 inches in breadth, tapering slightly towards the lower end. It bears a sword with straight guard in the centre of the stone, and the name James Ridoch on the blade. In the spaces on either side are a number of trade emblems—a square, an axe, an adze, a mallet and chisel, a millrind, an axe-pick of the kind used by millers for dressing the mill-stone, the coulter of a plough, a hammer and anvil (?), and an auger, indicating probably the various mechanical aptitudes of the deceased. The connection of the family of Reidheuchs or Ridochs with Strathearn began in 1502, when King James IV. granted a charter of confirmation of the lands of Tullychedile, Culturagane, &c., to his familiar servitor and steward, James Redeheuche, burgess of Stirling. In 1573, these and other lands acquired by him were erected into the Barony of Tullichiddil. In 1542, James Reidheuch of Tullichiddil is mentioned as dead, and it is not till 1610 that another James appears in the line of the Reidheuchs of Tullichiddil. The probability is that the stone here figured belongs to the seventeenth century, as it was only then that the name Reidheuche began to be spelt Ridoche. Of course, it is impossible to say whether this is the tomb-stone of the James Ridoche of 1610, or of a successor; but there seems to be nothing against the idea of the stone being as old at least as the date thus indicated."

Tullichettle must have been an old parish. Shortly after the Reformation, in the year 1572, it was served by John Edmeston, exhorter, and in 1574 by William Drummond, who had also under his charge Comrie, Monivaird, Monzie, and Crieff. The ruins of the church are still to be seen within the wall of the churchyard, but of the old manse there is no trace left now. We have often been asked the derivation of the word Ruchill, the name of the river, which, rising at the head of Glenartney, passes the graveyard of Tullichettle and falls into the Earn at the village of Comrie. It is compounded of two Gaelic words—*ruadh* (red), and *tuill* (flood). *Ruadhthuill*, therefore, is the red flood, and any one who has seen the red turgid waters of the Ruchill in time of flood will see that the name is significant of the thing itself. The word occurs in a shorter form—Ruel, a river in Argyllshire, which gives its name to the valley through which it flows—viz., Glendaruel. In the good old days when our Highland glens and straths were thickly populated, every hill and dale and crag and knoll had its name, and every strath and valley had its traditions. From many of our Highland glens the people are gone, and their traditions along with them. Sir Walter Scott, however, has rendered famous at least one of the glens at the head of Strathearn and preserved a few of its traditions. Who ever read that beautiful poem, "The Lady of the Lake," but knows something of Glenartney, Benvoirlich, and Uam-Var. Here the chase, which he sings in the first canto, begins:—

> "The stag at eve had drank his fill,
> When danced the moon on Monan's rill,
> And deep his midnight lair had made
> In lone Glenartney's hazel shade.
> * * * * *

Roused from his lair,
The antler'd monarch of the waste
Sprang from his heathery couch in haste.
*   *   *   *   *

With one brave bound the copse he clear'd,
And, stretching forward free and far,
Sought the wild heaths of Uam-Var."

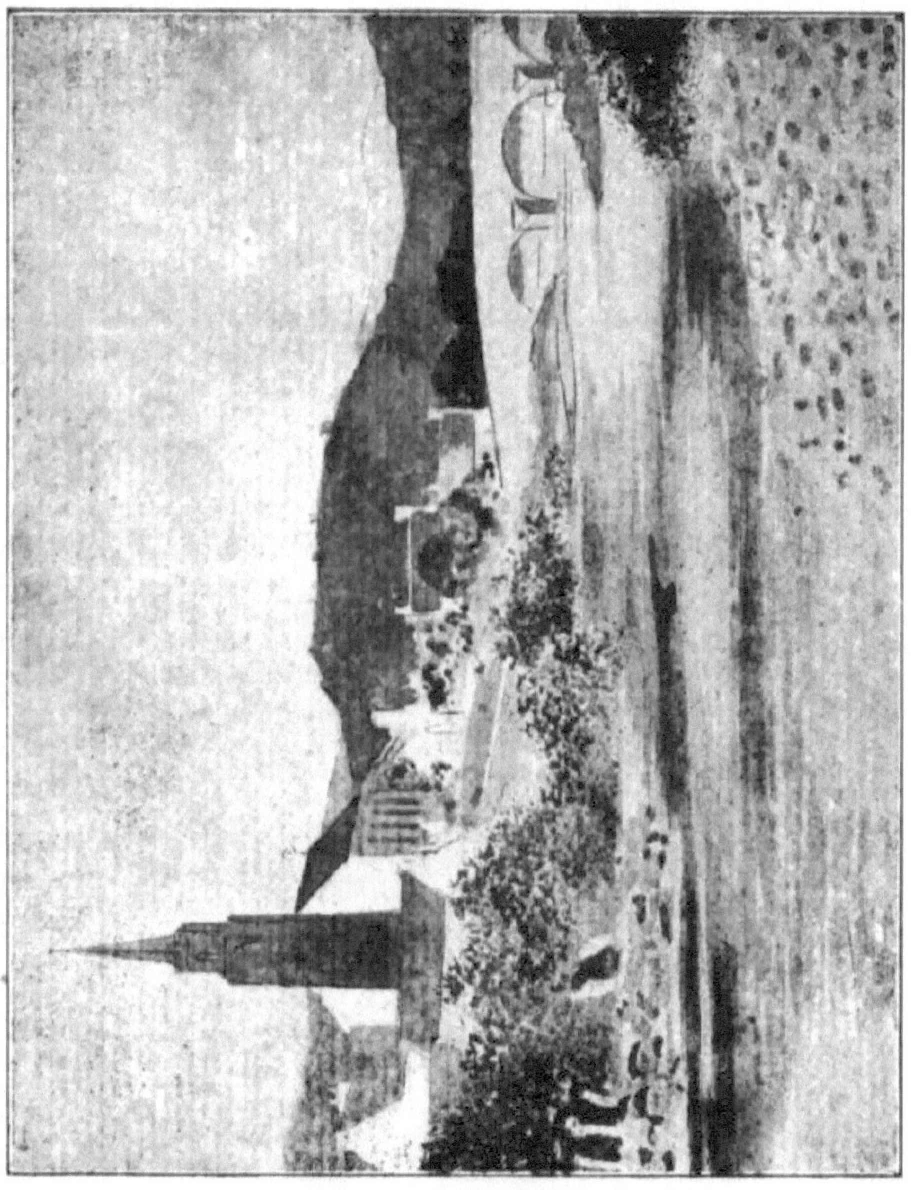

Church and Bridge, Comrie (Comrie Bridge and Kirk).

Uam-Var, which in Gaelic signifies large cave, is a mountain between Glenartney and Callander, and takes its name from a cave on the south side of it, said by tradition to have been inhabited by a giant centuries ago. Glenartney was a Royal forest, and a portion of it is still fenced off for the same purpose. On an eminence at the head of the glen stands Glenartney Lodge, belonging to the proprietor, the Earl of Ancaster. In the past as in the present the strict preservation of game seems to have been attended with dangers and difficulties. Some people seem to have an uncontrollable liking for hunting and poaching. In the sixteenth century Glenartney was the scene of a terrible tragedy. In the year 1588, John Drummond of Drummond-Ernoch was forester to King James VI. there. One day, according to one tradition, he discovered some of the Clan Macgregor trespassing in the Royal forest. He seized them and cropped off their ears. The Macgregors, incensed by the punishment inflicted upon their clansmen, vowed vengeance against Drummond-Ernoch. They made a raid upon the forest, seized the forester, and cut off his head, which they carried with them in a corner of one of their plaids. "In the full exultation of vengeance," says Sir Walter Scott in his introduction to the *Legend of Montrose*, "they stopped at the house of Ardvoirlich and demanded refreshments, which the lady, a sister of the murdered Drummond-Ernoch (her husband being absent), was afraid or unwilling to refuse. She caused bread and cheese to be placed before them, and gave directions for more substantial refreshments to be prepared. While she was absent with this hospitable intention the barbarians placed the head of her brother on the table, filling the mouth with bread and cheese, and bidding him eat, for many a merry meal he had eaten in that house. The poor woman, returning and beholding this dreadful sight, shrieked aloud and fled into the woods, where, as described in the romance, she roamed a raving maniac, and for some time secreted herself from all living society. Some remaining instinctive feeling brought her at length to steal a glance from a distance at the maidens while they milked the cows, which being observed, her husband, Ardvoirlich, had her conveyed back to her home, and detained her there till she gave birth to a child, of whom she had been pregnant, after which she was observed gradually to recover her mental faculties." Leaving Ardvoirlich, the Macgregors proceeded to Balquhidder, and at a meeting of the clan held in the church—the chief presiding—they placed their hands successively upon the dead man's head and swore to defend the author of the deed. At one time there was a large population in this glen. In 1745 the farm of Auchinnar alone had eight tenants. An interesting document in possession of the relatives of the M'Greuthers of Meiggar referring to the Rebellion of 1715 shows the power of the laird in those days, and the resources of the glen as far as fighting men were concerned. It is as follows:—

> "William M'Gruther, in Dalclaythick, you are hereby ordered to acquaint William M'Nivan, in the same town, and Alexander M'Gruther, in Dalchruwn, to go along with you as officers to command the company of our men that is to come out of your glen, and all the men are hereby ordered to obey your command on their highest peril, which you are to intimate to them, as you will be answerable to us, and this shall be your warrant.

"Given at Drummond Castle, the fifteenth day of August, one thousand seven hundred and thirteen years.

"See that none of the men of Auchinnear of whatever rank be absent, as they will be answerable, and all the men in good order.

"(Signed) DRUMMOND."

M'Gruther and his two neighbours obeyed the summons of the laird of Drummond, and took charge of the company of Highlanders raised in Glenartney; but the laird could not save them from the consequence of their obedience. When the Rebellion was quelled they were banished to America and sold as slaves. The two M'Gruthers managed to get back to their native country, but were doomed to spend seven long years in hiding.

The origin of place-names may not be of so much interest to the reader as it is to the writer of this article, but we cannot resist the temptation of recording a suggestion made to us years ago as to the origin of the word Glenartney, by Mr James Ferguson, the present keeper of the forest, and the worthy successor of old Drummond-Ernoch. It is this: *Gleann-àrd-an-fheidh*—"the high glen of the deer." This would certainly account for the last syllable of the modern name, and would also accord with the fact of the place being an ancient forest; but we prefer the derivation *Gleann-ardan*—"the glen of heights," and we think the last syllable has been added merely to suit the imperfection of the Saxon's vocal organs.

The mansion-houses of the head of Strathearn and their occupants are of some historical interest, but, as our space is limited, our reference to them must be brief, and confined to a few of the oldest. On the margin of Loch Earn stands Ardvoirlich House. The present occupant of the estate is Colonel John Stewart, who spent the first part of his life in India, and now resides upon the estate. With the exception of the Drummonds, who trace their ancestry back to Maurice, the Hungarian, who lived about the time of the Norman Conquest, the Stewarts of Ardvoirlich are the oldest family in the district. They lay claim not only to a long ancestral line, but also to Royal blood, through a son of Murdoch, Duke of Albany, Regent of Scotland, and son of Robert II. Among the antique curiosities of this family, it is said, there is a large gem called *clach dhearg*—red stone, seemingly white rock crystal, bound with four silver bands, which used to be regarded as a talisman, giving to water into which it is dipped virtue for the cure of all diseases of cattle. In recent times the Stewarts have been a family of soldiers who served in India. Their burying-place is within the old Chapel of Dundurn, but the monuments erected to the memory of members of the family recently deceased are in the Parish Church of Comrie. They are all handsome, and a great ornament to the interior of the Parish Church; but one of them is worthy of special notice on account of its artistic beauty. It is that erected by the Governor-General of India and other dignitaries and friends to commemorate the death of William Stewart, who, along with his wife and infant son, was murdered in the Indian Mutiny of 1857. It is a cenotaph of pure Carrara marble, with the figure of a Sepoy soldier with arms reversed on the one side, and a Hindoo in a kneeling posture on the other.

Dunira House is the seat of the Dundases. The present proprietor is Sir Sidney

James Dundas, the third baronet of Beechwood and Dunira, who succeeded his father, Sir David Dundas, Bart., in 1877. What is the word Dunira derived from? Is it like Dundurn, "the hill or fort upon the Earn"? or is it *Dun aoraidh*, "the hill of worship"? It is difficult to say; Gaelic words have been so much corrupted to suit the tongues of the Saxon. There is little doubt, however, that in ancient times the locality was intimately associated with divine worship. Not far from the east lodge there are to be seen large standing-stones, supposed, as already said, to be the remains of an old Druidical circle. On the hillside, above Dunira House, there is a place called Drumnakil, which signifies the "ridge of the chapel"; and farther to the north-east, near the hill of Dunmore, is Ballochintaggart, "the gap of the priest." At Drumnakil there is an old burying-ground, the grave-stones scarcely discernible among the rank grass; but all trace of the chapel, or monks' cell, if ever there was one, has disappeared. Dunira was once the property of Henry Dundas, Viscount Melville and Baron Dunira. He was son of Robert Dundas of Arniston, Lord President of the Court of Session. He was called to the bar in 1763, and elected member of Parliament for the County of Edinburgh in 1774, and after holding several important offices under the Crown, he retired with Pitt in 1801, and the following year he was raised to the Peerage. After his death his Perthshire friends paid a tribute to his memory and worth by erecting a monument on Dunmore Hill, at Comrie. It is an obelisk, 72 feet high, built in 1812 of Innergeldie granite. A better site could not have been chosen. From the top of Dunmore Hill there is a magnificent view of varied landscape. To the west you have a peep at Loch Earn, the Aberuchill Hills, and the old white-washed Castle nestling among its trees; to the south you have the village of Comrie and the strath, with the Earn and the Ruchill winding their way through the plain; to the east, Sir David Baird's Monument, the Knock of Crieff, Turleum, the Ochils, and one of the Lomonds of Fife; looking to the north, we see Glenlednock stretching far towards Loch Tay, with Spout Rollo at its head, and guarded on each side by the lofty peaks of the Grampians. This, like so many others of our Highland glens, has suffered much through depopulation during this century. An old Glenlednock farmer still living in the parish informs us that in his recollection there were thirty-six tenants with their cottars, where there are now five and a few shepherds. One cannot help admiring the industry, economy, and thrift of these old Highland farmers, who in such numbers could live and thrive and pay higher rents to the landlord than the few who are now in possession of the land.

Aberuchill Castle was for nearly three centuries the seat of the Campbells of Aberuchill and Kilbryde. It was originally built in 1602, but has since been modernised and enlarged. The Crown granted a charter of the lands of Aberuchill in 1596 to Colin Campbell, second son of Sir Colin Campbell of Lawers. His son James was made a baronet of Nova Scotia by Charles I. in 1627. He fell fighting for Charles II. at the Battle of Worcester in 1651. Sir Colin, only son of Sir James, succeeded him. He was the most distinguished of the family. Bred to the law, he rose to the position of Lord of Session with the title of Lord Aberuchill. Sir Colin was a Whig and a Presbyterian when the most of the gentry of Strathearn were either Episcopalians or Popish Jacobites. His name is associated with the massacre of Glencoe, inasmuch as he was a member of the Council that refused the certificate of the Sheriff-Depute of Argyle that M'Donald of Glencoe had taken the oath of allegiance to King William, unless they got a warrant to receive it from the King. From 1693 to 1702 he represented the County of Perth in the Scottish Parliament, and died in 1704. From the Campbells, the estate passed into the hands of the Drummonds. It is now the property of Captain Robert Dewhurst, son of George C. Dewhurst, Esq., lately deceased.

It would be unpardonable to write anything about Comrie without making allusion to the earthquakes which have made it famous. In the Statistical Account of Scotland, published in the year 1794, the Rev. Mr M'Diarmid, minister of the parish, gives an account of the first recorded earthquake in the district. During the autumn of 1789 loud noises, unaccompanied by any concussion, were heard by the inhabitants of Glenlednock; but on the 5th of November of that year they were alarmed by a loud rumbling noise, accompanied with a severe shock of earthquake, which was felt over a tract of country of more than twenty miles in extent. The Rev. Mr Mackenzie, successor to Mr M'Diarmid, writing in 1838, in the last Statistical Account, says that "at and after the time of the last Statistical Account the earthquakes were so frequent and violent, and accompanied with such noises, as to occasion great alarm, especially one which occurred on a Sabbath while the congregation was assembled." The year 1839, however, was the time of the great earthquakes. Writing in 1842 in the last Statistical Account, the Rev. John Ferguson, minister of Monzievaird, says:—"At this time they began to be frequently felt, nearly 20 shocks being occasionally experienced in 24 hours. The most violent one happened about ten o'clock on the evening of 23d October, 1839. The shock seemed to pass along through the parish of Monzievaird from north-west to south-east. For a second or two every house for miles around the village of Comrie was shaken from top to bottom; and while the motion was passing away to the eastward it was accompanied by a tremendous noise like the roar of 100 pieces of ordnance discharged at once and gradually dying away in the distance. This earthquake was partially felt throughout a great part of Scotland, as far as Inverness, Dunbar, Berwick, and the banks of Loch Awe. In this neighbourhood it was very alarming. Several individuals fainted, and most of the inhabitants of the village of Comrie spent the whole night in the streets, or in the churches, which were very properly opened for prayer. Many stone dykes were thrown down, walls of houses rent, and chimney-stalks shattered, the stones being frequently shifted from their places, but no serious damage was sustained. The shocks have again diminished both in frequency and violence since the autumn of 1839." Another severe shock occurred in November, 1846, but from that date they have decreased both in number and intensity. The cause of these subterranean commotions is in this as in similar cases a matter of conjecture, but there is good cause for thankfulness that they have hitherto been attended with no serious damage to life or property.

The Session records of some parishes in Scotland are of some historical value, but this is not so with those of Comrie. Beyond the perpetual reiteration of cases of discipline and doles to the poor, there is little to be found in them to throw light upon the Christian life and work of the parish. So meagrely kept were these records that until the year 1829 the Christian name and surname of the Moderator and Clerk never appear in the minutes—not even the Secession of 1843 is recorded, though the minister left the church with a great majority of the congregation to worship upon Tomachessock. The only exception to what we have just stated, perhaps, is a minute of Kirk-Session dated 17th November, 1772, recording the honour due to Patrick Campbell, Esq. of Monzie, then deceased, and the Rev. Robert Menzies, minister of the parish, for the active and benevolent part they took in the building of the Dalginross Bridge over the Earn. The bridge was built in 1756 at a cost of £230.

The Parish Church was erected in 1805, and holds 1044 sitters. The manse was built in 1784, and an addition was made to it in 1822. A new church was built in St. Fillans in connection with the Church of Scotland in 1878, and in March, 1895, it was endowed and erected into a parish *quoad sacra* under the old name of Dundurn. It is curious to note how the land has been changing hands during the last 180 years. In 1715, the heritors were the Earl of Perth, Duke of Athole, the proprietors of Aberuchill, Lawers, Monzie, Cultabraggan, Ardvoirlich, Comrie, Strowan, Drummond-Ernoch, and Balmacuin. At present they are the Earl of Ancaster, Marquis of Breadalbane, and the proprietors of Ardvoirlich, Dunira, Aberuchill, Strowan, Lawers, Dalchonzie, and Drumearn.

ON THE BANKS OF THE DEVON
BY REV. E. B. SPEIRS, B.D., GLENDEVON

Seeing that "St. Serf's Bridge" still spans the Devon at one part within the parish of Glendevon, and that the good Saint did not himself build the bridge, but, following a common practice, baptised and made Christian what was a Pagan structure, reared in this instance by the Imperial legionaries, it might be permissible for the local historian to go back at least to the times of the Roman occupation. After describing the camp and the Roman road which still exist in the mind's eye of the antiquaries, he might then go on to tell of holy St. Servan's feats in the way of detecting sheep-stealers by making them, like Speed under the influence of Proteus' reasoning, cry "Baa," or relate some such pretty human story as that of how he turned water into wine for the sake of a sick monk, or unfold the thrilling tale of how he fought the Dovan dragon, as Wyntoun sings, or at least says:—

> "In Dovyn of devotyoune
> And prayere, he slew a fell Dragoune,
> Quhare he was slayne, that place wes ay
> The Dragownys Den cald to this day."[35]

The more exact methods of writing history now in vogue, however, almost compel the chronicler to begin with the first certain mention of Glendevon in accredited records, and that belongs to the year 1521. On the eleventh of July of that year an interesting ceremony was gone through down at Cambuskenneth, on the banks of the Forth. Abbot Mylne, a man both of culture and character, who to a genuine love of letters added a love of art and architecture, and who was ultimately the first President of the Court of Session, had re-built the great altar, the chapter-house, and part of the cloister of his Abbey, and had laid out two new cemeteries. In order to signalise these notable additions and restorations he invited the Bishop of Dunblane to conduct a consecration and dedication service. The Bishop was directly assisted in this solemn function by three of his principal clergy—his archdeacon, George Newton; John Chesholme, prebendary of Kippane; and "Jacobus Wilson, prebandarius de Glendowane." John Tulydaf, warder of the Minorites of "Striueling" (Stirling), preached on the efficacy of dedication after the celebration of the Mass, and amongst those present were the "noble and powerful" Lord John Erskin, Jacobus Haldene of Glenegges (Gleneagles), Knight, and various others of the local clergy, nobility, and gentry, together with a large concourse of people from the surrounding district. The official account of what took place on this high

---

[35] Much of the legendary history of the Devon is given in the extraordinary poem "Glenochel," by Mr James Kennedy.

day when Glendowane, Glendovan, Glenduen, or Glendevon, first emerges into the light of history, is duly signed by Jacobus Blakwood, presbyter of the Diocese of Dunblane, public notary by apostolic authority, who was on the spot and saw everything properly done.[36] The name of Prebendary Wilson occurs in several documents both before and after this, all of which have reference to matters connected either with Cambuskenneth or Dunblane. He gets prominent mention in a paper dated from Cambuskenneth, June, 1530, in which he is styled "Canonicus Dunblanensis," heading a list of "venerable and discreet" gentlemen, including Alanus Balward, vicar of Kalender, and Andreas Sym, vicar of Cumry, but we cannot trace him further down than March of the following year. It is clear from this that Glendevon was attached to the "Kirk of Dunblane," and that the Parish Church was served from there, not, it is to be hoped, in the slovenly fashion characteristic of these times, when the stipend was too often fought for by different teind hunters in the shape of the bishop of the diocese and the abbot of some neighbouring monastery, a state of things to which Prebendary Wilson himself bears witness. There is something almost pathetic in the thought that less than forty years after that dedication service in which the Prebendary of Glendevon took part, these additions were to be pulled to pieces by the savage mob which wrecked, amongst other religious houses, the stately monastery on the Links of the Forth; and it is just possible that the great destroyer—spiritually at least—of what Canon Wilson helped to build up was in his parish in 1556. At any rate a spot is still pointed out on the glebe where, according to tradition, John Knox preached. We know from his own statement[37] that he spent some time in the early part of the summer of that year at Castle Campbell—which is only some four or five miles distant—"whare he taught certane dayis"; so it is at least not utterly improbable that he may have come through Glenquey past the Maiden's Well, and visited a possible congregation in Glendovan, exhorting them to "prayaris, to reading of the Scriptures, and mutuall conference unto such tyme as God should give unto them grettar libertie."[38]

The second direct mention of Glendevon in public records is of a somewhat unsavoury order, and affords a rather curious illustration of the beliefs of the people of Scotland in the seventeenth century. John Brughe, one of the most notorious necromancers and wizards of his day, was tried at Edinburgh on November 24th, 1643, for practising sorcery and other unholy arts, and amongst the charges brought against him was that he had met Satan thrice "in the kirkyeard of Glendovan at quhilkis tymes ther was taine up thrie severall dead corps, ane of thame being of ane servand man named Johne Chrystiesone; the uther corps, tane up at the Kirk of Mukhart, the flesch of the quhilk corps was put above the byre and stable-dure headis" of certain individuals in order to destroy their cattle.[39] John's

[36] See *Registrum Monasterii S. Marie De Cambuskenneth*, A.D. 1147-1535. Edinburgi: 1872; p. 122.

[37] *History of the Reformation*, Vol. I., p. 233.

[38] The parish was served by readers from 1568 to 1586, when the reader Symon Pawtoun was presented to the living, and, curiously enough, his successor, A. Marschell, after being minister for a year, was forced by the Presbytery to accept the lower position.

[39] See *The Darker Superstitions of Scotland*. By John Graham Dalyell. Glasgow: 1835; p. 579.

object in collecting Glendovan "muild" was, according to this indictment, not a beneficent one; but it is to be remembered to his credit that he used the powdered bones of the dead and other materials, notably "ane inchantit stane of the bignes of a dow egg,"[40] for the healing of man and beast, and we are told that for curing a number of oxen afflicted with the murrain by administering a pint of one of his patent medicines, accompanied with the invocation, "God put thame in their awin place," repeated thrice, he got "ellevin od schillings, with twa peckis of meill and thrie tailyeis of beiff." In those days, when not only human nature but Nature herself lay under the black shadow of one of the foulest of superstitions, the fair banks of the Devon were much frequented by the devil, who had whole "covins" of witches and wizards in his service, so that it is not surprising to hear that John was frequently in his company. "That John Brughe had been with the devil at the Rumbling Brigs and elsewhere was affirmed by Katherine Mitchell to be of veritie, at the tyme of hir criminall tryell at Culrose, and immediately befoir hir executione, the said John Brughe being confronted with hir at the tyme."[41] We can claim this renowned empiric not only for the Glendevon district, but in a sense for the Presbytery, since it was alleged against him that he had got his uncanny knowledge "from a wedow woman, named Neane Nikclerith, of threescoir years of age, quha wis sister dochter to Nik Neveding, that notorious infamous witche in Monzie, quha for her sorcerie and witchecraft was brunt fourscoir of yeir since or thereby." Spite of all he had done for the "bestiall," and all the testimonials he had from patients whom he had cured of their "seiknessis" by enchanted drinks, Glendovan and Mukhart mould, and sympathetic conjuring of "sarkis, coller bodies, beltis, and utheris pertaining als weill to men as to wemen," John was found guilty and condemned to be strangled and burned. These were the real Dark Ages, when intimations were frequently made from the Glendevon and other pulpits that the minister and session would be glad to receive information against suspected witches, and when the common pricker who pricked poor witches "with lang preins of thrie inches" to discover the marks of Satan, was specially busy in the vale of Devon, where in a record year no less than sixteen of the local "covin" were burned. In the Roll of Fugitives from kirk discipline drawn up by the Synod of Perth and Stirling in 1649, Glendevon was represented by a warlock, "Mart. Kennard, suspect of witchcraft," but of his fate we know nothing. In this connection it may be remarked that though the "Kirkyeard of Glendovan," immortalised by John Brughe's ghoulish visit, contains no epitaphs, humorous or otherwise, it possesses a "Plague Stone," a large rough slab, under which lie those who died of what is vaguely called the Plague (1645?), and the lifting of which was duly guarded against by a solemn curse pronounced over it on whoever would dare to remove it, for two hundred years ago a curse could break bones or "ryve the saull out of ye."

---

[40] Mr Wood Martin in his learned work, *Pagan Ireland* (London: 1895); describes similar usages still prevailing in Ireland.

[41] *Dalyell*, p. 671.

S Serf's Bridge, Glendevon.

Two years after John Brughe suffered at Edinburgh, the quiet of the usually peaceful valley of the Devon was broken by the clatter of cavalry and the skirling of the pipes, as Montrose, having in his usual brilliant fashion outwitted Baillie, marched through, burning and plundering as he passed, leaving Muckhart, Dollar, and, above all, Castle Campbell, the lowland hold of the detested Argyles, heaps of blackened ruins, a march which was to end in the bloody Battle of Kilsyth, that "braw day" when, as the Highlander with grim humour remarked, "at every stroke I gave with my broadsword I cut an ell o' tamn'd Covenanting breeks." When Chambers says[42] that "the Covenanting army marched close upon the track of Montrose *down Glendevon*, at the distance of about a day's march behind," he, of course, means down the Devon valley, and not down Glendevon proper, since it is pretty certain that Montrose, in making his descent from the north, entered the low country not by Gleneagles, but by the south-east end of the Ochils. Glendevon Castle—originally built, it is supposed, by the Crawfords[43] in the sixteenth century—thus escaped the fate which befel Castle Campbell[44] and Menstrie House, and other places in the Devon and Ochil district at this time, when the fierce strife was not merely between cavaliers and Covenanters, but quite as much, and specially during the Devon valley march, between the Ogilvies and Macleans on the one hand, and the Campbells and their friends on the other. It is, however, impossible, to say whether the Keep, which has been in the possession of the Rutherford family since 1766, was actually at this time in the hands of the Crawfords, and, indeed, the traditions regarding its ownership are so vague—one of them assigning it to the Douglases—that, in the absence of authentic records, it is impossible to make any really satisfactory statement regarding its origin and history.

Some years later the parish of Glendevon came prominently before the public in connection with the deposition and excommunication of its doughty true-blue Presbyterian minister, the Rev. William Spence, M.A., though it was not till he had been removed from his living that the really romantic part of his career began. He had graduated at St. Andrews in 1654, and after some years of schoolmastering[45] and probationership he was, in 1664, duly admitted on the new Black Prelatic conditions to the parish of Glendevon. Under the mild rule of Bishops Leighton and Ramsay he lived quietly there for fourteen years. His name occasionally appears on the Synod and Presbytery Committees during this period, and he seems to have done his best to get the brethren stirred up to "better the provision of Glendovan." The Bishop and Synod did actually order a "perambulation" to be made to see if anything could be annexed from the adjacent parishes, especially "Denying and Fossoquhy," so that, as Mr Spence put it, "ane augmentation proportionablie might be made to him out of the vacant teindes of the said paroches in respect of the poornes and meannes of his stipend for the present."[46] The perambulation, beyond affording a pleasant outing to the visitors in the long May days, does not seem to have had any practical result. Mr Spence had, however, been thinking of higher things than teinds and augmentation, and had been looking far beyond the bounds of his own parish, and, spite of the extreme gentleness of the somewhat

---

[42] *History of the Rebellions in Scotland.* By Robert Chambers. Vol. II., p. 87.

[43] *Statistical Account of 1794,* p. 234.

[44] *Memoirs of the Marquis of Montrose.* By M. Napier. Vol. II., p. 537.

[45] He was schoolmaster at Abernethy, and subsequently married the daughter of the parish minister. She died in 1708 at the age of 80.

[46] See *Register of the Diocesan Synod of Dunblane.* Edited by John Wilson, D.D. Edinburgh: 1877; page 91.

Before the passing of the Act of 1810 for augmenting parochial stipends in Scotland, the stipend was £21 17s 11d, the smallest in Scotland. 50 Geo. III., cap. 84.

mongrel Prelatic-Presbyterian rule under which he was, and the general atmosphere of conformity which he breathed, he began to have serious searchings of heart about the state of the "poor afflicted" Church. Accordingly, towards the end of 1678 he took the bold step of presenting a paper[47] to the Presbytery of Auchterarder drawing the attention of the Court to the sundry gross corruptions under which the Church was suffering and to the horrid defection from its first purity, obvious to every man who did not wilfully shut his eyes. The evils against which he asked the Court to testify were doctrinal, liturgical, disciplinary, moral, and what may be called ecclesiastical. He includes in the sweep of his very impartial denunciation not only the pernicious tenets of Pelagianism, Arminianism, Latitudinarianism, and Popish errors, but "the dotage of Quakers and other enthusiasts," human inventions in worship, and the private essays made to introduce or impose an unwarrantable liturgie of unsound and useless form, the loose spirit of atheism, profaneness, and ungodliness reigning in all corners of the kingdom, and the dreadful differences that prevailed, and calls for a return to sound doctrine, the practice of "the gude Kirk primitif," the exercise of a strict discipline, and the ways of peace. At the special meeting of Presbytery called to consider his paper he asked to have it back, apparently because he now thought its terms were not strong enough, and meanwhile a committee was appointed not to deal but to confer with him "until he should get full satisfaction of everything that was his scruple." He refused, however, to meet the Committee or attend the Presbytery, on the ground that he had not "clearness" as to the authority and constitution of a semi-prelatic Court. The Bishop and Presbytery thereupon suspended him, and he was summoned before the Synod in April, 1679, but did not attend, on account of "ane aguish distemper which had seized on him." A Synodal Committee with full powers was then appointed, before which he compeared in May, but spite of earnest entreaties of the Bishop he would withdraw nothing, and even added that he did not think the present Church government agreeable to Scriptural rules—a view shared by some of the Episcopalian bishops themselves. The Bishop and Committee recorded their opinion that the paper was contrived and adhered to for advancing some private interest against the unity and peace of the Church, and rather unfairly insinuated that Mr Spence was the more hardened therein by the late execrable murder of the Bishop of St. Andrews and the expectation of a Revolution to follow thereupon, and unanimously resolved that this unruly and unreasonable member be deposed. Mr Spence was quite prepared for this, and, "with some signs of choler in his countenance," handed a second paper to the Bishop, which turned out to be a protest against the sentence of the "pretended" Bishop and Synod of Dunblane passed on him. He was asked to retire for a little till they should consult, but he scornfully replied that he did not own their jurisdiction, and was making for the church-door when the Bishop ordered the beadle to lay hold of him, and carry him to his house, and desire the Baillie to keep him safely until he should find caution to answer before a competent judicatory. This was Mr Spence's first taste of imprisonment, of which he was to have a very large supply, of very different quality, too, later on. The good Bishop on his own responsibility sent three of the brethren that night to reason with him, but Mr Spence would

---

[47] *Diocesan Register*, p. 251.

not yield, and was let out on bail. He appeared at the next meeting of Synod, but, spite of the threat of excommunication, stuck to his guns and argued against his treatment on technical grounds, and on the following day, when, after being duly cited, he neither compeared nor pled "ane aguish distemper," the Bishop and Synod charged the Presbytery of Auchterarder to proceed with the excommunication, which after some bungling they did, and finally the superior Court ordered the intimation of the excommunication to be read from every pulpit in the Diocese on the first Sabbath of January, 1681, but no attempt was made to detain the unruly member, and the door of grace was left open to the very last, quite remarkable leniency when it is remembered that 1680 was the year of the Sanquhar Declaration and Airds Moss, and that the peroration of Mr Spence's protest would have done credit to Cuddy Headrigg's mother. "For these reasons specially, and many others I need not mention now, I, the said William Spence, protest against the sentence aforesaid, and disown the same, seeing the said inflicters have hereby proclaimed themselves to be the patrones and abettors of all the said corruptions, supplanters of the Gospel faction for Anti-christ, promoters of the powers of darkness, enemies to the kingdom of Jesus Christ, and such from whom all good Christians ought to separate because of their maintaining and defending soul-murdering heresies, and in persecuting with the utmost violence and rigour any man who darr open his mouth for the truth of Christ. (*Sic Subscribitur*), Mr William Spence."[48]

Mr Spence as yet was only an ecclesiastical rebel, and instead of going over to the extreme Covenanters, made his way to Holland, where he joined the colony of Scotch refugees. Ultimately he attached himself to the Earl of Argyle as a kind of secretary, and conducted part of the correspondence between the Earl and the English plotters. He was in London in 1683, apparently on the Earl's business, when he was arrested and imprisoned for some months, but as he could not be efficiently examined in England, where torture was not legal, he was finally sent down to Scotland along with Carstares and other suspects in His Majesty's "Kitchin Yaucht," which did not go at a royal pace, for the journey to Leith took thirteen days. They arrived late at night on November 14th, having left London on the 1st, and were taken straight to the Tolbooth.[49] A week after, orders came from London that Mr Spence should be put to the torture, but for some reason or other he was left alone till the April of the following year, being evidently in irons all the time, his close connection with Argyle rendering his imprisonment extra rigorous.[50] He was taken out of irons on the 25th of that month, but it was not till the 24th of July that he was ordered to appear before the Council and required to take an oath to answer all the questions put to him. He refused and protested, and was tortured in the boot, but, spite of the awful agony, remained "obstinate and disingenuous," whereupon the Privy Council "resolved to use all methods necessary to bring the said Mr William Spence to a true and ingenuous confession, and for expiscating the truth in so important a matter, do recommend to General Dalziel forthwith to call for the said Mr William Spence from the Magistrates of Edinburgh, and to cause such of His Majesty's forces, officers, and soldiers, as

[48] *Diocesan Register*, p. 150.

[49] *Historical Selections. From the MSS. of Sir John Lauder of Fountainhall.* Vol. I., p. 138.

[50] Wodrow's *History of The Sufferings of The Church of Scotland.* II., p. 386.

shall be found most trusty, to watch the said Mr William Spence by turns, and not to suffer him to sleep by night or by day, and for that end to use all effectual means for keeping him awake."[51] The "effectual means" were "pricking,"[52] and the intention was to induce raving, so that in his delirium the brave prisoner might perhaps reveal his secrets. The torture was continued for eight or nine nights, but Mr Spence did not rave, and tired his tormentors out. It was next resolved to try the "thumbkins" on him, and, indeed, Spence seems to have been one of the first regular prisoners to suffer this new Muscovy torture,[53] for the Act of Council authorising the use of "the new invention and engine called the thumbkins" was passed only a fortnight before; but the sanguine expectations of the Lords were not fulfilled in the present case, for though he sank under the agonising torment, he would not yield. Ten days later he was again threatened with the boot, and having meanwhile understood from his friends that the Government practically knew already all he could tell them, he promised to make a free and ingenuous confession on certain conditions—namely, that no new questions should be put to him, that he should not be obliged to be a witness against any person, and that he himself should be pardoned. Unfortunately, by a sheer accident in disclosing the meaning of some of the ciphers used in Argyle's correspondence, he put the Council on the track of the cipher[54] which expressed the name of his fellow-prisoner, the famous Carstares, who, however, does not in any way blame Mr Spence for what happened. He was sent back to prison, strict orders being given that he was not to be permitted to see Carstares, and when the Council adjourned for the holidays on September 13th, he was removed to Dumbarton Castle, and granted liberty within the walls. Whether he escaped, or was allowed to go out of the country, we cannot tell, but it is clear at any rate that he rejoined his old master in Holland, and the next we hear of him is that he was one of those who accompanied Argyle when he made his disastrous descent on Scotland in the spring of 1685. When the little fleet arrived off Kirkwall Mr Spence must needs go ashore to visit his uncle who lived there, along with one of the Earl's scouts. "Both," says Wodrow,[55] "were discovered and catched by the old bishop there. The Earl was peremptorily resolved to recover the two gentlemen, and ordered Sir Patrick Hume with a party of Fusileers to attack the town"; but the captains were obdurate and nervous, and gave the Earl time only to seize seven islanders and a vessel "lying ther with meall and money," when the ships sailed away, leaving the unfortunate secretary to his fate.[56] He was sent down to Edinburgh,[57] indicted for treason, and remitted in due form to the Assizes, tried, and found guilty, and we seem at last to be near his

[51] Wodrow II., p. 386.

[52] Graham Dunlop MSS., quoted in Story's *Carstares*, p. 80.

[53] See Fountainhall, p. 138.

[54] Story's *Carstares*, p. 82.

[55] History, II., p. 531.

[56] Fountainhall, p. 164.

[57] That his spirit was in no way cowed is obvious from the report of what he said and did when he was brought before the Privy Council and informed that "Argile was tane," and urged to tell everything. "He laugh't at them, and with a very obstinate and unbelieving carriage said—'If ye have the principall, what neids ye ask these questions at me.'"—Fountainhall, p. 187.

end when we read that the Lords ordained Mr William Spence to be taken to the Cross of Edinburgh on Wednesday next, July 22nd, and there to be hanged. Before that day arrived, however, he got a reprieve, and on August 17th he was allowed to remove to a chamber in Edinburgh because of sickness—quite unaccountable leniency at a time when the authorities did not scruple to hang dying men in their night-shirts. The Magistrates were made responsible for his safe keeping, and he undertook to re-enter the prison on the first of September. His reprieve was now continued till November 1st, and the last we hear of him was that in a letter from the King, dated October 14th, orders were given that he was to be kept a close prisoner. His master had been executed on June 30th, and had testified before his death that Mr William Spence had been to him a faithful friend and servant. It is impossible to say what became of him between this time and the Revolution, and unless he succeeded in escaping, it is highly probable that he remained in prison till the general clearance made by the alarmed authorities on the eve of that event. All we know for certain is that the General Assembly of 1690, amongst other items of business, declared his deposition null and void, and restored him to his old parish, the minister, Alexander Meldrum, having been deposed shortly before for not reading the Proclamation of the Estates, and not praying for their Majesties William and Mary. He remained in it only a few months, and in the autumn of 1691 he was translated to Fossoway, where he ended his days in peace in 1715,[58] at the age of 80, a clear proof that he was a man of iron constitution as well as of iron will and iron convictions.

We have to go forward something like a hundred years before the parish or its fair stream comes again into notice, though probably in the interval occurred the summary act of justice commemorated by the Glendevon "Gallows Knowe," on which some of the last Highland reivers were hung, and also the tragic event at "Paton's Fauld," a spot a short distance from the old drove road opposite the "Court Knowe," where two local gipsy families effectively settled their quarrel by practically annihilating each other.[59] It was in August, 1787, that Burns first made acquaintance with the Devon, which he has celebrated in three of his poems, though it is evident that both on his flying visit to Harvieston and during the longer stay he made in October of the same year he was more pleased with the human flowers that bloomed on its banks than with the awesome grandeur of the Rumbling Brig, and that Peggy Chalmers and Charlotte Hamilton were more intimately associated with his fond memories of the Devon valley than Caudron Linn and the Deil's Mill. Although the ladies at Harvieston were somewhat disappointed[60] that the more prominent local glories did not inspire the poet to an outburst, it is clear that the subtle softness of the Devon scenery made a deep impression on Burns, if the more aggressive beauty of its waterfalls and gorges left him cold. You feel this in all he has written about it, and it is significant that in one of his last songs, composed when he was down in body, mind, and estate, his thoughts

---

[58] *Fasti Ecclesia Scoticanae.* By Hew Scott, D.D. Vol. II., pp. 766-768.

[59] The ecclesiastical quarrel which began in 1765 when Mr Patrick Crichton was presented to the living, went on for several years, and only ended when the presentee, seeing that a peaceable settlement was impossible, retired.

[60] Chambers' *Life of Burns*, II., 144.

went back to the "crystal Devon, winding Devon," whose music seems to have got into his verse, and to the happy days he had spent on its "romantic banks" and amidst its "wild sequestered shades." It may be noted here that the "Holy Fair" was continued in Glendevon long after Burns' famous attack, and that down to 1835 the minister of the parish received an annual grant of five, and sometimes ten shillings, for grass destroyed at the Sacrament; while a handy parishioner also drew five shillings per annum for putting up the Communion tent on the glebe, and a little extra now and then for making a road to it.[61] It is impossible to say if Burns when at Harvieston was ever actually in Glendevon, but about thirty years later the home of the Taits, which the poet found so pleasant, is brought into close connection with the parish owing to an incident which had its own share in giving to the Church of England one of its wisest, if not one of its greatest, primates. It was in Glendevon House that young Archibald Campbell Tait, according to his own statement, which was found in his desk after his death, written on a sheet of foolscap, had an experience which he never forgot. His words are—"I had ridden over with my brother Crawfurd from Harvieston to Glendevon to visit old Miss Rutherford, and stayed the night in her house. I distinctly remember in the middle of the night awaking with a deep impression on my mind of the reality and nearness of the world unseen, *such as through God's mercy has never left me.*"[62] And with this fragment of spiritual history our local record comes to a close. If the parish of Glendevon, nestling, like Burns' Peggy, "where braving angry winter's storm the lofty Ochils rise," and its clear winding river, occupy but a lowly place in Scottish story, they have something better even than archaeological treasures and stirring memories—the abiding presence of that spirit of beauty, which is above all change, and which ever haunts

> "The green valleys
> Where Devon, sweet Devon, meandering flows."

---

[61] Glendevon Session Records.

[62] *Life of Archibald Campbell Tait.* By R. T. Davidson, D.D., and W. Bentham, D.D. 2 Vols. London: 1891.

BY THE WELL OF ST. FILLAN
BY REV. THOMAS ARMSTRONG, DUNDURN

"Harp of the North! that mouldering long hast hung
On the witch-elm that shades Saint Fillan's spring."

—Lady of the Lake.

Any one who has visited the scene hallowed in tradition as the sojourn of St. Fillan, can understand how the genius of Scott should have traced to Fillan's spring that draught of inspiration which conceived such a splendid poem as the "Lady of the Lake"; for it is here that the scenery of Upper Strathearn reaches its climax of beauty and grandeur.

Take St. Fillan's Hill as the point of vantage, and the view is most entrancing. Looking towards Comrie and Crieff, we have at our feet the richest and most beautifully wooded part of Strathearn—the valley interspersed in the most picturesque fashion, with knolls richly clad with larch, oak, or hazel; while here and there the gleam of the River Earn betrays her course, where she has emerged from sombre wood, or deep and rocky gorge. In spring-time the eye is delighted and refreshed with the varieties of green—from the deep and sombre shade of the Scotch pine and the almost yellow and brown of the young oak to the exquisite freshness and tender beauty of the larch. In autumn it is one blaze of colour. At our feet an avenue of beeches glowing red; everywhere masses of oak of russet brown—the rich and varied tints of the bracken contributing their share to the similitude of a glorious sunset; and the whole picture is rendered complete to the eye by being set in that massive rocky framework, known as the Aberuchill range, whose stern and rugged sides add to the feeling of the picturesque and beautiful the sense of the sublime.

Looking westward, we have within our immediate view a contrast in the form of a fine piece of pastoral scenery—green fields with cattle or sheep grazing, ploughed land and cornfield, farm-steading, and all that suggests the peaceful but laborious life of the hardy sons of toil.

Almost at our feet, in striking solitude, we discern the chapel and burying-ground of Dundurn. The peacefulness of the place, and the solemn grandeur of the mountains which soar above, and seem as if placed there to safeguard the seclusion, are all in harmony.

From the point of view already taken, that noble Ben, called Biron, forces itself upon our admiration—a mountain with what we might call character—not of any common order—not beaten into any shape by the ruthless elements, but with many determined points, which have survived the war with winds and frosts and rains—an old veteran, who, in spite of the scars where the shadows rest, has a look of triumph about him, especially when his peaks at evening catch the setting rays of the sun, or peer through a surrounding mist.

St. Fillan's Seat (S Fillan's Hill).

Although we are not at any great altitude on the top of St. Fillan's Hill, we are yet high enough to get a glimpse of that gem of Highland lochs—Loch Earn, set literally at the feet of the hills, its waters murmuring a never ceasing song, as if happy with their near presence, having wooed and kissed their steep and rugged sides into silver strands and gently curving bays from end to end; and, indeed, the very woods, as if drawn by this music and this wooing, have come to the very water's edge to bathe and to drink, and to watch their graceful forms mirrored in the bosom of the loch.

I need no apology for thus dwelling upon the romantic scenery of the place, for if, in these matter-of-fact times, the fame and reputed virtue of the Well of St. Fillans have departed, and the days of pilgrimage to its source are over, still the pure air, and perfect peace, and wild and romantic surroundings remain, to minister their undoubted healing powers to wearied minds and jaded bodies.

In writing about the Well of St. Fillans and other places of antiquarian interest in this neighbourhood, it almost goes without saying that much must be taken on trust. People are prone to believe that the dirty pool of stagnant water which still remains in the driest summer on the top of St. Fillan's Hill is the famous spring to which pilgrims at one time resorted. Any one who examines it will not fail to observe that it has all the appearance of an artificially built well, and must have been kept in order and preservation for a purpose. Tradition confirms the belief that this was at one time the well, but not always. The Rev. Mr M'Diarmid, minister of the parish of Comrie about the beginning of this century, gives us the following account of it:—

"This spring, tradition reports, reared its head on the top of Dun Fholain (Fillan's Hill) for a long time, doing much good, but in disgust (probably at the Reformation) it removed suddenly to the foot of a rock, a quarter of a mile to the southward, where it still remains, humbled, but not forsaken. It is still visited by valetudinary people, especially on the 1st of May and the 1st of August. No fewer than seventy persons visited it in May and August, 1791. The invalids, whether men, women, or children, walk or are carried round the well three times in a direction Deishal—that is from east to west, according to the course of the sun. They also drink of the water and bathe in it. These operations are accounted a certain remedy for various diseases. They are particularly efficacious for curing barrenness, on which account it is frequently visited by those who are very desirous of offspring. All the invalids throw a white stone on the Saint's cairn, and leave behind them as tokens of their gratitude and confidence some rags of linen or woollen cloth. The rock on the summit of the hill formed of itself a chair for the Saint, which still remains. Those who complain of rheumatism in the back must ascend the hill, sit in this chair, then lie down on their back, and be pulled down by the legs to the bottom of the hill. This operation is still performed, and reckoned very efficacious. At the foot of the hill there is a basin made by the

Saint on the top of a large stone, which seldom wants water even in the greatest drought, and all who are distressed with sore eyes must wash them three times with this water."

Of such holy wells, it may be interesting to learn that there were, previous to the Reformation, a great number throughout Scotland.[63] They were usually called after saints, because of the cells of saints being fixed near a spring. Hence these wells are usually in the vicinity of old ecclesiastical sites, and in many cases where the wells alone remain, they mark the place of those sites.

At these wells all diseases were supposed to be within the reach of cure. A student of the development theory might almost find traces of the growth of the specialist in them, for some of them acquired a fame for the cure of special diseases. The Well of St. Fillan, at Strathfillan, *e.g.*, was famous for the cure of insanity; the Well of St. Fillan, about which I write, as has already been noticed, was much resorted to for the cure of barrenness; and if we transfer the virtue of the waters to the credit of the Saint under whose auspices a cure was wrought, we might say of St. Servan that he was considered a great oculist; of St. Anthony, that he was an eminent specialist in the treatment of children's diseases; for to the Well of St. Servan the blind were led, to the Well of St. Anthony, sickly and "backgane bairns." In accounting for the popularity of these wells, the philosopher will reflect that there is a kernel of truth in most widespread error. The truth in the well is the truth that underlay the hydropathic treatment involved, also the treatment of fresh air and exercise, and the extra exertion, the stimulus of change, and the excitement associated with such pilgrimages, not to speak of the power of faith, based though it was on error. From this point of view we may in some respects regard the modern hydropathic establishment as in the line of development with the holy well of old.

It is a testimony to the universality and the popularity of the holy wells in this country, and to the persistency of the superstition, after it had been condemned by the Reformation, that a public statute had to be enacted in 1579 prohibiting these pilgrimages, and that this having been ignored or defied, they had again to be denounced in the strongest terms in 1679. "It seems not to be enough," says this edict, "that whole congregations were interdicted from the pulpit preceding the wonted period of resort, or that individuals humbled on their knees in public acknowledgment of their offence were rebuked or fined for disobedience. Now it was declared for the purpose of restraining the superstitious resort in pilgrimage to chappellis and wellis, which is so frequent and common in this kingdom, to the great offence of God, the scandall of the Kirk, and disgrace of His Majestie's government, that commissioners diligently search in all such pairts and places where this idolatrous superstition is used, and to take and apprehend all such persons, of whatsoever rank and quality, whom they sall deprehend going pilgrimage to chappellis or wellis, or whom they sall know themselves to be guilty of that cryme, and to commit them to waird until such measures should be adopted for their trial and punishment." It is further of especial interest to note the local effort made to suppress these pilgrimages. In the records of the Synod of Perth there is a minute to the following effect:—

---

[63] *Proceedings of the Antiquarian Society,* 1882-83.

"It is found that there is frequent repairing on certain days superstitiously to some wells within this province, as to one called Dumlorn, in Comrie. In the meantime the Synod ordains and entreats all the gentlemen of these bounds where these wells, or any other of that kind are, that they would use all diligence against these abuses as they may according to the Acts of Parliament made thereanent."

Those who have an antiquarian turn of mind will, on visiting the top of Dundurn, where the original well is supposed to have been, find themselves expatiating upon other features of interest surrounding them. The hill itself, it will be remarked, is covered all round, with the exception of the precipitous front facing the east, with piles of loose water-worn stones. At first view they appear only an irregular mass, and seem to be there only to make the ascent more slippery and difficult. Mr Skene, in his *Celtic Scotland*, points out that here we have the remains of an ancient fort. It is only recently, however, that the subject has come in for thorough investigation by Dr. Christison, one of the Rhind lecturers on Archaeology, who, by careful measurements and by the extensive knowledge which he has brought to bear on the subject, has quite established the fact. One sees that from the east side of the hill the position is by nature impregnable against attack; while on the south, west, and north sides, it is the triumph of the antiquarian's research and skill to re-build for us in imagination a series of fortified lines and enclosures, the original sites of which time has not altogether obliterated. The fortress was known in early days as Dundurn, and must have been a stronghold of considerable importance.[64]

Looking down upon the plain below, the little chapel at our feet, called the Chapel of St. Fillan, also takes us back to antiquity, though to a less remote one than the fortifications. It takes us back to pre-Reformation times. There is no record of the century to which it belongs, and the only relic that has been preserved to us from the pre-Reformation period is a holy water font. It stood in a niche in the wall of the chapel. When, however, it was deemed advisable to remove the tottering roof and to preserve what of the building would make a picturesque ruin, the font was taken in charge by Colonel Stewart of Ardvoirlich, and handed over by him to the Trustees of the Dundurn Parish Church. Placed on a suitable stand, and with an appropriate inscription, this font will represent an interesting link between the past and the present.

This old chapel, doubtless at one time a place of worship, was abandoned at the Reformation, and was taken possession of by the Stewart clan as a burial vault about the year 1580. For a long time this interesting old burying-ground was allowed to remain in a state of shameful neglect. There seemed to be no direct responsibility on the part of any heritor for its upkeep, and what seemed everybody's business became nobody's. This condition of *laissez faire* was confirmed by a sentimental though unreasonable objection to shifting into their right position a number of head-stones which time and weather had either displaced or Darwin's

---

[64] Fortrenn seems to have been the ancient name of a large district of Strathearn, of which Dundurn, or the fort of the Earn, was the capital.

worms had covered up. It was only five or six years ago that a Committee was formed, which in a regular manner, and with the consent of all parties interested, took in charge the upkeep of the burial-ground, with the aid of public subscription. A head-stone of great interest to antiquarians is one with figures of Adam and Eve sculptured in relief, while above these figures an angel is represented. The tree carved on the other side of the stone is evidently the tree of good and evil, and the whole represents in a crude way the expulsion of Adam and Eve from Paradise. This Adam and Eve stone is considered very rare, there being very few known throughout the country. This one differs from the others in the absence of the serpent, which is usually represented on them. Another monument of considerable interest is to be seen within the chapel. It is a memorial tablet recently erected by the present Laird of Ardvoirlich upon the wall of the east gable and containing the following inscription:—"This chapel, dedicated in early times to St. Fillan, the leper, has been, since the year 1586, the burial-place of the sept or clan of Stewart of Ardvoirlich." Here follow the names of those buried beneath, with the dates of their decease. On glancing over the names there recorded, one will notice the name of Major James Stewart, and will remember that it is to the same memory that a stone still stands erected on the south side of the loch, about three miles up. We there read that this Major James Stewart was temporarily interred, and thereafter removed to his final resting-place at Dundurn. This member of the clan seems to have been of a fiery, irascible, and adventurous nature, and Sir Walter Scott, while in this neighbourhood, found sufficient material in connection with this personage to reproduce his likeness in his Allan M'Aulay of the *Legend of Montrose*. In his introduction to this romance the author gives an interesting account of his character, and sets before us two different versions of the part he acted in the death of Lord Kilpont; indeed, one will look upon the romantic scenery of this district with redoubled interest after a perusal of this work of the great novelist. With reference to this Major Stewart's tomb-stone on the side of the loch, which has just been referred to, the legend is that the Major died a natural death at Ardvoirlich, and his body was being carried to Dundurn for burial, but the Drummonds and Murrays, who were at enmity with the clan, threatened to intercept the funeral, and a snowstorm coming on, they interred the body on the loch side near the spot where the stone is, and subsequently took it to the chapel.

Another head-stone of considerable interest is to be seen hear the entrance to the grounds of Ardvoirlich itself. It marks the place where the remains of seven of the Macdonalds were interred, the legend being that that clan, on their way to or from a raid on Glenartney Forest, attacked Ardvoirlich House, and the men of the clan being absent with their cattle on the hills, the lady of the house kept them at bay until the men came down, and then they slaughtered all the Macdonalds, except one man, and their bodies were buried in a hole on the loch side. Years after, on excavating to make a pond for cattle to drink from, a number of human bones were found, and the stone was erected to mark the spot.

Another object of considerable antiquarian interest in the possession of the Ardvoirlich family is the charm-stone. It is said by tradition to have been brought from the Holy Land at the time of the Crusades by the Fitz-Allans, who were progenitors of the Stewarts, and who were active Crusaders. It was considered a most holy stone, and had healing properties of a high order. It is a very perfect specimen of rock crystal; the silver setting is Saracenic in character, and said to be very old. Up to 1840, and even later, people used to come to Ardvoirlich from long distances to have the stone immersed in water, while a Gaelic incantation was repeated by the laird or lady. Then the water was carried home, and one condition was that the possessor of the water must not enter any house until home was reached; then if given to cattle to drink, or sprinkled over them, it acted as a perfect cure for any murrain or disease.

On the death of the laird in 1854, the stone was sent into a bank for safe custody, and then all the healing properties were destroyed. It was said also that the last lady of Ardvoirlich who used it, and who was a Maxtone of Cultoquhey, had no Gaelic, and was too lowland by birth to believe in it, and she most irreverently (not knowing the Gaelic incantation) just repeated—"If it'll dae ye nae guid, it'll dae ye nae hairm," and that also destroyed the charm.

Another object which does not fail to attract the attention of the visitor to St. Fillans is the picturesque little island at the east end of the loch, called the Neish Island, for it has its romantic story to tell. "It is uncertain" (says John Brown in his description of the place) when or by whom "the island in Loch Earn rose into form or importance; but that it was entirely the work of man (and certainly it was no contemptible undertaking) is evident from its circular shape, the nature of the bed on which it is raised and surrounding it, and the purpose to which it might be made subservient in lawless times. The ancestors of the present family of Ardvoirlich made it their occasional residence, at the remote period when they held the eight-mark land on which St. Fillans is now built, an endowment which continued annexed to the Chapel or Priory of Strathfillan till its dissolution at the Reformation." On the island there are the remains of what appear to have been a number of dwellings. That it was used as a haunt or refuge by raiders is certain from the tradition which gives it its name of Neish Island. According to the tradition, it was the refuge of the remnant of the Clan Neish who had been defeated in a bloody battle with the MacNabs. There the former carried on a kind of predatory warfare with the MacNabs, and on one occasion so roused the wrath of the latter that a speedy and terrible revenge followed. The stalwart sons of the MacNab, urged by their wrathful sire, whose hint in the words—"The night is the night if lads were but lads," almost amounted to a command, equipped themselves with dirk, pistol, and claymore, raised a boat on their shoulders, and carrying it by night all the way from Loch Tay across the hills by Glentarken, launched it stealthily on Loch Earn, and taking the Neishes by surprise are said to have killed them all, except one boy, who made good his escape. The following lines by the Rev. John Hunter, Crieff, give very appropriate expression and colouring to this interesting tradition:—

> Here sit we down on this fair sun-strewn bank,
> Beside this queen of lakes, whose loveliness
> From out of half-shut eyelids softly woos
> To sweet forgetfulness.
> Above, the wood, and interspersed knolls,

Made greener by the pat of fairy feet
And dancing moonbeams, fringe the rugged knees
Of scarred and bronzéd heights whose wind-notched crests
Look grandly down. Fair scene and home of peace
Ineffable; and yet not ever so,
For I have seen these scars run full and white,
And heard their trumpetings as they rush'd madly
      Adown the spray-sown steep, past wood and knoll,
To mingle with the waters of the lake
Vexed with the storm and sounding loud in sympathy.
      What have we here? What human trace of times
When hearts o'erflowed, and hand and steel were swift,
And red in the flashing of a hasty thought?
Ah me! these times, these woful times when word
And blow were wed, and none could sunder them,
And honour'd live! See yonder isle set single
In the lake, near by where Earn darts swiftly 'neath
The rustic bridge to bear the music of the place
To broader Tay, who murmurs from afar
In the rich harmony of his many streams—yon isle,
The haunt of lovers now, where hearts that touch
And thrill, cling closer in the eerie sense
Of fear that lurks amid the tumbled stones
Of robbers' lair. Here, once upon a time,
When might was right, and men made wrongful
Gain of Nature's fastnesses, a ruffian couched
And preyed upon his kind. Long time he throve,
But vengeance woke at length, and the heavy tread
Of frowning men from far Loch Tay—skiff-laden.
Adown the glen they came one moonless night,
Goaded by tingling sneer of white-hair'd sire.
They rest where Tarken pours his scanty tide,
Then silently—nor moon nor star appearing—
Launch forth upon the lake, and softly steal
Towards the caitiff's fire gleaming through the dark
Like blood-shot eye. All saving one, and he
Was left to skirt the shore and give the foe
Rough welcome should he 'scape to land. Who then
Fair-hair'd and young stood there in melting mood,
With all his mother in his swimming eyes,
Of abbot's line—with dirk half drawn, fearing,
Hoping, praying, as his gentler nature bade
That life and light would not go out together.
The hope seem'd vain. From out the gloom there came
The grinding keel—the tread of hurrying feet—
Clashing of words, of steel, and all was dark—

And all was still. But hark! a sound—the faint
Breathing of one who swims with pain, the plash
Of nerveless hands nearer and nearer comes,
Yet ever fainter. What boots it now to have
Escaped the vengeful swords that smote his kin?
The waves engulf him and his bubbling cry.
But unhoped help is near—a friendly word—
A plunge, then stroke on stroke, and timeously
A hand to save. Say not, ye thoughtless ones,
That yon grim head, clean sever'd from the trunk,
Was the chief trophy of that night. Nay;
For kindly thoughts endure, and the High Will
That holds all things within the ever-opening fold
Of His eternal purpose—that High Will
Look'd down with loving eyes that pierce the dark,
And bless'd the deeds that glorified MacNab,
The abbot's son—half-savage and half-saint.
Time sped; the deed was not forgot, and still
The tale is told when nights are long and the lone
Owl hoots upon the hill. And now there stands
Within bowshot of the isle—a house of God
That calls to prayer—a parish church—the fruit
Of kindly thoughts that stirr'd the watcher's heart,
And clomb to Heaven in mute appeal, that night
When vengeance smote and light and life went out together.

So much, then, for the prospect which an antiquarian standing by the Well of St. Fillan would embrace within the programme of his research. If we try to form a picture of the social condition of the people who lived in the midst of this fair vale of Earn in those early days, it is a scene of continual strife we conjure up—clan fighting with clan, and one feud succeeding another. These were the days of superstitious pilgrimages, days of rooted custom and unchanging faith. So much the better for the Saint. The halo of his sanctity shines out all the more against the background of ignorance and strife. If he were to re-visit those scenes now, how much would he have to deplore! No more pilgrimages, no more belief in miracles. What a downcome from his dignity to be the patron of a golf course or the chaplain of a curling club, instead of enjoying the fame and name of the holy well. *Requiescat in pace.*

The past was not all strife, however. Traces of agriculture lead us to picture this fine strath as at one time throng with peaceful and busy life. There were, no doubt, in those warlike times intervals of peace, when the inhabitants of the glen could tend their cattle and cultivate their potatoes and corn at leisure; and whether we look back upon this land of the "mountain and the flood" as having been the nursery of our best soldiers, or as having been peopled by a race rendered strong and manly by a simple mode of life, the present prospect of our Highland glens cannot but fill us with sad reflection when we behold the process of emigration and depopulation still going on, and when we see that ere long the only links with the past of a once strong and hardy race of people will be the mere traces of their cultivation, the ruins of their once populous hamlets, and the grave-stones in their old burying-grounds.

It is true there is a compensating process going on. For while one regrets the disappearance of the old thatched houses of the primitive village of St. Fillans and the migration of their youthful life to the city, the rise of the modern villa along the loch side speaks of the growth of a temporary population known as the "summer visitors." It is not likely that their peaceful pursuits—their climbing and pic-nic expeditions, their regattas and loch illuminations, will be considered to be as worthy to be recorded in a future "Book of Chronicles" as the feuds and raids of the past. Still, it is to be hoped that this land of "brown heath and shaggy wood" may even in this innocent way minister to the rearing of a healthy manhood and womanhood, and continue to be the nursery of that muscular body and brave spirit which in the past have made the name of Caledonia great.

THE PLAIN OF THE BARDS

BY REV. ARTHUR GORDON, M.A., MONZIEVAIRD

To supply even in brief outline a sketch of the united parishes of Monzie-vaird and Strowan is to cover many centuries and to recall some extraordinary events and remarkable persons. These parishes comprise an area of about eight miles long by six miles broad, and on the map somewhat resemble a pear. The scenery varies from the bare summit of Benchonzie, the limit on the north, where the highest elevation is reached at 3048 feet, and the wood-crowned Turleum, 1291 feet high, where "wind and water sheers," the southern boundary, down to the well-cultivated and nearly level carse, which lies all the way between Crieff and Comrie at about two hundred feet above the sea. The little hills abound with coigns of vantage, rewarding the pedestrian; while even the driving tourist finds a rich harvest for the eye in the wonderfully diversified landscape presented on all sides. The River Earn, if it lacks the majesty of the Tay and the impetuosity of the Garry, makes itself recognised as the dominating feature, whether in its quiet meandering moods or in the flooded temper, overflowing its banks and spreading its deposit of alluvial soil. Its tributaries—the Lednock, with its "Deil's Cauldron," and the Turret and Barvick, oft visited for their pleasing cascades, along with many another rivulet and spring—call up the Promised Land of old—"a land of hills and valleys which drinketh water of the rain of heaven." In climate, also, this part of Strathearn is singularly favoured, sheltered as it is from the biting east wind and fortified from the northern blasts by its mountain barriers. Its rainfall, also, is far from excessive; for many sky-piercing hill-tops tap the rain clouds from the Atlantic long before they reach Central Perthshire.

The name of the parish, now called Monzievaird, but formerly Monivaird, and anciently Moivaird, is believed to be Gaelic, and to signify, not the hill, but rather the "mossy plain" of the bards. It is difficult to say how far this carries us back. The Bards are not to be confounded with the Druids, a religious class from which they were quite distinct. The bards seem to have been the seanachies, antiquaries, poets, and genealogists. It was their special function to compose and to chant verses or rhymes in praise of their heroes or benefactors, and in the absence, so far as we know, of any method of recording past transactions or histories, we may believe that our ancestors transmitted orally, in lines composed by the bards, the memorable sayings and deeds which they wished to hand down to generations after them. How far they were worthy of credit, and how far they were subject to the vices of flattery or detraction we cannot tell, but we may be sure that those who were accounted great in these ancient times were anxious to have their doughty deeds immortalised, and perhaps were as sensitive to the tone of public criticism thus represented as is the statesman or warrior of to-day. What would we not give to hear from the living voice of one of those bards, were it only possible, the stores of traditionary lore of which they were the sole depositories! As it is, we can but lament the almost total absence of reliable information regarding their genius, perhaps also the jealous competition for the laureate's place in these pre-historic times.

Remains at the western end of the parish are supposed to represent two Druidical temples. Cairns and barrows have been numerous, and in one of these, on Ochtertyre, there was discovered, near the close of last century, a stone coffin, containing two coarse earthenware urns. One of these held burnt bones, and the other the bones of a head, having the lower jaw-bone and teeth in marvellous preservation. In the stone coffin was also found a stone hatchet about four inches long, bluish coloured, and of triangular shape, which evidently belonged to an age before iron was in use here. It is well known that the Romans had camps at Ardoch, Strageath, and Dalginross. Evidences of their presence in Monzievaird might, therefore, be expected, and they are not awanting. A Roman burial-ground of some extent, full of large slabs of stone, lies northeast of Clathick (hence perhaps the name), and is in a line between the camp at Dalginross—a circular burial-place near Victoria—and the Roman station on the Brae of Callander. In 1783 there was found in the plain of Monzievaird a bronze vessel resembling a coffee-pot, and in 1805 the bronze head of a spear was found in Ochtertyre Loch. In 1808 similar spear heads were found near the church, erected in 1804, which now serves the united parishes. These relics are pronounced by the best antiquarians to be undoubtedly Roman.

We now proceed to notice the first written account which history gives of Monzievaird. If there be any truth in the old chroniclers, a battle was fought here, and, after a long civil war, a contested succession to the Crown was settled by the slaughter of the reigning sovereign of Alban, a usurper who passes over the stage of history under the various names of "Gryme," "Girgh Mackinat Macduff," and reigned eight years. It may be worth while to give several references. John of Fordun's chronicle tells how Malcolm, son of Kenneth, strengthened by the favour of the people, and at the instigation of some of his chiefs, sent a message to the King, giving him the alternatives of either vacating the throne, or that they two should submit their cause to the just verdict of God by fighting, either man to man or accompanied by their warrior hosts. Gryme was very indignant at this defiance, while Malcolm, on the other hand, boldly advanced to meet him with a small but picked band, and reached a field called Auchnabard (the field of the bards), styled "a meet place for a battle." Here the two armies fought out a cruel engagement, till at length the King was mortally wounded, and, being led out of the battle by his men, died the same night. Thus Malcolm gained the victory and the kingdom. The register of St. Andrews calls the slain monarch "Kenneth (Grim)," and makes his death to be "at Moieghvard" in 1001. *The Chronykil of Scotland* calls this same place "Bardory," and in Latin "Campus Bardorum," which corresponds to Auchnabard. A cairn on a neighbouring height commemorates this conflict which made history;

but the slain King was not buried here, but

> "Carried to Colme-Kill;
> The sacred storehouse of his predecessors,
> And guardian of their bones."

The Church of Monzievaird was in all probability founded, by Saint Serf, and he was certainly its patron saint. If we are not compelled to postulate two saints of this name from the number of years covered by traditions which cannot all relate to the same person, we would incline to quit hold of the earlier and less definite tradition, and to consider Saint Serf as contemporary with Adamnan, the celebrated Abbot of Iona, and distinguished biographer of Saint Columba. St. Serf founded many churches, and his reputation in the Middle Ages for the neat and appropriate miracles attributed to him may be reckoned the measure of his eminence among Scotland's early evangelists. Wyntoun gives a quaint dialogue between St. Serf and the enemy of mankind, in which the Devil, plying the Saint with many knotty theological questions, wholly fails to overcome him, and suddenly departs. Another of these monkish miracles makes St. Serf discover the theft of a sheep by ordering it to bleat forth the story of its wrongs from the guilty stomach of the thief, and to redden his face with shame for having denied his crime! St. Serf's memory survives here in the well called after him, with its plentiful supply of water. As lately as 1760 the parishioners were wont to be drawn by a lurking superstition to drink of it on Lammas Day, leaving in it white stones, spoons, or rags, which they brought as remembrancers, just as devout Mohammedans still leave their prayer rags attached to the grating of the Mosque El-Aksa, at Jerusalem, or the lower branches of the giant oak that marks the site of the grove at Dan. St. Serf's festival and fair day long continued, and was kept on the 1st of July while the market lasted. The church itself was impropriated to the Abbey of Inchaffray, founded by the Earl of Strathearn about the beginning of the twelfth century, and was served by a vicar, to whom that monastery delegated the clerical duty, doubtless on the usual pittance of stipend.

The Tosachs, from the Gaelic word meaning "first" or "chief," were the old proprietors of Monzievaird. Their first residence was not at the old castle at Greenend, but at Balmuick, on the estate of Lawers, then called Fordie, and the foundation of the house was traceable at the close of last century. The chief of Monzievaird was accustomed to execute a man on the first day of every month, and this celebration of the almanac at Tom-an-Tosach was apparently designed to prevent the feudal rights of pit and gallows from falling into desuetude. The story runs that the last chief held nightly interviews with a fairy, a proceeding which aroused his wife's jealousy. She tracked him by a ball of worsted attached to his button, and, discovering him in conclave with the fairy, demanded her immediate destruction. Thereupon the fairy fled, and the power of the Tosach departed also. The inhabitants rose against him, and he had to seek refuge abroad.

Castle Cluggy, which stands on the peninsula on the north side of the Loch of Monzievaird, is undoubtedly very old, but how old no one can tell. A square tower, about 17 feet by 18 feet, with walls five or six feet thick, of tremendous strength, is all that now remains. It is said to have been a seat of the "Red Cumin," the rival of

Robert the Bruce for the throne of Scotland, slain at Dumfries before the high altar. The prison is sometimes said to have been on the island in the loch, but really the dungeon must be sought under the foundations of the tower. In the charter giving Ochtertyre to the Murrays, in the year 1467, it is even then described as an "ancient fortalice." The key of the tower was found about fifty years ago on the east side of the building. The old church of Monzievaird, now converted into a mausoleum, was the scene of a dreadful tragedy, characteristic of the spirit of feudal times. The Murrays and the Drummonds were but ill neighbours in the days of James IV. The collision between them in this instance has been ascribed to the levying of tithes, but without historic grounds; and the law of retaliation is even older than that of teinds, and far more widely practised. In a foray which began near Knock Mary the Murrays or their retainers were overpowered and driven westward. They kept up a running fight round the western base of Tomachastel, and an obstinate struggle took place in the hollow between Westerton and the Loch, where many men fell. The Murrays, however, succeeded in reaching the church, where 120 men able to bear arms, with their wives and children, took refuge. They were followed by the Drummonds, reinforced, as some say, by Campbell of Dunstaffhage, and thirsting for vengeance. Even then they might have escaped, had not one of the Murray clan indiscreetly revealed their hiding-place by aiming a successful shot at one of the Drummonds. The Drummonds now summoned them to surrender, but in vain, and then piled wood round the long, low, heather-thatched edifice, and consumed it with its human holocaust. One Murray alone, David by name, escaped, being aided by one of the Drummonds, who was attached to his sister. He in turn was hated and persecuted by his own clan, and forced to escape to Ireland. After some years he returned thence under the effectual protection of the powerful Abbot of Inchaffray, who was a Murray. He was settled on the Abbey lands, and the property which he received still bears the name of Drummond-Ernoch (of Erin).

The massacre of Monzievaird was sternly avenged by King James IV. The Master of Drummond, leader of the party, and some of his followers were executed at Stirling. The estate of Drummond was required to provide for the widows and orphans, and further to expiate their sacrilegious crime by re-building the church. Even then the house of prayer could scarcely be called the abode of peace. It is said to have been the scene of fierce bickerings, and that the gauntlet of the Murrays was for many years fastened on a small gallery of the church, and formal challenge made to anyone to remove it before divine service was allowed to begin. When the foundations of the present mausoleum were being dug a quantity of charred wood was found, and very many calcined bones—those nearer the door on the west being of larger size than the others towards the east, which were probably those of women and children. They must have been buried as they lay.

The Murrays of Ochtertyre come of the Tullibardine family, and the present proprietor is the fifteenth in descent from the first. The addition of Keith to the ancient "Moray," changed to Murray, arose from marriage with the heiress of Dunnottar Castle, in Kincardineshire. It is a singular fact that the succession has uniformly descended from father to son. The existing house of Ochtertyre was built by the great-grandfather of the present Baronet, and for prospect it would be hard to equal it. The old house stood near the great ash tree further west, and a yet older is proved by a family record, which narrates the births of generations at Quoig House, above the church. Robert Burns' visit to Ochtertyre in 1787 and the two poems he produced are too familiar to need mention here. In the reign of Charles I. a mortality greater even than that caused by war almost depopulated the bonnie braes of Ochtertyre. The dreaded Plague assumed alarming proportions, and many huts were erected for isolation near the west end of Monzievaird Loch. The dead were not buried in the churchyard, but in a large sepulchral mound near the Marle Lodge gate.

The Right Honourable Sir George Murray, G.C.B., perhaps the most distinguished member of the Ochtertyre family, after meritorious service in Egypt and the Peninsular War, was chief of the general staff under Wellington at Waterloo. He also served the State as a politician, six times representing Perthshire in Parliament, and attaining among many honours the office of Secretary of State for the Colonies in the Duke of Wellington's Government of 1828. The present Baronet is a worthy successor of an honoured line, and his generous consideration for the public in throwing open his grounds and granting the fullest facilities for their enjoyment deserves the highest praise. It is claimed for Glenturret that the two last wolves seen in Scotland were killed there. But a similar claim has been advanced for Nairnshire, and, with far more likelihood, for the wilds of the Moor of Rannoch. The glen, however, was long famous for its falcons. In few places is the bird-life more various or abundant than in the woods of bonnie Ochtertyre. And the rabbit, introduced there while the present century was young, has evidently come to stay and to multiply.

At Upper Quoig two reputed witches once dwelt, but whether from greater fear or greater enlightenment here than elsewhere, they were never called to endure the ordeal either by fire or by water. They hunted in couples apparently, for the story goes that two men at Clathick, rising early on a May morning, saw them coming up the burn-side, putting a tether across the stream, and saying, "Come all to me." This incantation succeeded in providing the witches' dairy with a double supply of milk, while their neighbours had none! Verily many poor old crones have lost their lives on as trivial a charge. Passing westward to the compact property of Clathick, now owned by Captain Campbell Colquhoun, we learn that it was given off from Ochtertyre in dowry with a Miss Mary Murray. It was a curious marriage contract provision that her initials should be cut upon each lintel, and men were living thirty years ago who had seen "M.M." carved on the stones of the old house.

The estate of Lawers conjures up from the deep oblivion of ages many stirring times. It was originally "Fordie," but was named Lawers after the Campbells from Loch Tayside came into possession. How different our quiet Christian Lord's Days and "kirk-yard cracks" from these Sunday and festival occasions of bloodshed,

> "When strangers from Breadalbane
> And clansmen from Loch Tay
> Brought to the priest their offerings,
> But fought each holy day!"

Still we may remark the ruined chapel almost smothered by the overturned yew trees that were planted, less, perhaps, to mark the "route" of the Mass carried in procession (hence "routine," corrupted into "Rotten Row,") than to furnish the twanging bow for these martial spirits. That great boulder-stone at the north-eastern end of the magnificent avenue opposite is, most likely, a Roman landmark, though it is customary to declare that the Earn once flowed past it. Colonel Campbell of Lawers was not only a sincere reformer, but John Knox's history tells us how he commanded a regiment raised to make good the cause of religious faith and freedom. His second successor was a yet more staunch and eminent Scotsman, knighted in 1620, and created Earl of Loudon in 1633. He proved himself a stout opponent of the arbitrary measures of Charles I. and Laud; was one of the most prominent actors in the Glasgow Assembly of 1638, and nominated to represent the Church of Scotland in the Westminster Assembly of Divines. He narrowly escaped being beheaded in the Tower of London, in spite of a safe conduct and without trial; but the fiat of the insensate monarch was recalled, and the warrant torn up by Charles a single day before the axe was doomed to fall, from fear of the odium and vengeance his death would have called forth. Not to remain Chancellor of Scotland (as he was for ten years) would he imperil the interests of religious liberty and national independence, just then threatened by Stuart absolutism; and yet he was a man of the type of the great Montrose, as loyal to the King as he was true to Church and people. Few deserve better to rank among "The Scots Worthies." He disponed Lawers estate to his brother, who, fighting against Cromwell at Inverkeithing, was badly beaten, and had his lands on the north of Loch Earn taken from him by an oppressive exaction put in force against him by the same Stuart dynasty, whose cause he had so faithfully championed.

A thrilling tale introduces the next laird of Lawers, son of the last named. He executed a punitive commission against his uncanny neighbours, the Macgregors, who determined on revenge. They surprised him at Lawers in bed, and threatened instant death, even in his wife's presence. He urged for time to pray, and that it might be for quietness in the chapel hard by, which request they granted. On the way thither he so played on their cupidity, offering them 10,000 merks if they would spare his life, that at last he prevailed. Faithful to his engagement, he raised this immense sum, much of it being gathered in halfpence, and carried on horseback to the appointed trysting-place. But Lawers was better than his word, for soldiers surrounded the house, and made the Macgregors prisoners. The game ended with checkmate, when the duped freebooters paid the death penalty in Edinburgh. Colonel David R. Williamson, the present laird of Lawers, has been long noted for his public spirit and eminent services to agriculture.

Tomachastel, the central wooded height of the parish, now surmounted by the monument, erected by his widow, in 1832, to the memory of General Sir David Baird of Ferntower, is marked out beyond all reasonable doubt as the site of the ancient Castle of Earn, for long the fortress dwelling of the great and powerful Earls of Strathearn. The title is now merged in the names of Royalty, like the Dukedoms of Rothesay and Albany. Our own beloved Queen's father was the Duke of Kent and Strathearn, as her third son is Duke of Connaught and Strathearn. No situation within the wide strath can compare with it in fair and far-reaching prospect, combined with facilities for defence; and the lighting of its beacon fire would be so universally observed over a wide domain that a personal summons, like that of the fiery cross, would scarcely be needed. Romance and gruesome horror are strangely blended here; for was it not from the walks in close proximity to the castle that the fair Lady Mary Graham, only daughter of stout old Malise, Earl of Strathearn, espied her future husband, John Moray of Drumshergart, fishing in the well-stocked pools below? And did he not find her society more engrossing than any (whole or half) scaly inhabitant of the mermaid's pool? The Morays of Abercairny estate (the fair lady's marriage portion) and many another territorial family claim descent from the union of these happy lovers. The rough hospitality, and swift, if not always impartial, administration of feudal justice are themes inviting to historic imagination; nor is the religious element wanting, for the Earls of Strathearn, besides founding Inchaffray Abbey, endowed the Bishopric of Dunblane with one-third of their domains. A sad and shameful story links the castle with the good King Robert the Bruce, and probably brought about its destruction. Joanna, only child of the seventh Earl, was Countess in her own right, and married to John de Warenne, Earl of Surrey, and English Governor of Scotland. The husband and wife had different minds and purposes. The lady was found guilty of conspiracy, with Lord Soulis of Hermitage Castle and others, against the life of the good King Robert. She confessed her offence, and was condemned to perpetual imprisonment within her own castle. Constant tradition affirms that it was set on fire and burnt to the ground, whether as the result of accident or a successful siege. One story tells how the Earl tried to save his wife, but failed from the irresistible power of the flames. The castle became a ruin, and was never re-built. Actual observation, after more than 500 years, has confirmed the truth, in this case stranger than fiction. Sir David Baird, the hero of the Nile, Cape of Good Hope, Corunna, and Seringapatam (remembered by the oldest folk for hunting with hawks, attended by a native Indian), having died at Ferntower in 1832, was first buried in Monzievaird Churchyard, and old people still recall the extraordinary storm of thunder and rain which signalised his funeral day. His widow prepared the massive monumental obelisk of granite, said to be exactly similar to Cleopatra's Needle, since struck by lightning in 1878, and badly rent, but now restored. It required foundations broad and deep. Most of the stones of the old castle had gone to form dykes in the neighbourhood. The workmen, thinking they had to deal with solid rock, proceeded to blast it, when to their amazement the charge of gunpowder, instead of only throwing stones and debris into the air, operated downward and revealed a dungeon cut in the solid rock. There lay all that remained of the proud and daring Joanna, Countess of Strathearn and Princess of the Orkneys. A few gold and silver bracelets and ornaments, belonging to a lady's dress, were found among the black rubbish with another trinket, teaching the old, old lesson, "Vanity of vanities, all is vanity."

Strowan Kirk.

It only remains to describe the antiquities of Strowan. There was a Thane of "Struin" in Strathearn, in very early times, when Thanes were servants of the King, holding their land in fee-farm for a certain "census," or feu-duty. Strowan, like Monzievaird, had a Celtic saint for founder—St. Ronan. He is not to be identified with the saint of that name, of whom the venerable Bede records that he championed the later Roman method of calculating the time of the Easter festival against Bishop Finan of Lindisfarne, who stoutly held the Columban rule. Rather may we count him the same with the Abbot of Kingarth, in Bute (died 737 A.D.), and founder of Kilmaronog, on Loch Etive, the parish of similar name in Dumbartonshire, and the Parish Church of Iona, called after him "Tempul Ronain." St. Ronan's name is to this day associated with his well, the pool that never failed to supply him with fish on Fridays; the ruins of the old church or chapel, and St. Ronan's bell. Tradition says that the Cross of Crieff was taken from Strowan to Crieff upwards of 200 years ago. The market cross of Strowan now stands on a small mound west from the old kirk and near the mansion-house. A fine old lime tree which shaded it succumbed to the unprecedented storm of November, 1893; and all who know the venerable Laird of Strowan hope that he may live to see the young lime sapling with which he lately replaced it grow up to cast its shade over the cross once more. The latter is Maltese in form; and has on it, besides the initials of the Latin inscription on the Saviour's cross, I.N.R.I., the Moray star, and other symbols. It was probably taken from the churchyard. The arches of the bridge, with its narrow roadway and parapet, and little cities of refuge for foot-passengers, are not of a hoary antiquity; but the pillars, on which at one time planks used to be laid for crossing, are much older. The Kirk-Session records contain many entries of sums paid to the boatman for ferrying parishioners from the north side to Strowan Church. Picturesque ruin though the church is, it is not 230 years old in any part, and public worship on alternate Sundays was performed there till the beginning of this century. In 1669 the previous church was still standing, and in such repair that an application was made to the Synod to require the lairds of Monzievaird, Ochtertyre, Fordie, Clathick, &c., to attend the Church of Strowan in consequence of Monzievaird Church having become ruinous and past repair. The Commissioners of Teinds had ordered one church to be built near the present site, but the heritors of each of the united parishes did their best to evade complying. Two graves are deserving of special mention. One is the resting-place of "fair Helen of Ardoch"; the other marks the place of repose of the eldest son of the House of Strowan, who laid down his life on the sands of Tel-el-Kebir, bravely advancing to the charge against the Egyptian lines.

St. Ronan's Bell is preserved at Strowan House. It is small, circular, and looks as if it had been made to be grasped by the hand. Tradition says it was rung under the bell-man's gown when mass was said in Romish times. The tongue is wanting. Some say it never had one, but was meant to be struck from without. It never could have been heard afar off. Close scrutiny proves it to be slightly cracked. But worthless for music, it is excellent for law! It is the symbol of tenure of Ballindewar or Dewarland. (Dewar is from the Gaelic for keeper). The Dewars were the hereditary beadles of Strowan, and keepers of St. Ronan's bell. They held their croft free of all cess, stipend, or public burden, as it still remains. When the present Laird of Strowan negotiated at a high price the purchase of this piece of land, he received with "the bellman's pendicle" the bell itself as the charter of the feu lands, and as custodier of all rights of the same.

The saddest feature in making this short survey of the united parish is the great and continuous decline of the population. In 1755 there were 1460 people; in 1793 there were 1025; in 1891 the number had sunk to 490. No doubt the livelier prospects of town life allure many. No doubt many have profited by the fact of removal. The agricultural outlook appears gloomier than ever, which tends to restrict the area under cultivation. But it cannot be gainsaid that many have had to remove from the mistaken policy of adding land to land and field to field. It is breaking down when viewed in the sole interest of the proprietor; how much more is it found wanting when viewed from the standpoint of the wider interests and welfare of our common country?

The minister of Monzievaird and Strowan most likely to achieve immortality is the Rev. William Robertson, the gifted versifier and author of Hymns 3—"Thee God we praise, Thee Lord confess," the Monzievaird *Te Deum*, and 311—"A little child the Saviour came," the first baptismal hymn, in the Scottish Hymnal. To him the account now given, incomplete as it is, owes more than to any other. He has also cast into verse that seems worth preserving his parish musings in the following lines:—

> A shady knoll o'erlooks a dale
> Where Earn meanders down the vale;
> A knoll enwreathed in oak and fern,
> The sweetest nook in all Strathearn.
> The morn there breaks with earliest ray,
> Here latest shines the lingering day,
> There summer reigns supremely fair,
> And winter ev'n is lovely there.
> Its eastern prospect looks entire
> Along the glades of Ochtertyre;
> Its south, a mountain forest shade
> By dark blue pine and larches made;
> While lone Glenartney in the west
> Lies cradled like a turtle's nest,
> And huge Benvoirlich crown'd with snow
> Defends the smiling glens below.
> Dear shady knoll, whose varied view
> Enfolds green field and mountain blue,
> How oft at morn and eventide
> I've strolled around thy stony side
> And listened to the artless song
> That swell'd the glorious vale along!
> Mark'd where the sunbeams kindliest fell
> On rocky ridge and heathery dell,
> And yielded all my soul to share
> The teachings of a scene so fair!
> In storm or calm, thy grateful shade
> My fond retreat was ever made.
> There have I marked the thunder cloud

Invest all heaven with sable shroud;
There heard the peal arouse again
The echoes of the Turret glen,
While Auchingarroch from afar
Rolled back the elemental war;
There have I watched wing'd lightning play
Adown Glenartney's rugged way,
Or gild each flinty summit hoar
From Callander to far Ken More;
There seen the Ruchill deluge foam,
And o'er the strath in eddies roam,
Sweeping beyond the power to save
A golden harvest on its wave.

    *   *   *   *   *

High on my left, unstained by storm,
An obelisk uprears its form;
Commemorates in fitting style
Heroic deeds upon the Nile,
When he who conquered in Mysore
To Afric's sands his legions bore,
And showed the trembling prince and slave
The gentleness of one that's brave.
Yet on that monumental stone
More feats of high renown are shown,
Where he a prisoner and enchained,
At last his noblest laurels gained:
Lived to avenge each treacherous wrong,
And triumph when he suffered long.
There, too, his brilliant tasks to cope,
'Tis told he seized the Cape of Hope;
And sad Corunna's bloody shore
But added to his fame the more.
A widow's love the warrior praised,
A widow's love the column raised;
And yet that column tall and bold,
Traced in the lines of Egypt old,
Arises as a new cut stone
Amid the dust of ages gone;
For while it tells of yesterday,
It stands upon the summit grey
Where stately tower and donjon stern
Were keep and tomb of fair Strathearn;
Where Wallace oft his prowess tried,
And royal Bruce in valour vied.
Talk we of Bruce? By yon dark wood

The Comyn's ancient fortress stood—
That traitor whose unhappy fate
Still on the monarch's conscience sate,
And urged him in a zeal divine
To send his heart to Palestine.

See where the waters dash aside,
And swiftly round the thicket glide,
Where mossy crag and fan-like bough
Inshade the torrent far below.
Within a towery wilderness
Of nature's wildest gorgeousness,
There rose in architecture quaint
The cell of Strowan's valiant saint—
A soldier-priest whose claymore long
Was more persuasive than his tongue;
Here stands his cross, there flows his well,
Here still is seen his holy hell;
Here, ivy-mantled, still remain
The ruins of the ancient fane,
Where once to heaven the anthem rose,
And silent now the loved repose.

On every side each scene has store
Of song and legendary lore;
Each stream has still its story true,
Each height some bloody conflict knew;
Each crag must give its meed to fame,
And consecrate a hero's name.
High o'er the rest, all bleak and dern,
Moulders the royal Kenneth's cairn,
Who for his crown his good sword bared,
And fell in fight at Monzievaird.
Even in their church, the doom of fire
Consumed the clan of Ochtertyre;
And in his home across the plain,
Old Drummond-Ernoch was slain;
Sons of the mist avenged their dead,
And bore away his grisly head.

Old tales like these, old legends true,
Spring up where'er I turn my view—
From Turret's glen and brawling wave,
From Tosach's keep and fairy grave,
From Ochtertyre's unfading bower,
From Comyn's lone and moated tower,
From where our chief with skilful eye
Watched wonders in the midnight sky,

From Tomachastel's haunted brow,
From cell for Ronan's prayer and vow,
From lordly Drummond's forest wall,
From Lochlane's grim empannelled hall,
From stately Turleum clothed in pine,
And every height surrounding mine.
'Twere idle then each tale to tell,
Of ancient feat by stream or dell,
From Benychonzie's snow-clad breast
To green Glenartney in the west,
Or round by sweet Dunira's den,
Where "bonnie Kilmanie gaed up the glen."
No need I ween of distant view
My sauntering footsteps hence to woo;
No need of song or knightly feat
To add new charm to my retreat.
Its own associations claim
Far better meed than modern fame,
With books and scenes and neighbours sage,
I commune with a former age.

BETWEEN STRATHALLAN
AND STRATHEARN

BY REV. JAMES MACGIBBON, B.D., BLACKFORD

I.

The name Blackford was given, according to tradition, by an ancient king of Caledonia, whose experience in passing the River Allan at this point was of the saddest. The stream spread itself out in those days, says the story, so as to be more lake than stream. When the king came to it with his queen and suite the waters were deep and the current strong. It must have been at night surely, if we are to have any faith in the tale, for the poor queen was carried away beyond help and hope. They drained the strath dry to recover the body; and a solitary knoll on the Allan's bank some way below the present village marks the place where they found and buried the remains of fair Queen Helen. Hence the name Blackford. In the days of the Roman occupation the legionaries frequented this upper part of Strathallan, and have left traces of their presence. Many of them, indeed, must have quartered near; for at the Loaninghead, about two miles east of the village, there is an undeniable Roman camp, an outpost of the great camp at Ardoch.

But the earliest historical reference to Blackford is in Blind Harry's "Acts and Deeds of Sir William Wallace." After taking the peel of Gargunnock, Wallace and his men passed up Strathallan on the way to Methven, and at Blackford met a party of the English, whom they slew, and threw their bodies into the Allan.

> "At yai Blackfurd, as at yai suld pass our,[65]
> A squeir come, and with hym bernys four.
> Till Doun suld ryd and wend at yai had beyne
> All Inglismen, at he befor had seyne.
> Tithings to sper he howid yaim amang.
> Wallace yarwith swyth with a suerd outswang.
> Apon ye hede he straik with so great ire,
> Throw bayne and brayne in sondyr schar ye swyr.
> Ye tothir four in hands sone wer hynt,
> Derfly to dede stekyt or yai wald stynt.
> Yar horss yai tuk, and quhat yaim likit best,

---

[65] Blind Harry's *Wallace*. Book iv., l. 309.

For this and other references and much valuable assistance the writer is indebted to the kindness of A. G. Reid, Esq., Auchterarder.

> Spoilzied yaim bar, syne in the brook yaim kest."

Further on in the same story, we learn that Wallace after slaying Fawdoune, and seeing his ghost at Gask Hall, rode south, hotly pursued by the English. He forded the Earn at Dalreoch, and crossed the Muir of Auchterarder. "Ye horss was gud," but the forced pace sorely taxed its strength; so "at ye Blackfurd" he alighted and walked. After he had gone a mile his pursuers overtook and harassed him. They had great advantage, being on horse, while he was on foot; yet Wallace beat back the foremost of them, recovered his seat, and fled towards Sheriffmuir.

> "Quhil yat he cum ye myrkest mur amang,[66]
> His horss gaiff our and wald no furthyr gang."

Then, rather than let the steed fall into the hands of the enemy,

> "His houch sennownnis he cuttyt all at anys,
> And left hym yus besyde ye standand stanys.
> For Southrone men no guid suld off hym wyn.
> In heith haddyr Wallace and yai can twyn."

In the year 1488, according to the Lord Treasurer's accounts, King James IV., returning from his coronation at Scone, halted at Blackford for refreshment:—"Item—Quhen the King cum forth to Sanct Johniston for a barrel of Ayll at the Blackfurd, xijs." Again, on November 7, 1496, on a journey from Methven to Stirling:—"Item—That samyn day at the Blackfurd quhaire the King baytit for corn to the horss, ii.s."; and the same year, on the way to Perth, March 12th—"Item—Giffen at the Blackfurde quhair the King drank as he raid by, xiiii.d." In 1498 there is the curious entry:—"Item—xxv March, to ane woman of the Blackfurde that brocht coppis to the King and at the Kingis command, xiij.s. iiii.d." These "coppis," probably wooden drinking cups or quaichs, were evidently of some value according to the reckoning of that day. A more quaint and artistic record of this monarch's doings was made later in Tullibardine. Pitscottie tells that in 1511 King James IV. built "ane very great monstrous schip," called "The Micheall." Nearly all the woods of Fife were cut down to provide the necessary timber, in addition to that brought from Norway. A year was spent in the building, and the cost to the King was £40,000. When complete she was manned by 300 sailors, 120 gunners, and 1000 "men of warre," besides officers. The dimensions of this leviathan were 240 feet long, 36 feet broad, and the sides 10 feet thick, "so that no cannon could doe at hir"; "and if any man believes that this schip was not as we have schowin, latt him pas to the place of Tullibardyne quhair he will find the breadth and length of hir sett with hawthorne."[67] Three of these thorn trees were standing in 1837; none of them exist now. A farmer, to improve his field, rooted them out, and did his best to fill up the hollow representing the hull; but spite of these obliterations, the plan of the great ship may be traced yet.

At what date the historic ford was superseded or assisted by a bridge we cannot tell. Some kind of primitive structure evidently existed about the year 1700; for in 1703 the Kirk-Session Records minute that Mr Archibald Moncrieff, the minis-

---

[66] Ib. Bk. v., l. 293.
[67] Lindsay of Pitscottie's *History of Scotland*. Vol., p. 256.

ter, caused his elders to make a collection throughout the parish, "being that when there came rain that did raise the waters a great many people were stopt from coming to ye kirk, and such as came behoved to wead if they wanted horse, which was very discouraging." Thereafter one James Waddel is commissioned "to repair the bridge upon Allan, and he is to bring hom some great trees from ye wood for helping ye same, and over each of ye two streams of ye water there is to be put four trees, at least three of greater size, and they are to be covered with fells and sand."

In 1715, being uncomfortably near the Sheriffmuir, Blackford was seriously disturbed. For four Sundays, between October 23d and November 27th, the church was closed, and again for eight Sundays between December 3rd, 1715, and February 5th, 1716. In the latter interval, as we learn from an account preserved by the Maitland Club, Blackford was burned to the ground by a party of Highlanders. The minister "had stayed at home, preached and prayed for King George and success to his arms, till he was threatened, and parties sent to seize him from the garrisons of Tullibardine and Braco, upon which he was forced to retire and shelter himself with some of his well affected friends." His wife remained, however, and had the presence of mind, so soon as she learned what had happened, to call for "a trusty servant, and by force of money and promises prevailed with him to go to Stirling ... to give ane account to the General and other officers there what was done and acted at Blackfoord." Such is the last eventful incident in the secular history of the parish.

II.

The Church of Blackford, beside the River Allan, was transplanted thither after the Reformation. In former days the name of the parish was Strageath, and the church stood by the Earn, seven miles from its present place. The ruins of the old church are yet standing, preserved from clean removal, doubtless, because the graveyard about them is still in use. Strageath Church has a very ancient origin, being founded by S. Fergus some time in the eighth century. According to the Breviary of Aberdeen, S. Fergus, after he had been Bishop in Ireland for many years, crossed over to Scotland with some companions and settled in Strageath. Finding the district favourable, he set to work and founded three churches—presumably Strageath, Struthill, and Blairinroar. Having appointed these as he best might, and put ministers in them, he quietly retreated to preach the word of God in further parts.[68]

Towards the end of the twelfth century, Gilbert, Earl of Strathearn, founded the Abbey of Inchaffray; and in the year 1200, moved to greater liberality by the death of a son who was buried there, he further endowed the abbey with five churches and additional teinds. One of these five was the Church of S. Patrick of Strageath. The gift is confirmed in a second charter, when the Earl added four other churches and more lands to the same abbey, and again in a charter of King Alexander.[69] Twenty-five or thirty years later the Church of S. Patrick was the scene of a somewhat significant ceremonial. Earl Robert, Gilbert's son, had evidently

---

[68] *Brevarium Aberdonense Pars Hyemalis.* Fol. 164.
[69] *Liber Insule Missarum,* pp. 4, 8, 18, 19.

offended against the powers spiritual, and sought, or was brought to seek, a reconciliation. A charter of his time records that Earl Robert, son of the aforesaid Gilbert, in presence of Abraham, Bishop of Dunblane, Gilbert, the archdeacon, and other notable witnesses, binds himself towards Innocent, the abbot, that he will never in all his life vex the said abbot or his convent unjustly, but will love and everywhere honour them as his most special friends, and will add to the possessions of their house whatever he may by the counsel of his friends. In particular, he confirms to them the Churches of Gask and Strageath. The Abbey of Inchaffray thus held the appointment to the parish of Strageath, and, in spite of many changes, the minister of the parish still receives part of his stipend from "the great vicarage teind of the Abbey of Inchaffray."

In pre-Reformation times there were two other ecclesiastical buildings in the parish besides the Church of Strageath—Tullibardine College and Gleneagles Chapel. The College Church of Tullibardine was founded in 1445 by Sir David Murray, who endowed it with a provost and four prebends, thus making provision not only for the wants of the people, but for younger sons of the family who might enter the service of the Church. Within the church, on the west end of the wall, are seen the arms of the founder and his lady, Dame Isabel Stewart, impaled,[70] the three stars within the bordure for Murray, and the galley for Stewart of Lorn, of which family this lady was a daughter. William Murray of Tullibardine, the son and successor of Sir David, enlarged the College of Tullibardine, and built that part where his arms and his lady's are impaled—the three stars within the tressure for Murray, and a cross ingrailed for Colquhoun, finely cut in stone on the outside of the wall. The Provostry was suppressed at the Reformation, but in the early years of the eighteenth century the Session Records frequently mention "sermon at Tullibardine, the Earle and his lady being there at present." Lord George Murray, though he favoured the Stewart cause, evidently encouraged Presbyterian worship, and occasionally showed his zeal by holding a court "for the fineing and punishing of any such persons as should be delated and found guilty of drinking themselves drunk or of profane swearing or Sabbath breaking or any such gross immoralities." The church, although no longer used for worship, is still excellently preserved, and is used as a burial-place for the Strathallan family.

Gleneagles Chapel is a small and unadorned building, standing near the present mansion-house. The old lairds of Gleneagles are buried within its walls, and the enclosed space about it has been used as a graveyard. The Session Records have an entry showing that the chapel was used as late as March 18, 1705—"Being that the Lady Gleneagles was brought to bed of a child, and the laird was desirous to have his child baptized on the Lord's Day, and was unwilling to bring him out so far as the kirk because of the seasons being yet cold and sometimes stormy. Therefor desired the minr. to preach at his chapel in the afternoon, and to baptize his child, which this day ye minr. did." As far back as 1149[71] there was a church in Gleneagles under the rule of Cambuskenneth Abbey; and, indeed, according to the most likely derivation, Gleneagles is the Gaelic rendering of the monastic *"Vallum Ecclesiae"*—Glen of the Church. The present chapel seems neither of age

[70] Nisbet's *Heraldry*. Vol. II., app. 188.

[71] *Chartulary of Cambuskenneth*. Walcot's *Scoto Monasticon*.

nor consequence enough to give a title. The first church, if it stood on the same site, must surely have been a larger building. A mile further up the glen, however, there rises a spring of the purest water, once believed to have virtue in curing certain diseases, and still called S. Mungo's Well. The saintly name and the fame of healing point to this spot as the more probable situation of the old church.

St Patrick's, Strageath.

Our only glimpse of Blackford at the Reformation shows slight resistance on the part of some to the orders of the new church government. On October 25,

1564, Sir Patrick Fergy—"sir" being equivalent to the modern "reverend"—was cited before the Kirk-Session of S. Andrews[72] as coming in place of the consistorial court, "to underlie diciplyn for takyng upon hand to prech and minister the sacraments withoutyn lawfull admission and for drawyng of the peopll to the Chapell of Tullbarne frae ther Paroche Kyrk." On the same day, "Schyr Johan Morrison efter his recantacion admittit reader in Mithyll, was delaytit and summoned for ministration of baptisme and mariaige efter the Papistical fasson, and that indifferently to all persones, and also for profanacion of the sacrament of the Lordis Supper, abusyng the sam in privat howsis, as also in the kirkyard about the kyrkyard dykis and resavying fra ilk person that communicat ane penne, and in speciall upon Pasche day last was, in the hows of Jhon Graham in Pannalis he ministrat to ane hundreth personis. He oft tymmis called nocht comperand beand of befoir divers tymmis monest to desist tharfra under panis of excommunicacion now wordely mentis the sam to be execut aganis hym and sa decretit to be used."

A relic of pre-Reformation days is the old church bell, which hung till recently in the belfry of old Blackford Church. The bell is inscribed with the words "O Mater S.D., O Mater S.D., O Mater S.D., I.S.," and the sign of a hammer. The thrice repeated phrase is evidently a contraction for "O Mater Sanctissima Domini"—"O Most Holy Mother of the Lord."

From the Book of the Assignation of Stipends, 1574, it appears that Strageath, Muthill, and Strowane were combined under the ministry of Alexander Gaw at a stipend of £60 Scots and kirk-lands, while Andro Drummond was reader at Strageath at a stipend of £20.

In 1617, the Parish Church was changed to Blackford by Act of Parliament:—

> "Our Soveraine Lord and Estaittis of this present Parliament understanding that ye kirk of the parochin of Strageth wes of auld situat and biggit upoun the newk and utmost pairt of the said parochin of Strageath, and the parochiners thereof found it nowayes to be meit to be the paroche kirk of the said parochin in respect of the wyidnes and gryit bonndis of the said parochin, they thairefore be the space of twentye-four yeiris or thairby biggit and foundit within the town of Blackfurde qlk lyis and is within ye middis of the said parochin, ane new kirk for the gryit ease of the parochoneris ... thairefore ... ordanis the samen kirk, now biggit within the said town of Blackfurde, to be ye principal kirk of ye said parochin of Strageath in all tyme cuming, and ordanis the haill parochoneris thairoff to resort thairto and ressave the benefit of ye kirk thairat."[73]

The year 1689 brought the Revolution, and the minister, Mr David Moray, A.M., refusing to conform with the new state of things, was deprived of his living by the Privy Council. He retired to Edinburgh, carrying with him the kirk bible as a memento of his ministry. When the Kirk-Session met in 1697 "it was recommended to the minister to use his endeavours to get the kirk bible from Mr

[72] *Register of Kirk-Session of S. Andrews. Scot. Hist. Society.*
[73] Thomson's *Scots Acts*, IV., 556.

Murray," and early in 1699 there appears the item—"To James Brown, the carrier, for bringing home the kirk bible out of Edenburgh from Mr David Murray, 9. 4."; and a fortnight later—"Twopence to James Brown for compleeting his payt. for bringing home of ye kirk bible."

The first minister after the Revolution was Mr Archibald Moncrieff, an admirable and faithful pastor, whose conscience forbade him to ask a manse from the heritors for several years, during which he lived at Stirling, and travelled to and from his work. He was succeeded in 1738 by his son, who became Sir William Moncrieff Wellwood. In that year the old kirk was burned in rather curious circumstances. The kirk was being used as the parish school, and was heated by a peat fire. In the master's absence one day the boys amused themselves by throwing about the lighted peats. The kirk caught fire, and was burned to the ground. Sir Henry Moncrieff succeeded his father in 1771, the sixth minister of the family in a lineal descent. He had not finished his University course when his father died, but the patron and parishioners waited for him. Sir Henry was too brilliant for Blackford, however, and in 1775 went to S. Cuthbert's, Edinburgh. The next minister, Mr John Stevenson, evidently did not please all. Three of the elders and a number of the congregation left the kirk. They met for some time in a stackyard beside the old ford, and eventually, with some like-minded ones in Auchterarder, formed the Relief congregation there. Mr Stevenson was followed, in 1815, by Mr John Clark—a splendid type of what was best in the reviled Moderates, an eloquent preacher, a true, large-hearted gentleman, a keen wit, and skilful farmer, as well as a faithful pastor. A new regime began with his worthy and lamented successor, the Rev. David Bonallo. The kirk on the brae-head was abandoned as insufficient and the present church, less prominent, but more convenient, was built at the east end of the village.

III.

Blackford has been the home of not a few distinguished families; but the old castles where they lived are, without exception, the most meagre ruins; of one, indeed (Tullibardine), not a stone remains to mark the site.

The chief heritor of the parish is Captain W. H. Drummond Moray of Abercairny, whose family, though old proprietors, seem never to have lived in the parish. Ogilvie Castle, a ruin on their lands, which originally belonged to the Montrose family, does not appear to have been ever occupied by the Morays.

In the south end of the parish stands Gleneagles, which Sir David Lyndsay, in his "Tale of Squire Meldrum," describes as "ane castell ... beside ane mountane in ane vaill," and a "triumphand plesand place." Gleneagles Castle was for many centuries the home of the Haldanes. They held the neighbouring lands of Frandie by charter of William the Lion, A.D. 1165-1214, and came into possession of Gleneagles about a century later. From time to time we find them taking an active and prominent part in the affairs of the kingdom. Sir John Haldane, in the reign of King James III., became "Lord Justice-General of Scotland benorth of the Forth"—a dignity next to that of Lord Chancellor; a later Sir John fought and fell at Flodden; another was one of the Lords of the Congregation. Sir John, in 1650, fell as a leader in the Presbyterian army against Cromwell at the Battle of Dunbar. Towards the end of the 17th century Mungo Haldane was an active member of the Scottish Parliament; his son John was member for Perth County in the last Scottish Parliament, and in the first British Parliament after the Union. At the beginning of the present century the estate passed into the hands of Viscount Duncan of Camperdown, and is now the property of his descendant, the Earl of Camperdown. The old castle, of solid walls, surrounded by a moat, was superseded in 1624 by the modern Place of Gleneagles, built from the ruins. Locally, the family is best remembered in one of its Presbyterian members, an ardent respecter of the Sabbath. He forbade the keeping of stalls and selling of wares on the Kirk Brae on the Lord's Day; and, finding his injunction slighted, was so roused that he went next Sunday with drawn sword, scattered the offending merchants down the brae, and tossed their wares into the lake beneath. There was no more Sunday trading at the kirk.

East of Gleneagles, overlooking its own deep wooded glen, stood Kincardine Castle, the residence of the noble family of Graham. The estate came to them from Malise, Earl of Strathearn, who granted it to his sister Amabil on her marriage with Sir David Graham, c. 1250.[74] The Grahams, as Earls, Marquises, and Dukes of Montrose, retained Kincardine till the beginning of this century, when it was sold to James Johnston, Esq. Many a fact and many a fancy attach to the old Kincardine. In 1579, the Earl of Atholl, Chancellor of Scotland, stayed at Kincardine on his way from Stirling, and suddenly took ill and died. The crime was never absolutely proved, but evidence went far to show that some rival had given him poisoned food at Stirling. During the boyhood of the great Marquis, Kincardine Castle was the principal residence of the family, and the young Lord James was a well-known figure in the neighbourhood. When his father died in 1626, the funeral took one month and nineteen days to accomplish; and the accomplishment was attended with such a consumpt of good things as makes it hard to see where room was left for mourning. When Montrose attended the General Assembly of 1638, he sat as commissioner for the Presbytery of Auchterarder, from which we may conclude that he was still closely associated with Kincardine. With the great Marquis the story of Kincardine Castle ends. In 1646, being Montrose's principal house, it was besieged and taken by Middleton, the Covenanter. We have a full account of the siege in Bishop Guthrie's Memoirs. Learning that the castle was fortified with a company of foot under Lord Napier, Middleton "brought a number of great ordnance from Sterlin Castle to batter the walls." After ten days the besieged were distressed from want of water. Lord Napier, guided by his page, who was a Graham, managed to escape. The rest surrendered, twelve being shot on the spot, and thirty-five taken prisoners to Edinburgh. "Then Middleton ordered the Castle of Kincardine to be burnt, which was done upon the 16th day of March."

---

[74] *Liber Insule Missarum,* p. xxxiii.

Tullibardine Kirk.

Close by the Church of Tullibardine used to stand Tullibardine Castle. Here lived for generations the family of Murray, who played many a part in the change-ful events of Scottish history. There was one Sir William Murray—the builder of part of the College Church—who is chiefly remembered as the father of seventeen stalwart sons. He took them one day to pay court to the King at Stirling. When the King saw their numbers he was angry, for an Act had been passed forbidding such formidable retinues. But when the Laird of Tullibardine explained that he brought only his sons, each with a single man attendant, the King's anger was turned to compliment, and he forthwith gifted an addition to the estate which grew so many men. There was a circular room in the castle, with a pillar in the centre, where all the seventeen sons are said to have slept—heads towards the wall, and feet at the pillar.[75] Fully a century later there was another Sir William Murray with the King at Stirling Castle. He so far forgot himself one day as to break the nose of the Earl of Argyll in the King's presence, for which double breach Sir William was exiled. But ere long the King felt need of him. Refractory subjects would not pay the King his mails and silver marts, and he was heard to sigh—"Oh that I had Will Murray again." The sigh was duly conveyed to the exile, who returned, and speedily regained the Royal favour by persuading the unwilling debtors to pay their dues. His son, Sir John, was educated with the young King at Stirling, and earned the title of Earl of Tullibardine in 1606. In 1670 the title went to the Earls of Atholl. Fortune was less kind to their descendant, better known as Lord George Murray. He took the Stewart side in 1745, and entertained Prince Charles Edward at Tullibardine Castle. Exile followed the disaster which overtook his cause; the old castle, abandoned as a dwelling-place, fell into decay; and a philistine farmer carted off the last stone of it to build field dykes.

In a M.S. book of Sir John Ogilvy, her Master of the Household, we learn that Queen Mary stayed at Kincardine and Tullibardine on a journey which she made to the North in 1562. Having left Edinburgh on August 11th, "she continued at Stirling until the 18th of August, when she set out from thence with a part of her train, and dined and supped at Kincardine. On the 19th she left Kincardine after dinner, and slept at St. Johnston." On the return journey, leaving St. Johnston on the 16th November, she "slept at Tulliebarne. On the 17th she proceeded after dinner to Drummond." Twenty years later these same castles were again favoured with a Royal visitor, King James VI. The visit to Tullibardine happened in August, 1584, and the motive of it was typical of that monarch's way. Moysie's Memoirs, which chronicle the visit, narrate that the King had been living ten days at Ruthven "or ever he knew there wes sex houssis infectit in Perthe, his seruandis being theare; and thairfoir with a few number the samyn nycht depairted to Tullibardin, and from that to Sterling, leavand his haill housald and seruandis encloisit in Ruthven." The visit to Kincardine is inferred from a letter written by Thomas, tutor of Cassillis, to the Laird of Barnbarroch, dated 10th October, 1585—"As for newis, it is trew my lord arrane was to have been in Kincarne upone Saterday last, and thair to have given his presens to the King, and the King thocht guid to stay him thereof for the ambassadouris causs being with his majestie, sua my lord hes nocht presentit the King as yit."

Early in this century the estate of Tullibardine was sold to Viscount Strathallan, who had married Amelia, daughter of the Duke of Atholl. Tullibardine thus became attached to the adjoining estate of Machany, long possessed by the Drummonds. The Laird of Machany and Viscount Strathallan were united first in William Drummond of Machany, who succeeded his cousin as fourth Viscount

[75] This and the anecdote about Mr Andrew Drummond are given by the kindness of Viscountess Strathallan.

Strathallan. True to the traditions of his House and title, the fourth Viscount was a loyal and devoted Jacobite. He fought in 1715, and again in 1745, when he was killed at Culloden. After his death the penalty of his ill-fated zeal descended on his family. His wife Margaret, daughter of Lord Nairne, was taken prisoner, and kept in Edinburgh Castle from February to September, 1746; his son James, who had attended his father at Culloden, suffered attainder, and for many years the title was withheld. There was more caution in the character of Andrew Drummond, brother to the fourth Viscount, who founded the Charing Cross Bank in London. He lent large sums to the Government; but his family connexion brought him under a suspicion of double dealing, which Sir Robert Walpole was inclined to believe. Learning, however, that the suspicion was unfounded, Sir Robert sought to conciliate the Drummond by warmly offering to shake hands with him when they encountered one day in the King's drawing-room. But Mr Andrew, proof against blandishment no less than against suspicion, met the advance by holding his hands behind his back. The ancestral spirit shone again in Andrew John Drummond, who should have been seventh Viscount. He died in 1812, a General in the British Army. The forfeited title was restored in 1824 to his cousin, James Drummond, Esq.

THE ABBEY OF INCHAFFRAY
BY REV. JAMES BROWN, M.A., MADERTY

To those who appreciate time and labour expended upon historical and anti-quarian research, there can be few—if, indeed, there be any—among our Scottish counties which present scope for their enthusiasm so extensive and so varied as that contained within the borders of Perthshire. Generally speaking, the attractions identify themselves. The Cathedral at Dunblane, the Round Tower at Abernethy, the Camp at Ardoch—these preserve still many of their original features and characteristic lineaments, and need hardly fail to arrest attention. But what chance traveller by road or by rail would, when midway between Crieff and Methven, dream that the bare, solitary column he sees in the valley below could prove other than the gable-end of a disused barn? Nay, did he approach and pass the remnant itself, he would probably wonder to learn that the gloomy, forsaken pile alone marks a spot once the centre of much holy rigour, educational zeal, and industrial activity; that thence sallied forth, six hundred years ago, the monk patriot, with whom the Scottish warriors knelt to pray upon the field before engaging in the memorable conflict whose issue achieved for them their country's independence. A ragged wall, an arched chamber, several solid heaps of fallen mason-work are all that remain of Inchaffray Abbey.

Perthshire owes largely to the ancient Earldom of Strathearn. Little is known concerning the line till Gilbert succeeded in 1171. Unlike his immediate predecessors, he manifested no hostility to the inroad of Norman and Saxon customs and usages. He was the first to adopt the wise precaution of obtaining charters for his lands, and rivalled the most ardent and obsequious followers of David I. in munificent gifts of these to the Church. Although it would be hazardous to accept as altogether faithful the statement of Fordun, the chronicler, that Earl Gilbert apportioned his whole estates—which extended in length from Newburgh to the west end of Balquhidder, and from the Ochils to the Grampians in breadth—equally between the See of Dunblane, the Abbey of Inchaffray, and himself with his heirs, we have yet sufficient reason to consider that his liberality to ecclesiastical settlements was handsome. It certainly reflects upon him high credit that, due to his pious devotion, the family of Strathearn were the only Scottish subjects (excepting possibly the Lords of Galloway) who established a bishopric and inherited its patronage.

About 1189 the King made over to Gilbert the lands of Maderty with all their feudal rights and privileges. In return, the Earl bound himself to contribute half a knight's service, and to secure that no part of these lands should ever be allowed to come again into the hands of their former owner, Gilliecolm Marischall, or any of his heirs. This Gilliecolm—elsewhere described as *arch-tyrannus et latronum principes*—had incurred his monarch's bitter displeasure by an act of felony, having betrayed the sovereign Castle of Earn to his Majesty's most mortal foes, and taken part with them to do him hurt to his power.

Not long after the transference, the Earl sought to signalise his estimate of the Royal favour by founding a religious house. He chose for a site the swamp-girt island which lay toward the northwestern corner of his lately acquired possession. So frequent were the liturgical celebrations there that the settlement received the name of *Inis Aifreen* (Celtic), *Insula Missarum* (Latin), Inchaffray—signifying "Island of Masses." He dedicated the monastery to God, St. Mary, and St. John Evangelist; deputed Malis, the hermit, to select Augustinian Canons from Scone, and granted his first charter, which bears the signatures of himself, his wife (Matilda), and his six sons. The edifice must have been completed by 1198, as Gilchrist, the heir, who died in that year, was interred within the building. Through this bereavement, the family's affections became more closely united to the place. "We love it so much," the parents are recorded to have said, "that we have chosen it as the place of sepulture for us and our heirs, and have already buried there our eldest son." Further and more extended benefactions followed. By the great charter, of date 1200, Inchaffray was endowed with the Churches of St. Kattanus of Abruthven, St. Ethernanus of Maderty, St. Patrick of Strogeath, St. Meckessok of Auchterarder, and St. Beanus of Kinkell; with tithe of the Earl's kain and rents of wheat, meal, malt, cheese, and all provisions throughout the year in his Court; with tithe of all fish brought into his kitchen, and of the produce of his hunting; with tithe of all the profits of his tribunals of justice and all offerings; with the liberty to its monks of fishing in the Peffer, of fishing and birding over all the Earl's lands, waters, and lakes; of taking timber for building and other uses from his woods, and pannage or mast feeding for pigs, as well as bark and firewood, in whatever places, and as much as they chose. Some years later an additional charter granted also the Church of St. Beanus of Foulis, with the dower land of the church and the common pasturage of the parish, and likewise the Church of the Holy Trinity of Gask, with the same privileges. To this document appends a fragment of the donor's knightly seal, which shows on the obverse side a mounted knight with drawn sword, and on the reverse side the inscription—"Secretum G. comitis, de Straderne."

Whatever may have been the demands of spiritual functions upon the time of the monks, they cannot fairly be charged with "agricultural indolence." Their glebe consisted entirely of marsh and bog when the Abbacy was created. By 1218—*i.e.*, in about twenty years—it had all been ditch-drained and reclaimed. The beneficial results of their labour are noticeable to-day. Fields immediately adjoining the ruin exhibit quite a different appearance in spring and yield quite an appreciable advantage in autumn compared with those more remote. No stronger evidence need be required than that the rental of the former doubles that of an equal area of the latter.

The detail of the great charter includes, as we said, "the tithe of the fines levied at the Earl's Court." Nowhere else throughout Scotland could a subject of the King exercise *jura regalia*. Perth was our only county, and the Earls of Strathearn our only Earls Palatine. When precisely this independent jurisdiction was bestowed and when revoked and abolished we have no clear account. But, according to the trustworthy evidence embodied in the above-mentioned deed of gift, we gather not only that the privilege existed in the thirteenth century, but that it operated favourably for the monks.

The source and reference of the name given to the parish has never been satisfactorily determined. Some have attempted to connect it with the dedication of Inchaffray. Now, whatever truth there might be in the view that part of the dedication—"to the Virgin"—was suggested by the name of the parish (Maderty being the English for the Celtic "mother of God"), there is certainly nothing whatever to support the opinion that the district took its style from the Abbey. Maderty was Maderty long before Inchaffray was Inchaffray.

Earl Gilbert died in 1223. Robert, his successor, maintained the like generous attitude which his father had borne toward the Church. We may, no doubt, feel disposed to conjecture some proof of estrangement having marred the hitherto peaceful relations between patron and clergy. But if such did arise, it can have been only temporary, for the very record which excites the suspicion assures us of even more devoted loyalty on his part. "In the Church of Strogeath, and in the presence of Abraham, Bishop of Dunblane, and others, Robert, Earl of Strathearn, bound himself toward the Abbot of Inchaffray that he would never in his life vex the said abbot or his convent unjustly—nay, would love and everywhere honour them as his most especial friends, and would add to the possessions of their house whatsoever he might by the counsel of his friends. He particularly confirmed to them the Churches at Gask and Strogeath."

The year 1240 witnessed Inchaffray narrowly becoming Chapter of the Diocese. "Clement, Bishop of Dunblane, went to Rome, and represented to Pope Gregory IX. how of old time his bishopric had been vacant upwards of a hundred years, during which period almost all the revenues had been seized by the seculars; and although in process of time there had been several bishops instituted, yet, by their simplicity or negligence, the former dilapidations were not recovered, but, on the contrary, the remainder were almost quite alienated; so that for ten years a proper person could not be found to accept of the charge; that the case having been laid before the Pope, he had committed the trust of supplying that vacancy to the Bishops of St. Andrews, Dunkeld, and Brechin, who made choice of this Clement; but he found his church so desolate that he had not where to lay his head in his cathedral. There was no college there, only a rural chaplain performed divine service in the church that had its roof uncovered; and the revenues of the See were so small that they could hardly afford him maintenance for one half of the year. To remedy these evils the Pope appointed William and Geoffrey, the Bishops of Glasgow and Dunkeld, to visit the Church of Dunblane, and if they should find these things to be as represented, he authorised them to cause the fourth part of the tithes of all the parish churches within that diocy to be assigned to the bishop thereof, who, after reserving out of these tithes so much as should be proper for his own sustenance, was by the advice of these two bishops and other expert persons to assign the rest to a dean and canons whom the Pope enjoined to be settled there, if these matters could be brought about without great offence; or, if otherwise, he ordered that the fourth of the tithes of all such churches of the diocy as were in the hands of seculars should be assigned to the bishop, and that the bishop's seat should be translated to St. John's Monastery of Canons-regular, (*i.e.*, Inchaffray), within that diocy, and appointed that these canons should have the election of the bishop when a vacancy should happen thereafter." Either "these things were found to be not so," or else the former part of the alternative was duly carried out, as the bishop's seat remained at Dunblane, and Inchaffray was denied its only opportunity of elevation to cathedral rank.

Inchaffray Abbey.

The next event of interest connected with the Abbey is the pilgrimage of the Abbot Maurice to Bannockburn. Every schoolboy can tell the story, for no annals of Scotland omit to record his presence and service when the rival hosts stood face to face for a huge trial of strength and valour. But probably it is not quite so well understood that much of the glorious success which crowned the Scottish arms was popularly attributed to the fact that the monk carried with him the arm of St. Fillan. A legend is that St. Fillan, when Abbot of Pittenweem, transcribed with his own hand the Holy Scriptures, and that his left arm became so luminous that it enabled him to proceed during darkness with his pious work. Lesly asserts that this wonderful limb afterwards came into the possession of Robert Bruce, who enclosed it in a silver shrine, which he commanded should be borne at the head of the army. Previous to the battle, a story has it, the King's chaplain (Maurice), with the view of preserving the treasure from all chance of abstraction by the English, had it removed and deposited in a place of security. While, however, the King, unaware of what had been done, was addressing his prayers to the empty casket, it was observed to open and shut suddenly. On inspection, the Saint was found to have himself returned his luminous member to its place as an assurance of victory. The writers of the Statistical Account of Maderty thus express themselves—"This relic might, indeed, have given some encouragement to the superstitious; but one arm of a brave Scotchman fighting in earnest for the liberty of his country had more effect in obtaining that memorable victory than could have been produced by the innate virtue of all the relics of the dead that could have been collected." If these critical authors had been less anxious to square truth with orthodoxy, and not orthodoxy with truth, they would have known that where the entire force was "superstitious" the influence of the sacred arm would enormously intensify soldierly enthusiasm, and that it is impossible to define its comparative share in the result. Robert Bruce, indeed, appears to have been sensibly impressed by the good offices of the sacred relic, and attested his gratitude in a substantial manner. He founded a priory at Strathfillan, on the Dochart, a stream in the Breadalbane district of Perthshire, and consecrated it to the Saint. At the dissolution of religious houses this priory with all its revenues and superiorities passed, by order of the King, to Campbell of Glenorchy, ancestor of the Lords of Breadalbane. Maurice's conduct on the field attracted the attention of others besides Bruce. Macleod of Scarinche, in Lewis, conceived a strong regard for the Abbot, and induced him to reside for a time at his western home, where he erected a monastery to St. Kattanus, whose bones lay buried there. Strathfillan, Scarinche, and Abernethy were cells of Inchaffray.

The Earls continued successively to be bountiful benefactors of the convent. One of them, Malise, in 1258, presented it with certain of his slaves (*nativi*)— namely, Gilmory, Gillendes, and John Starnes, the son of Thomas and grandson of Thore. Absolute serfdom was then a Scottish institution, comprising part of the labouring class, who were bought and sold with the land to which they were attached; and gifts of nativi by their masters to the religious establishments of those times are frequently recorded.

After the ancient line of Strathearn had failed in the direct male descent, and when Maurice de Moray, created Earl by David II., had met his death at Durham in 1346, leaving no issue, the King bestowed the Earldom upon his nephew, Robert, the High Steward, afterwards Robert II., who on his accession to the throne (1370) relinquished the Earldom in favour of his son David. Seventy years later the title and estates fell vacant and were merged in the Crown, the bishopric and temporalities being henceforth held in free barony of the Sovereign.

The intimate association of Inchaffray Abbey with the national and religious fortunes of Scotland receives further guarantee in 1513. Whether as chaplain or as common soldier, and under what designation, no available narrative declares. But certain it is that the stubborn fight which evoked Scotland's most waefu' dirge, no less than that which occasioned her immortal paean of victory, was graced by an abbot of this monastery. The respective fates of these two divines, however, were widely different. Not even monks, clad though they be in all the panoply of the Church, are safe from sword or arrow. He of Flodden never saw his northern charge again. Unknown, yet not unwept, he fell beneath the spoiler's weapon with the "flowers of the forest."

It is noteworthy that Abbots of Inchaffray, *ex-officio* prelates of Parliament, took little to do with public affairs. They do not seem to have shared at all extensively in the transactions which so often brought together the leaders of the various religious houses.

The subjoined list is fragmentary, but authoritative so far as it goes:—

MALIS—The Hermit—was present and acted as the head of the establishment at the beginning. Earl Gilbert must have considered him a person of trust, since he committed to him the important duty of selecting the necessary canons.

INNOCENT—The first Abbot—officiated during the lordship of Robert, 1223-1231.

ALAN—1258-1271.

HUGH—1284.

THOMAS—1296.

MAURICE—The Bannockburn celebrity—was promoted to the See of his own Diocese of Dunblane. Early in his Episcopate a dispute which arose concerning the lands of Airthrey was submitted to arbiters, one of whom was his successor in the Abbacy of Inchaffray, viz.:

CHRISTIAN.

WILLIAM appears to have acted for an unusually long term, or had a successor of the same name. On the Feast of Matthias, 1398, a deed of Janet Moray, wife of Alexander Moray of Abercairny, was witnessed by William the Abbot, John the prior, and the whole Convent of Inchaffray. On 25th January, 1468,

GEORGE obliged himself to make Lawrence, Lord Oliphant, his bailie for life of the lands of the monastery within twenty days after he should be admitted to the spirituality by the ordinary and by the King to the temporality of the said benefice. The family of Oliphant held this relation during the reign of James V., Mary, and James VI. In 1539,

GAVIN DUNBAR, Archbishop of Glasgow, had the Abbacy *in commendam*. On 15th May of that year he granted Anthony Murray a tack of 4 merk lands of the "Raith" "for furnishing of our bulls"—probably for the expense of his confirmation. Before the tack had run out the tenure was made perpetual by a free charter of the same lands of "Raith" and of the Moor of Maderty, granted by

ALEXANDER, styled Archbishop of Athens, postulate of the Isles, and perpetual commendator of the Monastery of Inchaffray, dated at Inchaffray, December 24th, 1554. This commendator was Alexander Gordon (brother of George, fourth Earl of Huntly), who was defeated in his hopes of the Archbishopric of Glasgow on the death of Gavin Dunbar, and imperfectly consoled by the high-sounding title of Archbishop of Athens *in partibus fidelium*, the poor See of the Isles, with, on November 26th, 1553, the Abbacy of Inchaffray *in commendam*, which last he held till 1564. In 1558 he was promoted to the See of Galloway. Nine years later he was accused before the General Assembly of the Kirk, and confessed to the indictment that he had not visited for three years part of the churches within his charge; that he had haunted Court too much; that he had purchased to be one of the Session and Privy Council, which cannot agree with the office of a pastor or a bishop; that he had resigned Inchaffray in favour of a young child, and set diverse lands in feu in prejudice of the Kirk. The young child was James Drummond of Innerpeffray, second son of David, second Lord Drummond. The Abbey was erected into a temporal lordship in his favour, and in 1609 he was created Lord Maderty. From him is descended the noble family of Strathallan.

And now the old Abbey fell on troublous times. The Reformation—that harbinger of good not unmixed with evil—closed the book of the monastery. It is strange and sad that ecclesiastical changes should partake so largely in the destruction of buildings and the spoliation of belongings. Never yet did religious fanaticism satisfy its own desires without simultaneously and obligingly ministering to the rapacity of the attendant greedy grabber. And so Inchaffray, experiencing the fate of other such establishments, had its walls torn down, its vessels strewn and broken, its canons put to flight or death, its revenues disposed by rude, regardless hands. The Earl of Kinnoull is the proprietor of the ruin and the few acres that surround it. These gave him the patronage of the seven parishes with which, we observed, the convent had been endowed.

Quite a crop of stories are told in connection with the demolition of Inchaffray. It is said, for instance, that long ago the ploughman-tenant of the dwelling contiguous to the convent discovered, while digging, the golden image "of a sow." This relic (for relic it was supposed to be of the abbey practices) he carefully secreted, but latterly converted into current coin, and became himself a very wealthy man. But perhaps the most reliable and authenticated is the following:—A Fowlis widower, lately bereaved, sought to find a grave-stone to honour his spouse's memory. Either he was too fastidious or too ungenerous, but he abstracted from Inchaffray a stone to be utilised for this solemn purpose. The writer quite lately identified the stone as the lid of the coffin of Abbot Maurice. There is the figure of a battle-axe engraved upon the slab.

And now we return to the point from which we started. All that the passer-by can see of this object is a chimney-crowned gable. Nearer approach shows an arched chamber. But the whole history of an interesting past appears to be covered with debris. It is impossible to fancy the feelings of Abbot or Earl were he to rise from his tomb and hear to what uses the fabric of his cherished house was being devoted. Pig-styes, barn-walls, fences—these comprise the objects to which the "holy stones" are set. *O tempora, O mores.*

If these words should meet the eye of antiquarian enthusiasts, and should happen to stir within them the desire of research, a welcome and a courteous lodging will be found at the Manse of Maderty.

A SOUTHERN OUTPOST ON THE EDGE OF THE HIGHLANDS

BY REV. HUGH M. JAMIESON, MONZIE

Monzie—a southern outpost on the edge of the Highlands—is said to derived from the Gaelic *Moeghe*, signifying "a good plain." It is a long, narrow, irregular parish, extending for nearly twelve miles up both sides of the River Almond, until it touches, on the north, the parishes of Dull, Weem, and Kenmore.

The vale of Monzie—the southern boundary of the parish—where stands the church, the hamlet, and the Castle of Monzie, extends for nearly three miles in a north-east direction, gradually rising to the height of several hundred feet. The most striking peculiarity of the surroundings of Monzie is the combination of wild and mountainous scenery with cultivation and picturesqueness. One of the finest views in the whole of Strathearn can be had from the Highland Road, to the east of the church. In the foreground are the luxuriant woods, the rich pastures, and the Castle of Monzie, and at a distance of seven or eight miles is the Aberuchill range, towering in majesty on the horizon, with the giant Ben Voirlich just visible over their heads. A little to the left is Turleum—a conical-shaped hill of respectable altitude; while Benchonzie and other off-shoots of the Grampians bound the view on the north. The general effect is exceedingly beautiful, and the mingling, within a short distance, of the sublime and the picturesque is probably not surpassed anywhere in Scotland.

There are three streams rising in the hills to the north that find their way into the vale. The Barvick, which runs for three or four miles along the western boundary of the parish, descends rapidly with leaps and bounds into a deep and rocky dell, until it terminates in the fall known as Spout Barvick. The Keltic, rising in the hills some four miles to the north, enters a rocky ravine fully a mile up from the turnpike road, and tumbling precipitously down a height of eighty feet it reaches the vale, skirts the castle grounds, and, joining the Shaggie, falls along with it into the Turret. The third stream—the Shaggie—rises to the north-east of the Keltie, and, threading its way for three miles between lofty banks covered with wood, it passes the village, and pursues its course beneath the old ivy-crowned Roman bridge, through the castle parks, until it becomes lost in the Turret.

The neighbourhood is peculiarly rich in trees. On the lawn behind Monzie Castle are three of five famous larches planted in the year 1738—the fourth one fell during the November gale of 1893. They rival those of the Duke of Athole at Dunkeld. There is a tradition that the Duke's gardener, on his way home with the seed, was hospitably entertained at Monzie, and planted them in remembrance of his visit. The gardener was sent annually to observe their growth and report to his master. "When this functionary returned and made his wonted report, that the larches at Monzie were leaving those of Dunkeld behind in the race, his Grace would jocularly allege that his servant had permitted General Campbell's good cheer to impair his powers of observation."[76] Altogether, the district is beautifully and bountifully wooded, and many a laird gathered to his fathers must have laid to heart some such advice as the laird of Dumbiedykes gave to his son—"Jock, when ye hae naething else tae dae, ye may be aye stickin' in a tree; it will be growin', Jock, when ye're sleepin'."

The valley of the Almond runs parallel to the vale of Monzie. Leaving the manse, and passing the church and the school, the Keppoch Road joins the road to Glenalmond, and after a walk of fully two miles the traveller finds himself at the entrance to what is known as the Sma' Glen—a romantic pass, stretching along the sides of the Almond for a distance of fully two miles. Standing half-way up the glen on a summer's day, looking northwards, the scenery is magnificent. Here, from the mountain's brow rushes a foaming stream; there, a clump of trees dressed in the most luxuriant green; here, mountains towering bleak and wild; there, a few spots of verdure growing amid the rocks; behind, the swift, pellucid Almond water; before, hills stretching on and on till they are lost in the azure sky.

The banks of the Almond along the vale are associated with much romance. Some time in the last century there lived at Corrivarlich a noted sheep-stealer named Alastair Bane. Little is known of his boyhood. He was supposed to have been brought to the district by Highlanders who were in the habit of bringing to Crieff cartloads of split pine from Rannoch Forest, which they sold to riddle-makers to make riddle rims. During one of those visits the child is supposed to have been left. He was called Alastair, owing to his supposed Highland descent, and Bane, because of his white hair. As he grew up to manhood he showed symptoms of a wandering disposition, and went frequently to Amulree and Falkirk, acting in the capacity of a drover. While pursuing this occupation he became acquainted with many of the ferocious caterans who were at that time following the same calling. How long Alastair continued a drover is not chronicled in oral tradition. After a time he associated himself with a band of bare-legged mountaineers, sixty in number, who located themselves under his leadership in a cave in the glen, to the great terror and annoyance of the district. It is said that the last combined effort of the band at cattle-lifting was at a farm situated in the moor between Fowlis-Wester and Buchanty. On this occasion dissension broke out amongst the thieves, which ultimately ended in the breaking up of the band. That Alastair Bane had his dwelling-place among the rocks in Wester Glenalmond was well known, but every effort to discover its whereabouts was in vain, until one night a shepherd, wandering on the hills, chanced to see a light shining through a crevice in the rocks. Creeping cautiously forward and peering through the opening, he observed the formidable thief sitting on the floor, amusing himself with an old fiddle and singing—

---

[76] *Statistical Account of Monzie*, by Mr Laurie.

> "Many a cow has lost her calf, many a sheep her lamb,
> But I'll sit on a stane, and sing at my den—
> The thief of Glenalmond will never be ta'en."

He was taken, however, and paid the full penalty of the law at Perth—hanging for sheep-stealing being in practice at that date. When on the scaffold he prophesied that "the water o' Almond runs ower mony a stane, but it'll ne'er run twa years withoot takin' ane." The prophecy has reference to the number of people drowned in the river, which is remarkable for the impetuosity of its floods.

At Fendoch—the entrance to the Sma' Glen—we tread on historical ground. Here, at Tom-an-Die—"Hill of God"—there is no reason to doubt, was one of the chief stations of the Romans, a standing camp, formed, not for a halt of a few days, but to be occupied for a considerable time. It was formed by Agricola in the year 84 A.D., in his seventh and last campaign, probably a little before the Battle of Mons Grampius. It had many advantages of situation, and we may well believe that it continued to be occupied by the Romans so long as they had possession of North Britain;—by Lollius Urbicus, who in the next century anew drove back the Caledonians to their fastnesses beyond the Grampians; and by the Emperor Severus in the beginning of the third century. So distinct were the traces of the camp in the year 1795, when the first Statistical Account of the parish was written, as to admit of its being measured. At that time the trenches were entire, and in some places six feet deep; but both rampart and trenches have disappeared under the operation of the plough. Though the camp covered upwards of fifty acres, nothing can now be seen but a small piece of breast-work facing the Almond.

At the mouth of the Sma' Glen there is a round knoll—Tom-an-Tighe—"the House of the Hill"—where Fingal, the father of Ossian, is said to have dwelt until his house was destroyed by Gara. The place is called Fendoch, a corruption of Finn-Tighe—"Finn's House." When Fendoch was burnt, Fingal built a fort on the summit of Dunmore, on the east side of the glen, where he and his father, Comhal, are said to be buried. The remains of this fort, still visible, show it to have been a place of retreat almost impregnable. That Comhal, his son, and grandson lived in the parish, the etymology of the place can scarcely leave a doubt. Not only have we Fingal's house, but on the moor contiguous to Fendoch we have Cairn-Comhal—"the cairn over the grave of Comhal"; while at Cultoquhey we have a camp called in Gaelic Comhal Cults—that is, "Comhal's battle"; and it is worthy of note that, towards the close of last century, some urns with ashes in them were dug up in this locality.

In the centre of the glen stands Clach-na-Ossian—"Ossian's Stone"—which tradition held to cover the mortal remains of Scotia's early bard. When the Government troops under General Wade were engaged in carrying a highway through the glen, they found it necessary to shift the position of Ossian's Stone. The detailed narrative of what took place is as follows:—

> "I have so lately mentioned Glenalmond, in the road from
> Crieff, northward, that I cannot forbear a digression, though at
> my first setting out, in relation to a piece of antiquity which hap-

pened to be discovered in that vale, not many hours before I went through it in one of my journeys southwards.

"A small part of the way through this glen having been marked out by two rows of camp-colours, placed at a good distance one from another, whereby to describe the line of the intended breadth and regularity of the road by the eye, there happened to lie directly in the way an exceedingly large stone, and, as it had been made a rule from the beginning to carry on the roads in straight lines, as far as the way would permit, not only to give them a better air, but to shorten the passenger's journey, it was resolved that the stone should be removed, if possible, although otherwise the work might have been carried along on either side of it.

"The soldiers, by vast labour, with their levers and jacks, or hand-screws, tumbled it over and over till they got it quite out of the way, although it was of such an enormous size that it might be matter of great wonder how it could ever be removed by human strength and art, especially to such who had never seen an operation of that kind; and upon their digging a little into that part of the ground where the centre of the stone had stood, there was found a small cavity, about two feet square, which was guarded from the outward earth, at the bottom, top, and sides, by square flat stones."[77]

"The people of the country," says Newte, who travelled through the district in 1791, "venerating the memory of the bard, rose with one consent, and with bagpipe music carried the sacred dust away by force, and buried it on the top of Dunmore, in the centre of his father's fort." Burns visited Ossian's grave. Writing to his brother, on his return to Edinburgh from the North, he says—"Being warm from Ossian's country, where I have seen his very grave, what care I for fertile plains and fishing villages?" Whether the dust of Ossian slumbers amidst these mountains or within this glen no one can say—we have but dim tradition to guide us; but surely no spot seems more suitable for the resting-place of the Caledonian bard. No monument is erected to perpetuate his memory, nor speaking stone whispers to each passer-by in the language of Wordsworth—

"In this still place remote from men
Sleeps Ossian in the narrow glen";

but it is surrounded by mountains torn and thunder-split, and it is laved by a stream as pellucid as his own Cona, which ever sings as it flows the lonely dirge of the bard who sang of battles and the breath of stormy war. "We feel a pride," says Fittis, writing of Ossian's tomb, "we feel a pride in cherishing the thought that the hoary bard's pilgrimage closed in Perthshire's 'narrow glen,' where the murmuring Almond sang his requiem, and that his ashes still rest not far from the banks of the stream."

[77] *Letters from a Gentleman in the North of Scotland*, 1732.

Innerpeffray, annexed *quoad civilia* to the parish of Monzie about the beginning of the seventeenth century, is one of its historic scenes. It derives its name from the Pow—a small stream which joins the Earn near this place. Inner-Pow-fray signifies the junction of two rivers. The name Powfray was given to it when the marshy grounds around the Abbey of Inchaffray were cut and drained, after the Battle of Bannockburn, by order of King Robert the Bruce, for the services of Maurice, Abbot of Inchaffray. In process of time "Powfray," or "Innerpowfray," became merged into "Innerpeffray," the name by which it has been known for many generations.

The first laird of Innerpeffray was Sir John Drummond. The lands were bequeathed to him by his father as his patrimony, and in 1508 he founded here a collegiate church, which he endowed with a revenue sufficient to maintain a provost and prebend. The ruins of the chapel, dedicated to Saint Mary, mentioned as early as 1342, are still to be seen. The chapel has one feature not observed in any ecclesiastical edifice—what is termed "a squint"—an oblique opening in the wall to allow those who were late in attendance to hear mass without attracting the attention of the officiating priest. Few traces of ornament are to be seen on the building, but at the eastern gable there is a niche in which a half life-size figure of the Saint may have been placed. The chapel was an off-shoot of the Abbey of Inchaffray, and part of it has been used for generations as the burial-place of the Earls of Perth.

Robert Mercer, the third laird of Innerpeffray, granted to the Abbot and Convent of Inchaffray the right to fish for eels in the water at Polpefery, within the lordship of Dullory. Eels, it appears, formed a favourite article of food among all classes of the people. During the season of Lent the monastic establishments throughout the country consumed large quantities. The fish were captured principally by means of weirs, the eel-skins being used for making bindings to flails. The licence to the Abbey of Inchaffray is dated 1454, and is as follows:—

> "To all who shall see or hear this charter, Robert Mercer of Innerpeffry wishes eternal salvation in the Lord. Be it known to your University that I, not led by force or by fear, nor fallen in error, but determined by my pure and spontaneous will, with consent and assent of Alexander Mercer, my heir, and with consent and assent of Andrew Mercer of Inchbrakie, are pledged for a certain sum of money, have given, granted, and by this my present charter have confirmed, in perpetual and pure charity, for the honour of Almighty God, and the glorious Virgin Mary, and the blessed John the Evangelist, for the salvation of my soul, and of the soul of Janet, my spouse, and that of Alexander, my heir aforesaid, and of all my successors, to the Abbot and Convent of Inchaffray, and their successors, serving, or that shall in future serve God in that place, entire liberty and perpetual licence of fishing, by means of enclosures, nets, or whatever instruments are necessary for catching eels and other fishes.... In witness whereof the seal of me, Robert Mercer, and the seal of Andrew Mercer, my uncle, are appended to my present charter, before these witnesses, Tristram of Gorty,

John Quhyston, Alexander Cardeny, William Bonar of Kelty, Alexander Sharp of Strathy, an John Crab, shield-bearer, with many others, on the twenty-fourth day of the month of June, in the year of our Lord one thousand four hundred and fifty-four."[78]

St Mary's, Innerpeffray (Innerpeffray Kirk and Library).

The Library of Innerpeffray was founded by David, third Lord Madertie, whose family is now represented by Viscount Strathallan. Lord Madertie's grand-

[78] *Liber Insule Missarum.*

father, James Drummond, was the second son of David, Lord Drummond, and was created Lord Madertie on 31st January, 1609. He was educated along with James VI., and was esteemed by that monarch as "a man of parts and learning," and became a special favourite of the Court. By his marriage with Jean, daughter of Sir James Chisholm of Cromlix, he obtained the Barony of Innerpeffray, which had been his mother's portion, and at his death, in 1623, his eldest son, John, succeeded to the title. John was married to Helen Leslie, eldest daughter of Patrick, Commendator of Lindores; and David Drummond, the founder of the Library, was their eldest son. His second wife was Lady Beatrix Graham, sister of the great Marquis of Montrose, and the intimate relationship betwixt the families accounts no doubt for the existence of several volumes that belonged to Montrose, which are now in the Library.

The Library was intended for the benefit of students, and any other persons in the district possessed of a literary turn of mind, or having a thirst for knowledge. By his will, dated 1680, David, third Lord Madertie, bequeathed the half of 6000 merks to be employed by Lord John Carmichael and John Haldane of Gleneagles for the maintenance of a library and schoolhouse which he had erected at the Chapel of Innerpeffray. The sum conveyed was in a heritable bond, which made the bequest inept; but in 1691 the nephew and heir of Lord Madertie executed a deed of mortification, having for its object the vesting of 5000 merks for the encouragement of learning and the good of the country; "and as a constant and perpetual stock for the preserving of the said library and maintaining a keeper and schoolmaster, and for augmenting the library and building a house; but under reservation of his rights and those of his successors to nominate the librarian and schoolmaster."[79] The endowment covered a school and library, but under the new scheme, instituted in 1888, the school has been taken over by Muthill School Board, and the present trustees are empowered, after paying £15 per annum for the maintenance of the school and the expenses of the trust, to pay over the remainder of the income, and to transfer the library to any town or village within five miles of Innerpeffray.

The Library is particularly rich in old Bibles. The oldest one in the collection, and one having a special interest of its own, is dated 1530. It is in black-letter French, the translation being by St. Jerome. It is a large folio copy, and contains initial letter illustrations and pictorial woodcuts, the title-page being in red and black ink. There is also a copy of what is popularly known as the Treacle Bible, so called because of the rendering given to the passage in Jeremiah viii. 22—"Is there not tryacle at Gylyad?" Two other peculiarities deserve passing notice. The seventh commandment reads—"Thou shalt not break wedlocke"; and Genesis xxxix. 2—"And God was with Joseph, and he became a lucky man." One of the smallest Bibles in the collection is one that is said to have been carried about by the Marquis of Montrose. It bears his autograph in more than one place, written in a bold plain hand. It seems to have been lost for a number of years, and only turned up after a more careful supervision was exercised. It was printed in the French language at Sedan in the year 1633. There are quite a number of mottoes or extracts copied by

---

[79] *Memorials and Queries*. Printed by Constable, Edinburgh, 1846.

the Marquis himself on the leaves of the Bible, taken from classical authors, showing that the book was one for close companionship. Three of these extracts freely translated may be here transcribed. The first is—"Honour to me is better than life"; the second, "Though the shattered universe o'erwhelm him, the ruins should find him untrembling"; and the third, under a pen-and-ink sketch of a mountain and a rose, "Roses grow not without thorns." Of psalm-books there are several very interesting examples. The oldest of these is an edition of Marot and Beza's Psalms, dated 1567, and having music set to many of the Psalms in staff and sol-fa notation. This copy is believed to be unique. It contains a great number of prayers. The volume of translations and paraphrases of the Psalms, which was published in 1630 as the work of James VI., is to be found in this collection. It is entitled "The Psalms of King David, translated by King James." It has portraits of King David on one side of the title-page and that of King James on the other—one of the portraits being, of course, apocryphal. Of prayer-books there is a copy of the "Booke of Common Prayer," printed by Barker in 1604; and also a copy of the book known as John Knox's "Confession and Declaration of Prayers," which was printed in 1554, and which lately gave rise to considerable discussion as to whether the early Reformed Church in Scotland used a liturgy. The oldest printed book in the Library is a copy of Barclay's "Ship of Fools," the date being 1508. Next in point of value as a specimen of typography is the famous Paris edition of Hector Boece's "Chronicles," printed in 1527; and of as much interest is the edition of Bellenden's translation of this work, printed by Thomas Davidson, of Edinburgh, in 1536. There is a specimen of early English printing shown in Fayban's "Chronicle," the copy at Innerpeffray being the extremely scarce first edition of 1533. The first edition of Holinshed's "Chronicles of Englande, Scotlande, and Ireland," which was printed in 1577; is also to be found here in good condition. Amongst other notable books may be mentioned:—"The AEneid," by Gavin Douglas, 1533; Bishop Lesley's "History of Scotland," in the original Latin, printed at Rome, 1578; Drummond of Hawthornden's "Flowres of Sion," 1630; the same author's "History of the Five Jameses," 1654; and also his "Miscellaneous Poems," 1656; Drayton's "Polyolbion"; Dr Donne's "Elegies"; Stowe's "Chronicles," 1580; Hitchcock's "Quintessence of Wit," 1590; John Major's "De Gestis Scotorum," 1536; Bacon's "Essays," 1639; and the first edition of Burton's "Anatomy of Melancholy." Students of warfare will find much to interest them in some of the military books of the sixteenth and seventeenth centuries—one of these especially, printed in the German language in 1620, being the work of John Jacobi von Wollhausen, and entitled *Kreigskunst*. It contains engravings showing the mode of pike exercise and the method of drill adopted for the management of the musket with rest and linstock as then used. Amongst the law books are numerous volumes of decisions by Kilkerran, Forbes, Durie, Dirleton, Maclaurin, and others; as well as textbooks on law by Grotius, Montesquien, Duffendorf, and other well-known writers.

Monzie is best known in connection with the burning of a witch. The traditionary story makes out Kate M'Niven to have been a nurse in the family of the Grammes of Inchbrakie, and as a proof that she was a member of the weird sisterhood, a story is told of her in connection with a visit which the Laird of Inchbrakie made to Dunning on the occasion of some festivity. According to the fashion of the time, he took with him his knife and fork. After he was seated at the dinner table he was subjected to annoyance similar to that which teased Uncle Toby—namely, the hovering of a bee about his head. To relieve himself from the tiny tormentor, he laid down his knife and fork, and attempted to beat off the insect with his hands. It soon flew out at the window; but behold! the laird's knife and fork had disappeared. They were searched for all over the table, and under the table; nowhere could they be found; but when their owner reached home and recounted his mysterious loss, Kate M'Niven, who was present, straightway went and produced both articles safe and sound from their accustomed repository. It was whispered that Kate had personated the bee.

Relieved of her duties in the house of Inchbrakie—as the result, it is said, of an attempt to poison the young laird—Kate M'Niven returned to her old home at the Kirkton of Monzie, where she acquired an "uncanny" reputation. Evidence of her sorceries was collected or suborned, and through the machinations of the young laird of Inchbrakie, she was apprehended and brought to trial on a charge of witchcraft, and her guilt being conclusively established, sentence of death was pronounced against her. The stake was pitched and the faggots piled on the summit of the Knock of Crieff, and thither was the sorceress dragged, to suffer in presence of an immense multitude gathered from all the surrounding country.

> "From Fowlis and Logiealmond, even from Perth,
> The rabble-multitude poured thick and fast,
> Until it seemed as if the conscious earth
> Believed this spectacle might be the last
> Of fire and faggot she would e'er behold,
> Lighted by *legal cruelty and crime.*
> For never did such hosts of young and old,
> Of tottering crones, and women in their prime,
> Of high and low, of poor men and of rich,
> Assemble at the burning of a witch."[80]

The Inchbrakie family tradition is much more reliable than the traditionary story as related by Dr. Marshall and Rev. Mr Blair. Writing under date November 25, 1895, Miss L Graeme says:—"My mother was the wife of the second son of Inchbrakie, and I have over and over again heard her relate how, on her home-coming as a bride, my grandfather on one occasion told her the story. He spoke of Monzie having brought a witch to the notice of the authorities. She was being burnt on the Knock of Crieff, above Monzie, when the Inchbrakie of the day,[81] riding past, did all in his power to try and prevent the matter from being concluded, without avail. Just as the pile was being lit she bit a blue bead from off her necklet, and spitting it at Inchbrakie, bade him guard it carefully, for so long as it was kept at Inchbrakie the lands should pass from father to son. Kate then cursed the Laird of Monzie.

"My grandfather had the ring[82] carefully kept in a casket, and his own daugh-

---

[80] *The Holocaust.* By Rev. George Blair. Edinburgh: 1845.

[81] The first Graeme of Inchbrakie was a son of the first Earl of Montrose. His father gave him a charter to it, and to Aberuthven, dated June, 1513.

[82] The stone had been honoured by being set in a gold ring.

ter was not allowed to touch it—only the daughters-in-law. On my mother presenting my grandfather with his first grandson, he bade her slip it on her finger, as the mother of an heir. Nearly forty years after, when I was a young girl, I well remember my mother's horror and dismay when my cousin Patrick—the head of the family—after his majority, opened at our house a box of papers which, during the family's absence abroad, had been left in my mother's care; for there was the ring in which the stone was set—no longer guarded within the walls of Inchbrakie. A few years after this the first acres of the old Barony of Inchbrakie and Aberuthven were sold; now there is not one of them left.

"The ring is still retained among the family papers—such, at least, as were left after the burning of the castle by Cromwell. It is a moonstone sapphire, set in two brilliants of different shape. There is a curious bluish enamel on part of the gold, which is embossed half-way round. There is also a charm, which is said to have belonged to Kate M'Niven. It is a slight iron chain with a black heart, having two cross bones in gold on the back, bearing the words 'cruelle death' on it, and attached to it a death's-head in the shape of a serpent's head with curious enamel."

The first statute in Scotland against witchcraft was passed in the year 1563, during the reign of Queen Mary, and is here inserted as a sample of the simple and concise enactments which were passed in these days:—

"Queen Marie—Ninth Parliment
IV. of June, 1563.
73. Anentis Witchcraftes.

> Item—For sa meikle as the Queen's Majesty, and the three estates in this present Parliament, being informed that the heavie and abominable superstition used by divers of the lieges of this realm, by using of witchcrafts, sorcerie, and necromancie, and credence given thereto in times by-gone, against the law of God; and for avoiding and away-putting of all such vain superstition in times to come, it is statute, and ordained by the Queen's Majesty, and the three estates aforesaid—that no manner of persone or persones, of what-sum-ever estait, degree, or condition they be of, take upon hand in onie times hereafter to use onie manner of witchcraft, sorcerie, or necromancie, nor give themselves forth to have onie such craft or knowledge thereof, their-throw abusan the people; nor that onie persone seek onie help, response, or consultation at onie such users or abusers foresaid, of witchcraft, sorcerie, or necromancie, under the pain of death, as well to be execute against the user, abuser, as the seeker of the response or consultation. And this is to be put in execution by the justice, sheriffs, stewards, bailies, lords of regalites and royalties, their deputies, and other ordinary judges competent within this realm, with all vigour, and they have power to execute the same."[83]

That Kate Nike Neiving—not M'Niven, as her name is generally pronounced—

---

[83] *Waverley Anecdotes*, p. 190.

was among the first to suffer as the result of the passing of this statute, is clearly proved by referring to the case of John Brughe, the notorious Glendevon wizard, who was tried at Edinburgh on November 24th, 1643, for practising sorcery and other unholy arts. It was alleged against him that he had obtained his knowledge "from a wedow woman, named Neane Nikclerith, of threescoir years of age, quha wis sister dochter to Nike Neveing, that notorious infamous witche in Monzie, quha for her sorcerie and witchcraft was brunt fourscoir of yeir since or thereby."[84]

That the date of the burning of the witch at Monzie took place in the year 1563, and not, as is generally supposed, in the year 1715 is not only proved by the recorded evidence in the case of John Brughe already referred to, it also receives confirmation from the fact that although reference is made over and over again in the Session Records to public events, there is no mention made of the witch. An additional argument for the earlier date is also found in the fact that Patrick Graeme, younger of Inchbrakie (referred to by Dr. Marshall as the person who brought Kate to the stake, and by Mr Blair as the man who would prove the means of her death), had been for over twenty years in exile. Having slain John, the Master of Rollo, when returning homewards from a revel at Invermay, he escaped abroad, and it was not till the year 1720 that he procured remission of his sentence and returned to Inchbrakie. That he did return is proved by the fact that he was a witness to a feu-charter, granted by Anthony Murray of Dollary, to Donald Fisher, taylzior in Crieff, dated "at Dollary," January 13th, 1725.

An attempt has been made not only to fix the date as 1715, but also to give a list of the "understanding gentlemen, magistrates, and ministers of the neighbourhood," who acted as judges on the occasion; and in particular the then minister of Monzie—Mr Bowie—is singled out as one of those who are said to have been bitter against the witch, and because of the part he is supposed to have taken in bringing her to justice, not only was a curse pronounced upon the parish, but for rhyming purposes a curse is also pronounced on Mr Bowie and his successors in office—

> "Yon bonnie manse shall ne'er a tenant see
> Who shall not yet this bitter day abye," —

a curse which has not been realised, so far as we know, in the case of any of those who have ministered in holy things in the parish. If there is any honour attached to the work of burning witches, we conclude that the parish can claim the honour of being the first to obey the law enacted on the 4th of June, 1563, and if the evidence given at the trial of John Brughe be at all reliable—as we have no reason to doubt—the real name of the witch was Kate Nike Neiving.

Fifty years ago, Monzie was a flourishing village of one hundred and twenty inhabitants, while in the immediate neighbourhood there would be perhaps two hundred and thirty more. Now, the population over the same area is not above a fourth of that number. The few cottages that remain speak of other days, and the old churchyard, and the jougs—an iron collar in which offenders were pil-

---

[84] *The Darker Superstitions of Scotland.* By John Graham Dalziel. Glasgow: 1835, p. 579.

loried—fastened to the porch of the church, bring back the long-forgotten past. Many changes have taken place during the last fifty years. Pendicles have been swept into large farms; the industry of weaving and spinning has disappeared. But the natural aspect of Monzie is unchanged: the Almond and the Shaggie still run sunny and clear from the everlasting hills through her silent vales, which look upon the lover of nature with a face of beauty as fresh and entrancing as ever.

THE CASTLE, BARONY, AND SHERIFFDOM OF AUCHTERARDER

BY A. G. REID, F.S.A., SCOT., AUCHTERARDER

Tradition asserts that the Castle of Auchterarder was one of the seats of the Scottish Kings and the residence of King Malcolm Canmore, who granted the Common Muir to the neighbouring burgh. The Barony was originally a Crown possession. Being situated on the road from the Royal Palaces of Scone and Forteviot to Stirling, and the principal manor place of a Barony belonging to the Crown, there is every probability that the tradition of its having been a royal palace is correct, and that the warlike Malcolm and the sainted Margaret abode within its walls.

Auchterarder was one of the Royal Burghs of Scotland. It may be said that no charter of erection is in existence, but its absence is explained by the fact that the proximity of a royal seat gave the neighbouring town the status of a Royal Burgh. Whether or not Auchterarder got a charter of erection from the Sovereign, no doubt can exist that at a very early period it was one of the Royal Burghs of Scotland. In the charter of William, the son of Malise, of the lands within or outside the town of Auchterarder, still known as the Abbey lands, granted to the Canons of Inchaffray, which lands he had bought from John, the son of Baltin, he not only appended his own seal to the writing, but, for greater security and fuller evidence, procured to be appended thereto the common seal of the Burgh of Auchterarder.

The Barony of Auchterarder remained Crown property until the time of King Robert the Bruce. King Alexander II., by charter, dated at Cluny, the 13th day of August, in the eleventh year of his reign (1227), granted to the Canons of the Abbey of Inchaffray the teind of his duties of Auchterarder to be drawn yearly by the hands of his tacksmen and bailies of Auchterarder.

In 1296, Edward I. invaded Scotland with 5000 armed horse and 30,000 footmen. He passed the River Tweed on 28th March, and continued his progress until 24th April, when he routed the Scots at Dunbar with great slaughter. He continued his triumphant progress northwards, resting at various places. We are told that "on the Thursday he went to Stirling, and they who were within the Castle fled, and none remained but the porter, who surrendered the Castle, and there came the Earl of Strathearn 'to the peace,' and there tarried the King five days. On the Wednesday before the Feast of St. John (20th June) the King passed the Scottish sea, and lay at Auchterarder, his Castle; on the Thursday, at St. John of Perth, a good town, and there abode Friday, Saturday, and Sunday; this same day was John the

Baptist's Day." His progress and the places at which he stayed are circumstantially narrated in the Itinerary from which we quote. He returned to Berwick on 22nd August, and the chronicler adds—"And he conquered the realm of Scotland, and searched it, as is above written, within twenty-one weeks without any more."[85]

Attention is directed to the terms of the words of the Norman French Itinerary in reference to the King having taken up his residence in Auchterarder Castle. *"Le Mescredy devaunt Seint Johne passa le roi le Mere d'Escoce et jut â Outreard, son chastelle."* Reference is made in the narrative to many other castles in which the King lay, but only in this instance is the castle stated to have belonged to him. This is conclusive evidence that the Castle was the property of the Crown, and that the King took up his abode in it as such.

The halting of Edward I. with his army at Auchterarder was not the only occasion upon which Auchterarder received an embattled host. In 1332 the Scottish army of Donald, the Earl of Mar, 30,000 strong, lay at Auchterarder previous to the disastrous Battle of Dupplin,[86] and in 1559 the army of the Dowager Queen Mary, under the Duke of Hamilton and Monsieur d'Osel, lay there, prepared to encounter the Lords of the Congregation.[87] The most disastrous military visit and the last was when the Earl of Mar, in 1716, burnt the town.

Auchterarder being the only Royal Burgh in Strathearn, was the head burgh of that County Palatine and the seat of a Sheriffdom, the area of which was probably co-extensive with Strathearn. In the interregnum after the death of Alexander III. the office of Sheriff was vested in Malcolm of Innerpeffray, who, in the *compotus* of the extent of all the King's lands of Scotland for the period between 25th April, 1304, and 28th February, 1305, accounted as "Sheriff of Uthrardor of its issues, iocs."; and again, "from said Sir Malcolm of the issues of the Sheriffdom of Uthrardor and the farms of Glendowiche, £58."[88]

The Sheriff figures in a transaction in the Scottish War of Independence. There was an Inquisition at Perth held on 1st September, 1305, before Malise, Earl of Stratherne, lieutenant of the warden north of Forth, and Malcolm de Inverpeffray, Knight, Deputy of John de Sandale, Chamberlain, and William de Bevercotts, Chancellor of Scotland, on certain articles touching the person of Michael de Miggal by Gilbert de Hay, David de Graham, and others; "who say on oath in Michael's presence that he had been lately taken prisoner forcibly against his will by William le Waleys, that he twice escaped, but was followed and brought back, and he was told if he tried to get away a third time he should lose his life. Thus, it appears, he remained with William through fear of death and not of his own will." The following deliverance is endorsed:—"The Chamberlain is 'commanded to give him his goods and chattels of the King's special grace.'"[89] The Sheriff, as Chamberlain, no doubt favourably represented to the King Michael's excuse, as the subsequent conduct of both the Earl of Strathearn and himself showed a fel-

---

[85] M.S. in the Imperial Library at Paris. Fonds Lat., 6049, folio 30 b.
[86] Buchanani Hist.
[87] Knox's *History of the Reformation.*
[88] *Calendar of Documents relating to Scotland.* Vol. II.; 1689.
[89] *Calendar of Documents relating to Scotland.* Vol II.; 1646.

low-feeling, and that, like Michael, they had been acting under constraint.

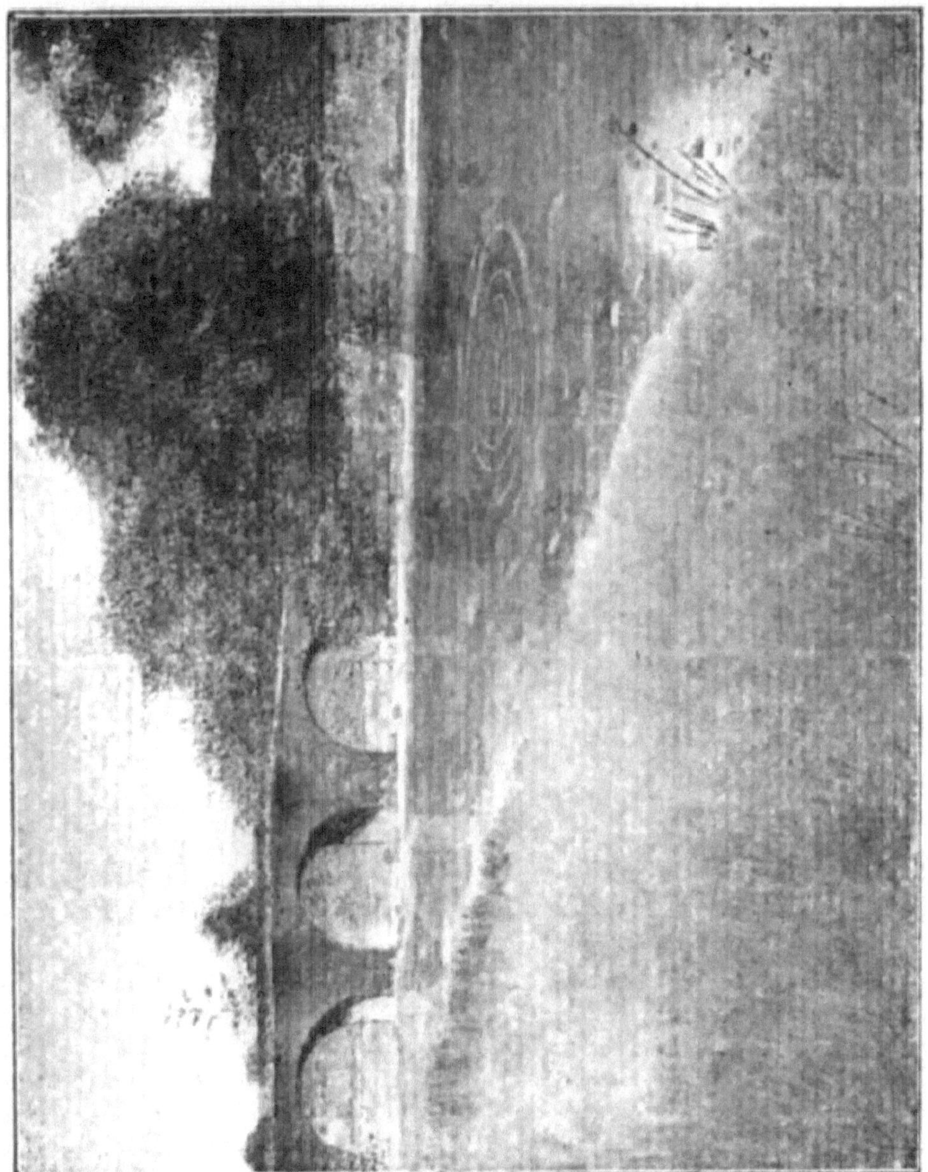

Kinkell Bridge.

On 15th September, 1305, King Edward I., with the concurrence of ten Scots and twenty-two English Commissioners to his Parliament, made an ordinance containing certain regulations "for the settlement of Scotland." Amongst these regulations was the following:—"That there should be Sheriffs natives either of Scotland or England, to be appointed or removed by the Lieutenant or the Chamberlain, at discretion, who should execute the office of escheatry as usual, and that none should be appointed but the most sufficient men and most profitable for the King, and people, and the maintenance of peace." Sir Malcolm de Innerpeffer was appointed, or rather continued, in office of Sheriff of Auchterarder, and he was at same time appointed Sheriff of the shire of Clackmannan.[90] The appointment did not, however, extinguish the Sheriff's patriotism, as the next thing we hear of him is:—

> "The King sends to Walter, Bishop of Chester, the Treasurer, Malcolm de Innerpeffrei, Knight, who at the time of this last 'riote' of the Scots was the King's Sheriff of Clackmannan and Auchterarder, but nevertheless was one of the first to join Sir Robert de Brus, and wickedly allotted the Earls of Menteth and Strathern in aiding said Robert; also fought against the King at the Battle of Seint Johan de Perth, and has done all the damage he could, commanding that he be secured in some strong castle, not in irons, but body for body."

"Whereon said Malcolm was at once delivered to the Constable of the Tower of London, on the 7th of December."

Another writ follows regarding Sir Malcolm's two horses, which the King permits him to make profit of at pleasure.[91]

We do not know the result of the proceedings against the Sheriff of Auchterarder, but as his two horses were restored to him, he seems to have been treated leniently. In regard to the Earl, we find that in November, 1306, he presented a memorial to the King and Council, showing that he was compelled to join Sir Robert de Brus through fear of his life.

The Castle and Barony of Auchterarder appear to have been Crown possessions until the reign of Robert the Bruce, when they became the property of Sir William de Montfichet or Montifex, appointed Justiciar of Scotland in 1332. The family was of Norman extraction. They had possessions in England, and a branch for some time settled in Scotland, Robert Montfichet being a witness to a charter of William the Lion in 1184. In Robertson's *Index of Ancient Charters* there occurs an old official inventory, compiled, apparently, about the close of the sixteenth century, in which mention is made of a charter—"Wilhelmo de Montefixo of the lands of Auchterarder with the town duty." Sir William Montfichet or de Montifex had large possessions, being not only proprietor of the Barony of Auchterarder, but of Cargill and Kincardine in Menteith, and other lands in Perthshire; and also of Kilmahew, in Dumbartonshire, and other lands. He had three daughters, who became his heirs-portioners. To his eldest daughter Marie he left the estates of Auchterarder, Cargill (or Stobhall), and Kincardine in Menteith. She married Sir John Drummond, the seventh Thane of Lennox. Sir John Drummond's eldest daughter was Annabella Drummond, Queen to Robert III. Our present Gracious Sovereign Queen Victoria is a lineal descendant of Marie Montifex of the Castle of

---

[90] *Calendar ut supra;* 1691.
[91] *Calendar;* 1858.

Auchterarder.[92]

In the reign of David II. mention is made of the Burgh of Auchterarder in the account of the Great Chamberlain for 1366 as being in arrear of the contribution for payment of the King's ransom, being due the sum of thirty-one shillings.[93] In 1374, the Chamberlain debits himself with thirty-three shillings and fourpence received from the bailies of Auchterarder for contribution; and there are two different entries in the rolls of 1390, both relating to a debt owing by the Crown to the community of Auchterarder on account of certain services to the late King Robert II. There is also another entry in the Chamberlain Rolls, under date 1435, in which it appears that the services to the Crown had not been uplifted by the Chamberlain from the burgesses of Cromarty, Dingwall, and Ochterardor, because no Chamberlain aires had been held within those burghs at the time when the account was made up. Under date August, 1569, in the accounts of the High Treasurer there is an entry, where the "customaries of Ochterairder" are mentioned along with those of St. Andrews.

On 14th August, 1565, by Act of the Privy Council, in name of Henry and Mary, it was ordained "that lettres be direct to officiaris of armes chargeing thame to pas to the mercat croces of the Burrowis of Edinburgh, Hadingtoun, Linlythquow, Striviling, Clakmannane, Kinross, Uchterardour, Perth, Cowper, and all utheris places needful, and thair be oppin proclamation in thair Majesteis' name and autoritie to charge all and sindrie Earlis, Lordis, Baronis, frehalderis, landit men, and substantious gentilmen dwelland within the bundis (*inter alia* of the Stewartrie of Stratherne), with their houshaldis, honest friendis, and servandis weil bodin in feir of weir, and providit for xv. days after thair comin, to convene and meet the King and Quenis Majesteis at the places and upon the days respective efter following— that is to say, the inhabitantis of Stratherne to meit thair hieneises at Striviling Brig upon Sounday the xii. day of August instant."[94]

Not only is there thus evidence of Auchterarder being assessed in dues and exercising the privileges of a Royal Burgh, but, what is of more importance, as showing its burghal character, is, that there are three separate precepts of Parliament—in 1570, 1581, and 1600—summoning Commissioners to Parliament from the Burgh. No doubt the names of the Commissioners do not appear in the Rolls of Parliament, but that did not derogate from the right of the Burgh to send them; and the probable cause of their not having been sent, and of the infrequency of Auchterarder appearing in the public records, arose from its being completely inland, and without foreign trade, on which the great customs were levied, and consequently being one of what were called dry burghs. Owing to this, and being much exposed to predatory incursions, it had fallen into an unprosperous and decayed state, which would well account for the fact common enough to Royal Burghs of its not sending any Commissioners to Parliament.

This state of matters is quaintly described in the Act of Parliament of 30th November, 1581, entitled "Ratification of the Fair of Vchterardour," which had

---

[92] *History of the House of Drummond.* By Viscount Strathallan.

[93] *Rotuli Camerarii Scotiae.*

[94] *Register of the Privy Council of Scotland.* Vol. I., p. 348.

been obtained with a view to restore the prosperity of the burgh. The Act is in the following terms:—

> "Oure Souerane Lord and three estaites of this p'nt Parliament, understanding that the burgh of Vchtirardour is of auld erectit in ane frie burgh regall, and that the samin is far distant fra the say portis, and hes not usit faires nor m'cat dayis; the samin is becum decayit, and the inhabitantis thereof pure sua that thai ar not abill to intertene the civill ordor of ane frie burgh, nor zit execute sic justice as thay micht in the cu'trie about being opressit dyvers tymes be broken men and lymmeris, quha makis incursiones, and hereis mony cu'trey men and manassies aftymes the inhabitantis of the said town and burgh; and thairfoir said Souerane Lord wt. auise foirsaid, for help of the comoun welth of the said burgh, and support of the inhabitantis thairof, hes given and grantit lyk as his heires wt. auise forsaidis, gevis and grantis license, fredome, and libertie to the provost, bailleis, inhabitantis, and communitie of the said burgh of Vchtirardour to hald zeirlie ane trie fair and m'cat day upoun the 25th day of November nix to cum, and to cotinew zeirlie thairefter in all tymes cu'ing, declarand expresslie be thir p'ntis that all or Souerane Lordis liegis may resort and repair thairto for bying and selling of all guidis and m'chendice thairintill, quhairby the policie of the said burgh may the better incres, and that the liegeis also may haif the better eisement and intertertenigment for decora'un of the realme; and ordainis l'res of publica'un to be direct hereupon in form as effeiris."

This fair—the date being transferred by the change of style to 6th December— though shorn of its former importance, is still held. It was the day for reckoning and paying yearly accounts in the town and district, and was until lately a large cattle market.

After the Act of Parliament establishing the fair there is little reference in contemporary records to Auchterarder. The Castle and Barony continued in possession of the noble family of Perth, which during the eventful years of 1715 and 1745 exercised its influence, not without effect, in the district in favour of the exiled family. One of the most memorable events in the history of Auchterarder was the burning of the town in January, 1716, by the Earl of Mar, after the Battle of Sheriffmuir, in order to prevent shelter to the Duke of Argyll's army, which in pursuit had to encamp amidst the scene of desolation. This was an impolitic act, and calculated to exasperate the public mind against the exiled family. The burning was accompanied by great hardship, having been done during the depth of winter in a snow storm. The sufferers, after great delay and protracted litigation, succeeded in obtaining payment from the Exchequer of a pecuniary consideration, called the "burning money," in respect of their losses.

After the Act for the abolition of the heritable jurisdictions in 1748 the portion of Auchterarder strictly burghal ceased to have titles completed in the burgage form. Until that date titles were made up on burgage holding and resignations made in favour of the bailies of Auchterarder, who probably received their appointment from the family of Perth, the proprietors of the adjoining Barony. No burgh register existed, and the instruments were somewhat anomalously recorded in the Particular Register of Sasines. A difficulty was presented as to completing titles when there were no bailies to give infeftments or receive resignations; and so late as 1832 a petition was presented to the Court of Session praying the Court to appoint bailies to the burgh of Auchterarder to give infeftment. The then proprietor of the Barony, conceiving this was derogatory to his rights as alleged superior, entered appearance, and the petition was withdrawn on the superior offering to give a charter of the lands in question to complete the title.

The Barony of Auchterarder continued in the possession of the Perth family until its attainder after the death of James, Duke of Perth, when the lands passed into the hands of the Commissioners of the Annexed Estates. Under their administration a good deal was done for the improvement of the place. The Commissioners encouraged the manufacture of linen, and they laid out the lands of Borland Park into convenient divisions, erecting cot-houses thereon for the soldiers who had been engaged in the German War. They also made a grant of the Girnal House of Auchterarder for the benefit of the inhabitants. The lands were restored to the Perth family in 1784, and were disposed of by Lord Perth shortly thereafter; the Castle and the adjoining lands of Castlemains becoming the property of the late John Malcolm, Esq., while the remainder of the Barony was purchased by the Hon. Basil Cochrane, by whose trustees it was sold in 1831 to the late Lieutenant-Colonel James Hunter, who erected a mansion-house thereon. He died in 1874, leaving the estate to his nephew, Major Patrick Hunter, who in 1887 sold it to the late James Reid, Esq., Lord Dean of Guild of Glasgow, and it is now possessed by his trustees.

The Castle of Auchterarder, which is situated about a quarter of a mile to the north of the town, though not of large dimensions, must have been a place of considerable strength. It was surrounded by a moat, the traces of which are still visible. The only remaining fragment is a part of the donjon keep. A carved stone is built into the wall. Through exposure it is very much defaced, but it represents a warrior seated in a chariot, and is supposed to be Roman. The wall is nine feet thick. Some years ago the draw-well of the Castle, built around with masonry, and of considerable depth, was discovered. The Castle is said to have been entire until the end of last century, when a vandal farmer took it down to build farm offices.

A Common of upwards of two hundred acres in extent is situated to the west of the town, over which the inhabitants from time immemorial exercised a right of pasturage. A Process of Division was raised before the Court of Session in 1808 by the Honourable Basil Cochrane, then proprietor of the Barony. This process was wakened in 1814, and again in 1841. Defences were lodged for the portioners and feuars, and thereafter by the inhabitants, on the ground that, as the Common was a pertinent of a royal burgh, it was indivisible, and the Act for division of commons did not apply. Litigation followed, and ultimately in 1860 a Bill was brought into Parliament and carried through for the vesting of the Common for the benefit of the town in a set of Commissioners. Under the Muir Improvement Act, 1860, the Common was reclaimed by the Commissioners, being drained, trenched, and fenced. The debt incurred in the reclamation is nearly wiped out, and it now forms a valuable source of public revenue. The careful and economic conduct of the Commissioners since the Act was passed, by which such a favourable result has been attained, is deserving of all praise, and the gratitude of future generations.

In 1894 the ratepayers resolved to adopt the Burgh Police Act, and the affairs and management of the town are now entrusted to Police Commissioners.

Having given this retrospect of the civil history of Auchterarder, we shall now advert to a few prominent facts in its ecclesiastical annals.

The first notice we have of the Church of Auchterarder is in the foundation charter by Gilbert, Earl of Strathearn, dated in 1198, in favour of the Abbey of Inchaffray. By that charter he granted the Church of St. Meckessock of Eochterardeour, and the four other Churches of Aberuthven, Madderty, Strageath, and Kinkell. This grant was subsequently confirmed, and the additional churches added thereto of Dunning, Monzievaird, Fowlis, and Kilbryde.[95]

As already stated, King Alexander II. granted the teind of his duties of Auchterarder, and, by a subsequent charter, amongst other grants he confirmed the grant of these churches to Inchaffray.

William the Lion executed a similar confirmation of the grant of the Churches of Madderty, Kinkell, and Auchterarder.

In virtue of these grants the teinds of the Church of Auchterarder were drawn by the Abbey of Inchaffray, but, as a condition, the Abbey had to provide divine ordinances in the Parish Church, and the cure accordingly was served by a vicar. The church and parish were within the Diocese of Dunblane. The old parish church is situated about half a mile to the north of the town, and, though roofless, is standing nearly entire. It is a long, narrow building with no architectural beauty. The foundation cross—a long slab with a Latin cross thereon—was, a number of years ago, exhumed, and now stands within the walls; while the baptismal font, which until lately stood at the western entrance, was recently removed for safe custody to the new parish church within the town. The old bell is also there. Although small, it gives forth a very sweet and clear sound, and bears the impress of antiquity.

The Church of Auchterarder was dedicated to St. Mackessog, who was also the patron saint of Luss and Comrie. He flourished in the sixth century, and his day was the tenth of March. His legend and office are given under that date in the Breviary of Aberdeen. Southward from the church a few hundred yards there is a perennial spring still bearing the name of Mackessog's Well, and which until recent times was resorted to for the healing virtue of its waters. After the Reformation the Saint's day was kept on the 10th of March, O.S., as one of the principal fairs of the town, and so continued until a recent period.

The old church appears to have been used as a place of worship until about

---

[95] *Liber Insule Missarum.*

the time of Charles I. The tradition is that the roof fell in on a Sunday after the congregation had left and were returning on the Brae of Powhillock to Auchterarder. While the old church continued to be the church of the parish, there was at an early period, and anterior to the Reformation, a chapel in the town of Auchterarder where the present parish church stands. The croft at the back is still named the Chapel Croft. The northern part of the present parish church and the steeple were erected about the middle of the seventeenth century, the steeple being built of stones taken from the old Castle of Kincardine, dismantled after the siege in 1646. The southern portion of the church was added in 1784.

St Mackessocks, Auchterarder (S. Mackessog's, Auchterarder).

There is incorporated with the parish of Auchterarder the eastern portion of the parish of Aberuthven. Aberuthven was one of the earliest ecclesiastical foundations in Scotland. It was dedicated to St. Cathan, Bishop and Confessor, who flourished in the sixth century. His festival was held on the 17th of May. The Churches of Kilchattan, in Bute, and Fortingall, in Perthshire, were also dedicated to him. Aberuthven was one of the churches appropriated to the Abbey of Inchaffray by the foundation charter of Gilbert, Earl of Strathearn, before referred to. The cure was served by a vicar appointed by that house. In the charter it is named *"Ecclesia Sancti Kattani de Abbyrrothueuen."* This charter was confirmed, and other churches granted by a subsequent charter of the Earl Gilbert. Alexander II. confirmed this last charter. Earl Malise confirmed by charter the gifts of his grandfather, Gilbert, and the confirmation of his father, Robert, Earl of Strathearn, and granted four merks of the rents of his lands of Aberuthven, which the Canons of Inchaffray were accustomed to receive previous to the year 1247.

Aberuthven continued a separate parish from Auchterarder until some time after the Reformation. It was united to Auchterarder prior to 21st February, 1618, and the minister for some time thereafter occupied the manse and glebe of Aberuthven. The parish of Aberuthven included the Brae of Foswell, south of the Ruthven, now partly situated in the parish of Auchterarder and partly in Blackford. Kincardine Castle, the seat of the Earls of Montrose, was within the bounds. Aberuthven was the parish church where that family worshipped and where their remains were interred. The walls of the Church of Aberuthven—a long, narrow building like that of Auchterarder—are still standing. On the south side, and partly within the area, a four-square building named "the Aisle" has been erected as a mausoleum for the ducal family of Montrose. The last received within its walls was James, Duke of Montrose, who died in 1836. This aisle was designed by Adam, the eminent architect. At the east end of the church, on the gospel side of the site of the high altar, there is a recess in the wall, forming an ambry of elegant form. It is evident there has been a door upon it, from the iron sockets which still remain. This was probably used for holding the church utensils. Worship was continued in Aberuthven Church until the end of the seventeenth century, as the funeral sermon of the Marchioness of Montrose was preached in it on 23rd January, 1673, by the Rev. Arthur Ross, the then parson of Glasgow, afterwards Archbishop of St. Andrews. His daughter, Anna, Lady Balmerino, was the mother of the gallant Lord Balmerino who was beheaded on Tower Hill in 1746.

Sir David Cardney was vicar of the Parish Church of Auchterarder in 1527.

After the Reformation it was proposed by the General Assembly, in 1581, that the Presbytery should be erected as the Presbytery of Crieff. The Assembly, on 8th April, 1593, "ordaines the Presbyterie of Dumblane to be transportit to Ochtirardour, and ordainis the Presbyteries of Stirling and Perth to establishe the said Presbyterie in Auchtirardour upon Thursday come xv. days," being 19th April, 1593. It was changed to Muthill prior to 18th January, 1633, but Auchterarder was resumed before 1638.

At the Reformation the parish of Auchterarder was supplied by David Murye, reader, in 1567. The first Protestant minister in Auchterarder was John Hamyll. He was previously vicar of Dunning, having succeeded there to his uncle, Sir John Hamyll, who from his title was likely vicar of Dunning in the old church and conformed to the new opinions. John Hamyll was presented by King James VI. to the Vicarage of Auchterarder on 28th June, 1568, and to the Vicarage of Aberuthven on 1st March, 1582. He had also charge of Kinkell and Dunning.

John Graham was minister of Auchterarder in 1636. He was a member of the General Assembly at Glasgow, in 1638, at which the famous James, Marquis of Montrose, was representative elder from the Presbytery of Auchterarder, he being then on the Covenanting side. Mr Graham was deposed by the Commission of the Assembly on 27th November, 1644, for speaking once to the Marquis of Montrose.[96] The sentence was taken off by the Assembly, 8th February, 1645; but he was again deposed by the Assembly, 6th July, 1649. His prelatic predilections were attributed to his wife being a descendant of John Hamilton, the last Catholic Archbishop of St. Andrews.

James Drummond, son of the Rev. James Drummond, minister of Fowlis, and a near relative of the Earl of Perth, was successively incumbent of Auchterarder and of Muthill. He was consecrated Bishop of Brechin on Christmas Day, 1684, in the Chapel Royal of Holyrood. He is reported to have been a man of strict Protestant principles, and a decided opponent of King James' interference with the Church, though he, like most of his brethren, was a keen supporter of hereditary monarchy, and took a decided part with King James when the most of his courtiers deserted him. Bishop Drummond was deprived of his bishopric at the Revolution, having preached at Brechin for the last time on Sunday, 18th April, 1688.[97]

David Freebairn was minister of Auchterarder from 1680 to 1686, when he became minister of Dunning. He was deprived by the Privy Council, 4th September, 1689. He went to Edinburgh, and was consecrated a bishop of the Scottish Episcopal Church, 7th October, 1722, and died Primus and the oldest Presbyter in Scotland, 24th December, 1739, in his eighty-seventh year and sixty-fourth of his ministry. "He was of blameless conversation and sweet temper, while he was a vigilant preacher and a successful physician." His son Robert was a bookseller and printer in Edinburgh, and a staunch adherent of the Stuart family.

Andrew Duncan, D.D., was minister of Auchterarder from 1781 to 1802, when he was translated to Ratho. He was Principal Clerk to the General Assembly, and Moderator of the Assembly in 1824.

Robert Young was presented to the church by the Earl of Kinnoull, 14th September, 1834. Objections were taken to him under the Veto Act, and his settlement was delayed till 1843. He died 15th September, 1865. He was an excellent scholar, an able preacher, and a faithful pastor.

In conclusion, let us express a hope that Auchterarder may long flourish and increase in prosperity, and that the sentiment contained in its motto may continue to be verified—*Non potest civitas abscondi supra montem posita.*

---

[96] *Guthrie's Memoirs.*
[97] *History of Brechin.* By David D. Black (pp. 97-98.)

AT THE GATE OF THE HIGHLANDS
BY REV. JOHN HUNTER, M.A., CRIEFF

The title describes admirably the position of the town of Crieff, planted as it is on the Knock, at the base of which the main road from Stirling and the South splits into two portions—the one running by way of Monzievaird and Comrie, the other by Monzie and the Sma' Glen, into the Western and Northern Highlands.

Crieff has had a long history. The most probable meaning of the name is "Tree-town," from *Craobh*—Gaelic for "tree"—a fact that carries us back into a remote age. Fifty or sixty years ago, the Breadalbane Highlanders spoke of Crieff as the "town of the tree." In early historical times the fame of Crieff was overshadowed by that of Foulis, near by which was the Castletown—the principal residence of the Earls Palatine of Strathearn—not the Celtic Earls whose home was at Tom-a-chastel, but the Stewarts, and afterwards the Grahams, who rose into place and power in Strathearn upon the ruins of the ancient line, which seems to have had no family name.

Treasonable practices against the life of Robert the Bruce brought about the downfall of the Celtic Earls. The Black Parliament, which sat at Scone in August, 1320, condemned Joanna, daughter of Malise, the last Earl, to perpetual imprisonment. She had married Warrenne, Earl of Surrey—appointed Guardian of Scotland by Edward I. in 1296—and in 1334 her father resigned his Earldom of Strathearn to his son-in-law. For the doing of this he was forfeited and attainted, in 1345, "as an enemy to the King and Kingdom of Scotland." The fief reverted to the Crown. Next year was fought the Battle of Durham, and David II. was carried captive to London, where he remained for eleven years. While in England he bestowed the forfeited Earldom of Strathearn upon his nephew, Robert, the High Steward of Scotland, afterwards King Robert II. On his accession to the throne, in 1370, Robert II. transferred the Earldom to David, the eldest son of his second marriage to Euphemia Ross, the widow of Randolph, Earl of Moray. Earl David took the title, Earl Palatine, in 1375, and his only daughter, Euphemia, who succeeded him in 1389, styled herself "*Senescalli Comitissa Palatina de Strathearn.*" She married Patrick Graham, who was killed at Ferntower, in 1413, by Sir John Drummond of Concraig, Steward of Strathearn, and kinsman of James I., whose mother was Annabella Drummond. The only son of Patrick Graham and his wife, Euphemia, was Malise Graham, who, as Earl of Strathearn, became security along with twenty-seven others for the payment of the ransom of James I. He was detained as a hostage in England for thirty years, and meantime his estates and title were resumed by the King, on the ground that they did not descend to the heir-female. To compensate him for this, he was created Earl of Menteith. The annual rental of his estates as Earl of Strathearn was set down in the Durham Schedule at 500 merks. The schedule was drawn up in the year 1424.

Even in the time of the old Earls, Crieff held an important position in public affairs. It will hardly do to say that it was the capital of Strathearn. As a Royal Burgh of the foundation of Malcolm Canmore, perhaps Auchterarder was entitled to claim the premier rank. But it would seem that the business of the ancient Earldom was transacted here. So early as 1218, Earl Gilbert, the founder of the religious house of Inchaffray, granted a charter of "six marcis of Abercarnich, dated apud Crefe die Santi Ambrosii." Fifty years later, Earl Malise, who was the first of his race to show fondness for English ways—sending his sons, Gilbert and Robert, to be educated in the English Court—granted, to the Convent of Inchaffray, permission to quarry stones within his lands at Nether Gask. The permission was dated at Crieff, 1266. Later traces are a narration by Robert, the Steward of Scotland and Earl of Strathearn, of the proceedings of his Court, held at Crieff on May 8th, 1358; and the fact that on May 7th, 1491, William, Lord Ruthven, moved King James IV. and his Council for a return of the record of "ane justiceayr holden at the Skait of Creif on the penult day of July, 1443."

The Steward's Court of Strathearn was held in the open air. The site was included within the park of Broich. It was a circular mound, twelve yards across, and was recognisable up to the year 1860. A "fail" dyke surrounded the spot, and two aged larch trees threw their shadows upon it. A certain reverential feeling, due to a site from which had gone forth the issues of life and death, kept the place intact. But in that year vandalism scored a regrettable triumph. The site was trenched and levelled. Two cists were discovered of the rudest construction. Human remains were found within one of them, bearing traces of fire action; also an urn, which measured 5 inches in height and 5 inches across. Here, then, was the stayt, or skait, or skeat of Crieff. The Court continued in the full vigour of its energy for more than a hundred years, dispensing justice both in civil and criminal cases. Originating in the claim of Earl David in 1375 to be Earl Palatine, its jurisdiction continued in unimpaired strength and scope down to the year 1483—well on into the reign of James III., and exactly thirty years before the disastrous Battle of Flodden. This latter date is interesting to us, seeing that it marks the turning point in the fortunes of Crieff. With the decay of the power of the Court of the Earl Palatine of Strathearn Crieff also decayed, and sank into the position of an ordinary kirktown. The period of decaying prosperity lasted for 200 years—on to 1683, when a forward impulse was given by George Drummond of Milnab, who in that year became Lord Provost of Edinburgh. By giving off pieces of his lands, in feu, he offered an inducement to settle in Crieff, which was taken advantage of to some small extent. Others have taken up the lead of the enterprising Laird of Milnab, and Crieff is now a town of feuars, holding mainly of the Perth Estate, Dollerie, and Broich. But this is modern history, and we have not yet done with the old. I have still to relate as briefly as may be how it came about that the Court of the Earls Palatine lost power and influence.

The result was due in great measure to the jealousies and dissensions of the rival families of the Murrays and the Drummonds. The people of Crieff, in the period of its decadence, may well have anticipated Shakespeare's "A plague on both your houses," as applied to the Capulets and the Montagues. The hereditary office of Steward of Strathearn was a prime bone of contention. In the days of the Celtic Earls the office was usually held by a younger son, or other near relation. The last of these Seneschals of the old line was Malise, who had married Murialla, the widow of Fergus, son of Gilbert, Earl of Strathearn, the benefactor of Inchaffray. He got with her the lands of Tullibardine in dower. A son, Henry, and a daughter, Ada, were born to them. The daughter married Sir William Murray, who got the lands of Tullibardine conveyed to him, in 1284, by his mother-in-law, and confirmed, for his greater security, by his brother-in-law, Henry. This Sir William Murray was one of those who were summoned to Berwick by Edward I. in 1292 to hear the advocacy of the claims of Bruce and Balliol. Henry, the brother-in-law, became Steward of Strathearn on the death of his father, Malise. His only daughter married Sir Maurice Drummond of Concraig, and carried with her the office and lands held by her father. Sir Maurice was the first Drummond who was Steward of Strathearn. Both he and his wife were buried within the choir of the Church of Muthill. It is not to libel human nature to say that the Tullibardine Murrays looked with disfavour upon the passing of the Stewardship to the Drummonds of Concraig. The latter, however, were legally in possession, and the Murrays had to bide their time. The opportunity was not long in coming. King Robert II. died in 1390. He is described by Froissart as a man "not valiant, with red, bleared eyes, who would rather lie still than ride." His reign was prosperous but at his death "every man did what seemed right in his own eyes." His third son, nicknamed the Wolf of Badenoch, quarrelled with the Bishop of Moray and burned his Cathedral of Elgin. The Duke of Rothesay, heir to the throne on the death of his father, Robert III., was starved to death in Falkland Palace by his uncle, the Duke of Albany in 1401. In these wild days Strathearn had its own troubles. In or about the year 1391 the Stewardship was held by Sir John Drummond of Concraig the grandson of Sir Maurice, who lies buried in the choir of Muthill Church. Sir John married Matilda Graham, the sister of Sir Patrick Graham who subsequently became Earl of Strathearn in right of his wife Euphemia, the daughter of Earl David, first Earl Palatine. It was his duty, as Steward of Strathearn, to try Sir Alexander Murray of Ogilvy for the murder of William de Spalding. This was specially unfortunate, seeing that Sir Alexander Murray's father had got the Barony of Ogilvy in compensation for the loss of the Earldom of Strathearn, when it was assumed by Robert Stewart, afterwards King Robert II. He was at the bar of a Court over which he doubtless thought he had a right to preside. The Court sat at Foulis. Upon the bench were Sir John and Maurice Drummond, deputies of the High Justiciar, the Lord of Brechin. The accused pled the privilege of one who was within the ninth degree of kin and "bluid" to Macduff, some time Earl of Fife, stating that he had gone to the Cross of Macduff, near Newburgh, and "given nine kye and ane colpindach (young cow), and was therefore free of the slaucher committed by him." His counsel were Sir Bernardo de Hawden, Knight of Gleneagles, and Sir John de Logy of Logiealmond. The judges referred the matter to the High Justiciar, who decided that Sir Alexander should make his defence before the Court at Foulis. He submitted, and got off easily, "not with such severities and rigours of law as might have been shown."

Gateway, Foulis Church (Church Gate at Foulis).

This affair made matters worse between the Murrays and the Drummonds. Sir Alexander and his friends set about trying to emancipate themselves from the jurisdiction of the Stewards of Strathearn. They found an aider and abettor in Sir Patrick Graham, who had assumed the title of Earl of Strathearn in right of his wife. Sir John Drummond of Concraig, the Steward, was his brother-in-law, but disposed to stand stiffly upon his position as hereditary Steward. He declined to resign his office into the hands of the Earl of Strathearn as superior. Upon this there ensued a bitter personal quarrel between the Earl and the Steward. The Murray party saw their advantage and took it. The wife of the Laird of Ogilvy was grand-niece to the second wife of the Earl of Strathearn, and through this connection or otherwise he was induced to give a pledge that he should either have power to dispose of the Steward's office or not be Earl of Strathearn. He set out from Methven Castle with the intention of breaking up the Steward's Court at the Stayt of Crieff. Sir John and his friends encountered him in the park of Ferntower at a place still marked by a large standing-stone. The Earl was killed, and Sir John and his friends fled to Ireland. Fordun states that none of them were brought to justice, except William and Walter Oliphant. These were probably sons or grandsons of Sir Walter Oliphant of Gask, who married Elizabeth, the youngest daughter of Robert the Bruce, on 11th Jan., 1364. This fatal encounter in the park of Ferntower took place in 1413, during the regency of Albany, who succeeded to power in 1406, after the death of his brother, King Robert III. Sir John had secured the succession to his lands and offices in favour of his son, Malcolm, so that the outlawry decreed against him affected himself only. He died in Ireland. But misfortune dogged his House. Even in the time of his grandson, the family historian states "that ever since the killing of the Earl of Strathearn the family had no settled peace, but were forced to keep house to so many friends and servants for their security that it brought a consumption upon their fortune, ingadged it in burdens, and made him pairt with many of his lands to relieve his debts." In 1474 the laird of the time, Maurice Keir Drummond, sold lands and his office of Steward to his chief, John Drummond of Cargill, afterwards Lord Drummond.

Thus the Murrays had gained their object, so far. The family of Concraig was ruined. But they were foiled in their attempt upon the Stewardship. They had tried for that many ways. In 1441, Sir David Murray of Tullibardine had attempted "to wind himself once in possession of the Stewartrie" by proposing a marriage alliance between his daughter, Isabella, and Malcolm Drummond, son of Sir John. The scheme fell through somehow. Meantime, King James I. had put new life into the central governing body. Parliament was now waking up to a sense of its rights and duties. The actual reign of James I. only lasted for thirteen years (1424-1437), but he held no fewer than thirteen Parliaments during these years. It was his object to break the power of the nobles and local dignitaries. The unique position of the Earldom of Strathearn and the hereditary Stewardships which had grown up alongside of it attracted his attention. The Earldom was the only Palatinate within the bounds of Scotland; the only Earldom possessing Royal privileges. King James I. was a reformer of the "hot-haste" school. The execution of a plan of action followed hard upon the heels of the conception of it. An Act of his first Parliament directed an inquest to be made by the Sheriff—"what lands pertain to the King, or has pertained during the reign of the last three kings, and in whose hands they now are." In terms of this statute, King James I. resumed the Earldom of Strathearn on the ground that it was a male fee, and did not pass to the wife of Patrick Graham, the heir-female. This happened in 1436, and it cost the King his life the following year at the hands of Robert Graham, uncle and tutor of the young heir, Malise, who was still detained as a hostage in England in security for the payment of the King's ransom. But the impulse had been given; though dead, the reformer King still spoke to the nation, and in 1442 James II, and his Parliament declared that the Earldom had fallen to the Crown. In 1455 it was enacted that all regalities in the King's hands should be annexed to the royalty, and subject to the King's Court. This action in Scotland had the support of the Murray faction. They had come to see the futility of any attempt upon the Stewardship. In the year 1474—the very year in which Maurice Keir Drummond of Concraig had parted with lands and office to his kinsman, the Laird of Cargill—Sir William Murray of Tullibardine obtained from King James III. a discharge or dishonouration of the Seneschalship of Strathearn. The effect of this was that his person and his lands were emancipated from the jurisdiction of the Steward's Court. This example was followed by the Laird of Abercairny, who held a tack of the lands of Tullichettle, which Sir William Stirling of Keir, the granter, was called on to warrant. In 1483, the Laird of Abercairny, Humphrey Murray, appeared at the Stayt of Crieff and withdrew his suit—"*Levavit sectam suam de predicta curia*," which was transferred by Crown charter to the King's Sheriff Court at Perth. Thus terminated the jurisdiction of the Earls Palatine of Strathearn. It was followed up by a declaration of date 16th February, 1505, to the effect that "the Baroneys of new create and maid within the King's Earldom of Strathearn within thir three years bipast" were released of all service in the Steward Court of the King's Earldom of Strathearn. Such service was now due to the King's Sheriff Court of Perth "in all times to cum."

In giving this rapid sketch of the early history of Crieff, I have followed mainly the guidance of the writer of a historical introduction to a little book entitled *The Beauties of Upper Strathearn*. For the short account of the Skait of Crieff, I am indebted to one or two articles in the *Strathearn Herald*, written by the late H. B. Farnie, on the 17th and 24th days of November, 1860, just when the trenching and levelling were in full swing. We must now turn to the later period during which Crieff tasted the sweet uses of adversity. It suffered eclipse for 200 years—from the year 1483, when the jurisdiction of the Earl Palatine terminated, down to 1683, when a citizen of Crieff—George Drummond of Milnab—became Lord Provost of Edinburgh. During these long years, Crieff was an ordinary kirk-town, nowise distinguished among its fellows. It had its Gothic Church, which seems to have dated from a very remote period. When it was demolished, in 1787, forty gold coins of Robert I. were found in a hole in the wall six feet from the ground. There was a law plea for the possession of these coins between the Crown and James Gentle, the purchaser of the old walls, which was decided in favour of the Crown. The houses of Crieff were clustered round this old church—mainly east and north and south. Crieff had no west end beyond the Cross until after 1731, when the Master of Drummond made good his title to the Perth Estate, after the forfeiture which ensued upon the proceedings of 1715. It was burned to the ground in this year, but, thanks to the Master of Drummond, it had reached a thriving condition as a market town for the midland and western districts of Scotland, when the Highlanders broke loose again in 1745. It suffered no second burning, though the Highlanders had possession of it, and Prince Charlie held a stormy council of war in the old Drummond Arms, at the foot of Hill's Wynd. Since then, Crieff has become a "braw toon" without the other "singe" its Highland neighbours destined for it. The coming of the railway in 1856, and the adoption of the Police Act in 1864, have done wonders, enabling it to take full advantage of its many attractions. It was loyal to the Hanoverian dynasty during the troubles of the "'15" and the "'45"; but one hundred years before the last outbreak it gave a kindly welcome to Montrose, who entrenched himself very securely at Callum's Hill, having doubtless his headquarters at the house of his kinsman, Inchbrakie.

We come now to look more closely at Crieff, when it set out upon its comparatively undistinguished career as a kirk-town. No doubt it felt the loss of the Court of the Steward of the Earl Palatine of Strathearn, just as the whole strath felt the want of the sunshine of the Royal favour after the murder of King James I. in the Blackfriars Monastery of Perth, at Christmastide, 1437. But though, doubtless, many forsook it, some remained, and there were kirk-lands near by for the maintenance of the Gospel. Conflicting interests began to stir in connection with these lands. When they come under our notice the kirk-lands of Crieff are attached to the Chapel Royal at Stirling. In "Ane Index of Rights of the Chappell and of their Bulls or Patents" we read, as one of the contents, "Applicatio prima fructuum de Air, Kincardin, Crieff, et Pettie Brachley." This seems to have been sanctioned by a Bull of Alexander VI., of date May 16th, 1502; and surely it is interesting to know that the kirk-lands of Crieff, Ayr, Kincardine, and Pettie Brachley—wherever that was—were allocated to the Chapel Royal at Stirling by the Borgia Pope, Alexander VI., one of the prime disgraces of the Chair of St. Peter. But the allocation did not pass unchallenged. Crieff had its perpetual pensionary vicar in those days, and naturally enough he could see neither rhyme nor reason in the arrangement which a Pope had no doubt sanctioned, but which completely ignored his interests. The name of the worthy vicar was Master John Broune,[98] a discreet man, as he is called in the public instrument in which the process is recorded, by means of which he got an augmentation of stipend. The instrument begins in this way:—

> "In the name of God. Amen. By this present public instrument, be it evidently known to all men, that in the year of the Incarnation of our Lord, 1511, on the 5th day of March, the 15th year of the Indiction, being the 9th year of the Pontificate of the Most Holy Father in Christ, and Master of our Master, Julius II., Pope by the Divine Providence. Compeared in person, in Court, Master John Broune, perpetual pensionary vicar of the parish of Crieff, in Stratherne, on the one part, and on the other, Masters William Sterheid and John Goldsmyth, Canons of the said Chapel Royal and Prebendaries of the same Church of Crieff."

The President of the Court was Master David Abercrummy, principal official of Candida Casa and of the Chapel Royal, Stirling, also sub-deacon of the same Chapel Royal. A notary public was also present and certain subscribing witnesses.

[98] Vicars of Crieff at an earlier date were Bricius, who was a witness to the reconciliation of Earl Robert and Innocent, Abbot of Inchaffray, in the Church of Strogeth. The entry is—"*Bricio persona de Creffe, et Malisio filio ejus,*" showing that celibacy was not the universal clerical custom; and Nicholas, who in one charter, of date 1258, is called "*Camerario Comitis*" (Malise); and in another, "*Meo filio,*" by "*Malisius filius Gilberti quondam Comitis de Stratherne.*" Hence he was a cousin of the Malise to whom he was "*camerarius.*"

Master John Broune, the vicar, stoutly maintained that the pension was too small and mean (*exigua parva et exilis*) for his proper maintenance, and strengthened his plea by the production of two documents—one subscribed by the proper hand of the most excellent Prince and Master of our Master, James IV., the most illustrious King of the Scots; the other subscribed by the proper hand of the reverend Father in Christ, and Master of our Master, David, by the Divine compassion, Bishop of Candida Casa and of the Chapel Royal, Stirling. Then follows the King's letter in "braid Scots":—

> "We, as patrone of the Kyrk of Creyf, gyffis our full consent and assent to thir ouyr lettres that the Bishop of ouyr Chapel Rial erec and mak the vicar's pension of the said kyrk equivalent to the utheris vicaris pensionarys of the Kyrks of Balmaclellene, Suthwyth, and Kellys, unit and erectit to our said chappell with ane manse, yard, and gleyb of twa akaris of the kyrk-land of Creyf, callyt 'For,' next adjacent to the said kyrk, to the sustentacion of the vicar thairof to serve the cuyr, payand procuragis and synnagis, and mak the dene rural expensys in visitacion as efferys, and ordains that this be done be the Bishop of ouyr Chapell Ryal and official tharof by tharis dyscrecionys, the quantyte of the cuyr beyng consyderit.

> "Subscrivit with ouyr hand at Edynbrugh, the xxv. daye of September, and of our reng the xxiiij.or zeir, 1512. *Et sequitir subscripcio manualis*. Rex James."

There is a slight discrepancy in the above record; for whereas the Royal letter is dated the 25th day of September, 1512, it is stated to have been produced by the vicar before the Court of Master David Abercrummy on the 5th day of March, 1511. The explanation may be that it was found difficult to grit the augmentation out of the clutches of the Stirling Canons, even after the Bishop of Candida Casa (Whithorn) had decreed in the vicar's favour, and that the Royal authority had again to be invoked to give effect to it. However this may be, it is certain that Master John Broune gained his point, as will appear from the following document, also in "braid Scots":—

> "Schyr official, forsamekyll as the vicarage of the Kyrk of Creyf, is nocht contenyt, in the erectioun of our Souerane lordis Chapell Rial as the layf of the vicarages that are incorporat tharto, this is, tharfor, that ze assygne and mak ouyr vicar of Creyf als meikle zeyrly to his pensioun of the fructis o' the sayd vicarage to sustene him and serve the cuyr as ony of the vicarages of Balmaclellene, Suchwych, or Kellis has, with ane manse, zard, and gleyb and twa akaris of the kyrk-land callyt 'For,' next adjacent to the sayd kyrk, wyth certain gress soums for gudying of the sayd gleyb, according to the extent of the sayd kyrk-land, he payand of the samyn procurage and synnage aucht and wount and makand the deyne rurale expense quhen he vesiis the sayd kyrk.

"Alanerlye, for that our Souerane lordis, patroun of the sayd Kyrk of Creyf, has consentyt heirto, and commendit us to hys writtings to do the samyn, keip this our mandment for your warand, and cause the samyn to be fulfyllyt, sa that we heir na complant tharof in tymys cuming. Subscrivit wyth our hand at Edinbrugh, the v. day of March, the zer of God im. vc. xi. zeris. *Et sequitur subscripcio manualis dicti Episcopi D. Candide Case et Cappelle Regie Striuelingensis Episcopus.*"

Then follows a narrative of proceedings in monk Latin, which I have been at some pains to translate thus:—

"Certain relevant documents having been publicly examined and shown in open Court, the said vicar immediately demanded from the judge that he should proceed with the augmentation of his annual pension of the said perpetual vicarage according to the tenor of the said two documents, especially because no reasonable bar had been alleged in Court why the augmentation in this kind should not be granted. And Master Abercrummy, the foresaid judge, having carefully examined the two documents and the foundation of the foresaid Chapel Royal, Stirling, particularly in that point where it treats of the erection of perpetual vicarages and of their annual pensions, as in the case of the Parish Churches of Suchwych (Southwick), Kellis (Kells), and Balmaclellan, belonging to the said Chapel Royal, augmented the annual pension of the perpetual vicarage of Crieff in the manner which follows, and ordained—viz., that the perpetual vicar of the Church of Crieff, in Strathearn, who has had, *pro tempore*, shall have in perpetuity of the fruits of that Church of Crieff for his own sustenance and for those dependent on him, wherewith he may be able to live in comfort, twenty-four merks of the usual money of Scotland and two acres of arable land adjacent to the said church of the town, which is called 'For,' pertaining to the same church and (origin?) the house built upon it, along with pasture for his own animals according to the congruency (convenience?) of the same said acres, and with 'hearth-rights in the muirs and marshes of the said town' (focalibus competentinus in moris et marresiis ejusdem villae.) [The Latin is barbarous, and may mean anything; but it does seem to have some connection with the right of digging peats.] And besides, that the forenamed vicar, who has been bound, *pro tempore*, so, hereafter is, in perpetuity, bound to pay annually to the bishop in ordinary of the place the procurations aucht and wount on behalf of the said church, the synodal moneys and expense in ordinary for the Dean of Christianity who has annually visited the said Church of Crieff, in Strathearn, and the parish thereof; and that the payment of the pension, as regards the said 24 merks, shall be made to the said vicar of Crieff for the time being, at the four usual annual terms, in equal portions, to be lifted annually out of the fruits of the said Church of Crieff—viz., at the Festivals of the Finding of the Holy Cross; of St. Peter of the Chain; of All Saints; and of the Purification of our Lady.

"Upon which premises—all and single—the foresaid John Broune, perpetual pensionary vicar of the said parochial Church of Crieff, in Strathearn, asked the present public instruments to be executed for him by me, notary public undersigned. These deeds were lodged in the Chapel Royal, near the town of Edinburgh, in the consistory of the same, at the twelfth hour before mid-day, or thereby, in the year, day, month, indiction, and pontificate as above, there being present discreet men, Masters Ninian Spottiswoode, Archdeacon of the furesaid Chapel Royal, Stirling; John Tod, Alexander Painter, William Atkyn, Nicholas Buchan, all of the Chapel; James Aikman, burgess of Edinburgh; John Abercrummy, and Alexander Ramsay, with divers others, witnesses to the premises.

(Signed) "J. PRYMROIS."

It would appear from all this that there was a deal of trouble in connection with the erection of the Church of Crieff. One is apt to get confused among the Popes, Bishops, principal officials, and notaries public who were all concerned in the erection. We seem to reach the close of the long process on the first day of September, 1537, the year of the marriage of James V. to Madeleine of France, the year which lies almost exactly midway between the Battle of Flodden and the outbreak of the Reformation in 1560. Upon the second day of December, 1537, "the reverend father in Christ, Henry, by the Divine compassion, Bishop of the forenamed Chapel and of Candida Casa, from the tribunal with the consent of his brother canons, or at all events of the greater part of them, being assembled in Chapter, and as a memorial of a perpetual thing, ordered, ordained, and decreed that the erection of the Vicar Church of Crieff should be registered by Master John Lambert, Prebendary of the sacred Chapel and scribe of the foresaid Chapter, and to be inscribed and placed upon the books of the Registrars of the oft-mentioned Chapel."

I am greatly indebted to A. G. Reid, Esq., Auchterarder, for kindly furnishing me with the above valuable extracts, and I bring the paper to a close with a word or two about the Crieff of a later time. The annals of Crieff as a kirk-town are a dreary waste in the judgment of one who assures us that he has waded through the records of services from 1549 to 1700. One incident, however, took place between these dates which may be mentioned as being the last expiring flicker of the old jurisdiction exercised by the Stewards of Strathearn. The Earl of Perth discharged the duties of the office—what remained of them—down to the abolition of heritable jurisdictions in 1748. In the year 1682, the minister of Trinity-Gask, by name Richard Duncan, was condemned to death for the murder of a child which was found concealed under his own hearth-stone. Lord Fountainhall reports that he was convicted on very insufficient evidence, and the country people took the same view of the case. He was hanged on the "kind gallows of Crieff," on the knoll near the Cemetery, still marked by a solitary tree. The story goes that a messenger was seen and heard approaching, bearing a reprieve, but he came too late. Local sympathy asserted that the hour of execution was anticipated to gratify the spite of some one in authority. However this may be, the hanging of the Episcopal minister of Trinity-Gask was the last exercise of criminal jurisdiction on the part of the Steward of Strathearn. This was the last time the "kind gallows of Crieff" bore its ghastly fruit. The Highlanders' salutation to it is familiar to everybody.

A pleasanter sight by far than a string of dangling caterans was the great annual tryst, or Michaelmas Market. It was largely frequented, as being the only market of any consequence between Stirling and Inverness. We have it on the authority of Macky, a Government secret agent, who visited Scotland in 1723, that no fewer than thirty thousand cattle were sold to English dealers for thirty thousand guineas. He came from Stirling expressly to see the market, and here is his graphic description of what he saw:—

> "The Highland gentlemen were mighty civil, dressed in their slash'd short waistcoats, a trousing (which is breechen and stockings of one piece of striped stuff), with a plaid for a cloak and a blue bonnet. They have a ponyard knife and a fork in one sheath, hanging at one side of their belt, their pistol at the other, and their snuff-mull before, with a great broadsword by their side. Their attendance was very numerous, all in belted plaids, girt like women's petticoats down to the knee, their thighs and half of the leg all bare. They had each also their broadsword and poynard, and spake all Irish, an unintelligible language to the English. However, these poor creatures hired themselves out for a shilling a day to drive cattle to England, and to return home at their own charge. There was no leaving anything loose here but it would have been stolen."

The Michaelmas Market was shorn of its glory and its picturesque aspect by the transference of the cattle tryst to Falkirk in 1770. There was occasional bloodshed at these gatherings, the peace being with difficulty preserved by the authority of the Lord of Drummond, who collected the customs of the fairs of Crieff and Foulis. These customs amounted, in 1734, to nearly £600 Scots. The Lochaber axes carried by the guardians of the peace may still be seen in the armoury at Drummond Castle. This last shred of baronial supervision—the ghost of the ancient Stewardship—disappeared in 1831. But perhaps the most interesting memorial of the Crieff Michaelmas Tryst is a poem written by one of the Highland drovers, whose appearance moved the compassion of Macky, the tourist of 1723. His name is Robert Doun or Donn. He had left his heart behind him in his native glen, as people will do, drovers as well as others. There is a ring of genuine poetry in the verses in which he expresses his love-sickness—his desire to go upon the wings of the wind as it whistles northward, northward:—

> "Easy is my bed—it is easy,
> But it is not to sleep that I incline.
> The wind whistles northwards, northwards,

And my thoughts move with it.
More pleasant were it to be with thee
In the little glen of calves
Than to be counting of droves
In the enclosures of Crieff."

Mention of the name of Robert Doun brings up recollections of another literary name—that of David Mallet, or Malloch, who is said to have been born in Crieff. He has the honour of being mentioned several times in Boswell's *Life of Johnson*. The latter had no great respect for him, though, perhaps, he did not mean all he said in his famous criticism of Lord Bolingbroke's philosophy, which Mallet published after the author's death. "Sir, he was a scoundrel and a coward—a scoundrel, for charging a blunderbuss against religion and morality; a coward, because he had no resolution to fire it off himself, but left half-a-crown to a beggarly Scotchman to fire it off after his death." It has been disputed whether Mallet, or Thomson of the "Seasons," wrote "Rule Britannia." I do not care to enter into it. After all, David Mallet was a lesser light in the literary firmament. It more concerns the literary honour of Crieff that John Cunningham, the historian of the Church of Scotland, did his life-work here; and that in the year 1793, Rachel Barlas, daughter of the Secession minister of Crieff, went to Comrie as wife of Samuel Gilfillan and became the mother of George Gilfillan, late of Dundee, a man of fine gifts and of glowing imagination—somewhat loosely controlled, who wrote much—too much; but unfortunately left nothing worthy of the reputation he had among his intimates.

APPENDIX

ROLL OF MINISTERS WITHIN THE PRESBYTERY OF AUCHTERARDER FROM THE REFORMATION TO THE PRESENT TIME

BY REV. GEORGE D. MACNAUGHTAN, B.D., ARDOCH

ARDOCH

(Chapel opened for Worship, 25th March, 1781.)

1781-1788—DAVID SIMPSON, tr. to Tulliallan.

1788-1792—GEORGE ERSKINE, tr. to Monzie.

1793-1802—GBORGE LOGAN, tr. to Eastwood.

1803-1812—LAURENCE MILLER, tr. to Abdie.

1813-1822—THOMAS YOUNG, tr. to Gask.

1823-1833—JOHN MACFARLANE, tr. to Collessie. Mr Macfarlane afterwards joined. the Free Church; received degree of D.D., and died Free Church minister at Dalkeith in 1875.

1833-1839—ALEX. OSWALD LAIRD, tr. to Abbotshall. Afterwards joined Free Church; became minister of St. John's, Dundee; died in Crieff, 1891.

1840-1843—SAMUEL GRANT. Seceded in 1843, afterwards tr. to Aberdeen.

1843-1844—Chapel vacant.

1844-1858—DAVID BONALLO, tr. to Blackford.

Ardoch erected into parish *quoad omnia*, 21st February, 1855.

1858-1864—JOHN ROBERT CAMPBELL, tr. to Monzievaird.

1865-1869—WILLIAM MAIR, A.M., tr. to Earlston; now D.D., and author of "Digest of Church Laws."

1869-1874—CHARLES M'GREGOR, tr. to Dornoch. Since minister of East Church, Aberdeen; now of Lady Yester's, Edinburgh; also D.D.

1874-????—GEO. D. MACNAUGHTAN, B.D.

AUCHTERARDER

(Before Reformation belonged to Abbey of Arbroath.)

1568-1585—JOHN HAMMYL, returned to Dunning.

1591-1593—PATRICK DAVIDSON, A.M.

1594-1599—JOHN CLERK, A.M.

1601-1607—ROBERT SINCLAIR, A.M., returned to Madderty.

1607-1617—JOHN MONTEATH, A.M., tr. to Monzie.

1617-1623—HENRY ROLLOCK, tr. to Kilconquhar. Nephew of Principal Pollock, Edinburgh.

163?-1649—JOHN GRAHAME, deposed as a Royalist.

16??-1658—JAMES DRUMMOND, A.M., tr. to Muthill.

1655-1680—ARCHD. DRUMMOND, A.M., died.

1680-1686—DAVID FREEBAIRN, A.M., tr. to Dunning.

1686-1688—JOHN RATTRAY, A.M. Ousted for not praying for William and Mary; died 1712.

1700-1705—JAMES MITCHELL, A.M., died July.

1709-1718—JOHN STEDMAN, A.M., died January. Took part in drawing up "Auchterarder Creed," and prepared Presbytery's defence before Commission.

1718-1729—DAVID SHAW, A.M., died 28th September.

1730-1770—ROBERT DRUMMOND, died 15th September; son of John Drummond, of Crieff.

1770-1781—JAMES CAMPBELL, A.M., died 1st January.

1781-1803—ANDREW DUNCAN, tr. to Ratho.

1803-1834—CHARLES STEWART, died 31st August.

1834-1843—Parish vacant pending settlement of "Auchterarder Case," Presbytery refusing, in obedience to Veto Act, to take Robert Young on trials.

1843-1865—ROBERT YOUNG, died 14th September. "His congregation greatly increased in numbers, and many who had once been his bitter opponents became his warmest supporters and best friends. When the day of his death came all mourned him with unfeigned grief." —*Presbytery tribute to his memory.*

1865-????—WILLIAM GIBSON. In 1871 Mr Gibson was judicially declared to be insane, and the parish has since been served, in terms of the Belhaven Act, by a series of ordained assistants.

1871-1878—WM. SIMPSON. Appointed to Bonhill.

1878-1888—CHARLES SHORT, died 2nd June.

1888-????—Archibald Jamieson, M.A.

ABERUTHVEN

(*Supplied with Readers from 1567-1591, but united to Auchterarder before 1618.*)

BLACKFORD

(*Formerly Strageyth.*)

1574-1576—Alex. Gall, tr. to Trinity-Gask.

1576-1589—Wm. Drummond.

1590-1591—Wm. Striuiling.

1592-1606—James Brandon, tr. to Muthill. Protested against introduction of Episcopacy.

1607-1613—Andrew Allan, A.M.

1613-1651—James Govane, A.M., died in August.

1660-1683—David Littlejohn, A.M., died in May.

1683-1689—David Moray, A.M. Ousted at Revolution.

1697-1739—Archibald Moncrieff, A.M., died in August.

1738-1767—William Moncrieff, A.M., died 9th December. Succeeded in 1744 to the Baronetcy of Tullibole. Parish vacant till 1771, appointment of minister being delayed till his son was licensed.

1771-1775—Sir Henry Moncrieff Wellwood, tr. to West Kirk (St. Cuthbert's), Edinburgh. Afterwards well-known Church leader.

1777-1815—John Stevenson, died 5th April.

1815-1861—John Clark, died 31st December. A Moderate of the old school, and a man of great shrewdness and humour, many of whose sayings have lived.

1858-1889—David Bonallo, died 27th August. Translated from Ardoch as assistant and successor to Mr Clark.

1890-????—James MacGibbon, B.D.

BLAIRINGONE

(*Chapel erected in 1838.*)

1841-1843—Andrew Noble. Seceded.

1843-1848—Chapel vacant.

1849-1854—Wm. Ferguson, tr. to Fossoway.

1855-????—Alex. M'Whannel.

Disjoined in 1856 to form part of new Presbytery of Kinross.

COMRIE

(Conjoined with Comrie is old Parish of Tullichettle.)

1585-????—ALEX. CHISHOLME, tr. to Lecropt.

1588-????—JOHN DAVIDSON, A.M., rem. to Muthill.

1598-1607—JOHN MONTEATH, A.M., tr. to Auchterarder.

1607-1614—GEORGE CALLUM or M'CALLUM, rem. to Balquhidder.

1618-1619—ANDREW YOUNG, died.

1635-1660—JAMES GRAHAME, A.M. Suspended 1649-1651 for adhering to the Engagement.

1656-1665—HUGH GORDON, A.M., tr. to Row.

1668-1689—JOHN PHILP, A.M. Ousted at Revolution.

1693-1698—JOHN M'KERCHER, A.M., tr. to Dull.

1702-1709—JOHN M'CALLUM, tr. to Callander.

1711-1719—DUGALD CAMPBELL, tr. to Lismore and Appin.

1721-1722—PATRICK M'ADAM, A.M., died in March.

1723-1731—ANDREW MUSCHET, died.

1733-1742—AENEAS SHAW, tr. to Pettie.

1743-1780—ROBERT MENZIES, A.M., died 12th Nov.

1781-1801—HUGH M'DIARMID, died 4th November.

1802-1829—PATRICK M'ISAAC, died 25th January.

1829-1841—WM. MACKENZIE, tr. to Dunblane. Took active part in Non-Intrusion Controversy. Seceded in 1843. Became minister of North Leith Free Church. Died on voyage home from Australia, and was buried in the Red Sea.

1841-1843—JAMES GARMENT, A.M. Seceded.

1843-1875—JOHN M'DONALD, D.D., died 17th January. "Left Church at Comrie strong and flourishing, and his memory deeply stamped on hearts of people. Possessed of a clear and vigorous intellect, a ready eloquence, and a good knowledge of ecclesiastical law and forms of procedure, he always took an interest in Presbytery business, and was recognised as one of the leaders of the Court." —*Pres. tribute.*

1875-????—JOHN MACPHERSON. Formerly minister of Gaelic Church, Greenock.

CRIEFF

1563-????—THOMAS DRUMMOND.

1592-1636—DAVID DRUMMOND, A.M. Demitted.

1635-????—DAVID DRUMMOND, junr., A.M.; probably deposed. Died in 1676, aged 64.

1658-1682—GILBERT MURRAY, A.M. Demitted.

1682-1689—WILLIAM MURRAY, A.M. Succeeded his father at Revolution; read thanksgiving after Battle of Killiecrankie; was ousted.

1699-1754—JOHN DRUMMOND, died 26th July. A good man, but no scholar. No Dissent in his time except Episcopacy.

1755-1767—THOMAS STEWART, A.M. Deposed for drunkenness.

1771-1813—ROBERT STIRLING, died 16th December.

1815-????—ALEX. M'INTYRE, died 15th November. A disputed settlement, which so affected the minister's health that he died the same year.

1816-1845—WILLIAM LAING, died 16th March. A brother of Dr. David Laing, the well-known antiquarian.

1840-1843—R. HORNE STEVENSON, tr. to St. George's, Edinburgh; afterwards D.D. and Moderator of General Assembly of 1871. Mr Stevenson was assistant and successor to Mr Laing, and after his translation, Mr Laing resumed the full duties of his office until his death.

1845-1887—JOHN CUNNINGHAM, D.D., LL.D., resigned 16th May. Author of "Church History of Scotland" and other works. Moderator of General Assembly of 1886. Resigned on his appointment as Principal of St. Mary's College, St. Andrews. Died September, 1893.

1887-1894—WILLIAM P. PATERSON, B.D., resigned 2nd November on appointment as Professor of Systematic Theology in Aberdeen University.

1895-????—ANDREW CAMPBELL.

CRIEFF WEST

(West Church, Crieff, opened for Worship in 1838.)

1839-1843—FINLAY MACALISTER. Seceded.

1843-1848—Chapel closed.

For some years afterwards served by licentiates.

1856-1862—MATTHEW RODGER, tr. to St. Leonard's, St. Andrews. Now D.D.

1862-1878—ARCHIBALD HART, A.M., resigned 6th June.

Crieff West was erected into parish *quoad sacra* on 20th July, 1864.

1878-????—JOHN HUNTER, M.A.

DUNDURN

(St. Fillans Chapel, opened for Worship, 1879.)

1879-1881—JAMES W. BLAKE, tr. to Temple.

1881-????—THOMAS ARMSTRONG.

Erected into parish *quoad sacra*, called Dundurn, on 15th March, 1895.

DUNNING

(Church dedicated to S. Servanus.)

1562-1564—ANDREW SYMSON, tr. to Dunbar. Became Protestant by reading Sir David Lindsay's Poems.

1568-1594—JOHN HAMYLL. Deposed for baptising an adulterous child.

1586-1607—JOHN EDMISTON.

1610-1651—GEORGE MUSCHIT, A.M., deposed. Member of Glasgow Assembly, 1638.

1652-1668—ANDREW ROLLO, A.M., died in May.

1669-1672—ROBERT HUNTER, A.M., tr. to Bo'ness.

1673-1682—JAMES HUNTER, A.M., tr. to Stirling.

1682-1686—THOMAS CHRYSTIE, A.M., died in January.

1686-1689—DAVID FREEISAIRN, A.M. Ousted at Revolution. Afterwards became Bishop of Scotch Episcopal Church, and latterly Primus. Died 24th December, 1739.

1691-1716—WILLIAM REID, A.M., died 28th January. Preached at Auchterarder on 18th September, 1715, with pistol hanging at his breast, while rebels in possession of town. They afterwards burned Dunning, the minister being just dead. Thorn-tree planted in commemoration.

1716-1725—LAUCHLAN M'INTOSH, A.M., tr. to Errol.

1728-1761—ANDREW SMYTH, died 20th February.

1761-1768—ALEXANDER SMYTH, died 20th February, Son of previous minister.

1769-1782—LEWIS DUNBAR, tr. to Kinnoull.

1783-1812—JOHN BAIRD, died 7th August.

1813-1814—CHARLES WILKIE HARDY, died 6th February. Son of Dr. Hardy, Edinburgh. Waylaid and hung by heels over a bridge, which hastened his death.

1814-1818—JOHN GRIERSON, A.M., tr. to Dunblane.

1818-1860—JAMES RUSSELL, D.D., died 8th October. A man of peculiar temperament.

1848-1860—PATON JAMES GLOAG, tr. to Blantyre. Assistant and successor to Dr. Russell; afterwards D.D., minister of Galashiels, Moderator of General Assembly of 1889. Author of "Commentary on Acts of Apostles," and other works.

1861-1878—JOHN WILSON, D.D., died 1st March. Author of "Index to Acts of Assembly," "Presbytery of Perth," "Register of the Diocese of Dunblane." "A man emi-nently fitted to win affection and respect."

1878-????—PETER THOMSON, B.D. Formerly minister of Kelvinhaugh, Glasgow. Author of "The Greek Tenses in New Testament."

FOSSOWAY AND TULLIBOLE

Tullibole was supplied with Readers from 1567, and had as Ministers:—

1576-1578—JOHN EDMONSTOUN, tr. to Crail.

1578-1580-3—THOMAS SWINTON, tr. to Muckhart. Was united to Fossoway about 1614, but had service every third Sabbath till 1729.

MINISTERS OF FOSSOWAY

1585-1588—ADAM MARSCHELL, removed to Glendevon.

1589-1590—RICHARD WRIGHT, tr. to Clackmannan.

1590-????-ALEX. WALLACE, A.M.

1607-1652—LAURENCE MERCER, A.M., died in October.

1647-1657—LAURENCE MERCER, jun., A.M. Son of previous minister.

1659-1689—ALEX. RELAND, A.M. Deposed for "gross immorality and oppression." In 1691 tried to intrude with malignants on kirk, but was driven back.

1691-1715—WM. SPENCE, A.M., died 19th March. Formerly minister of Glendevon.

1712-1716—ALEX. BARTON, A.M., died 12th June. Ordained assistant and successor to Mr Spence.

1717-1742—ANDREW URE, died 7th April. Got church built for united parish in 1729.

1743-1778—JOHN STORER, died 8th June.

1780-1803—WILLIAM GRAHAM, died 14th February.

1803-1824—GEORGE GRAHAM, A.M., died 4th July. Son of previous minister.

1825-1845—PETER BRYDIE, died 30th October. Seceded in 1843, but came back.

1846-1852—DUNCAN CAMPBELL, tr. to Luss. Latterly D.D. Died March 23, 1896.

1852-1854—ALEX. COSENS, tr. to Broughton.

1854-????—WM. FERGUSON.

Parish disjoined in 1856 to form part of new Presbytery of Kinross.

FOWLIS-WESTER

1567-????—THOMAS MAKGIBBUN.

1574-????—WILLIAM MELROSS.

1576-1578—ANDREW YOUNG.

1586-1592—JAMES BURDOUN, tr. to Strageyth.

1593-1603-7—Wm. Buchanan, A.M., tr. to Methven.

1607-????—John Young, A.M.

1619-1634—James Drummond, A.M., died in February.

1635-1645—John Fyff. Deposed 11th February. A Royalist.

1646-1675—George Murray, A.M., died 11th April. A Protester, all the other members of Presbytery being Resolutioners.

1674-1689—John Drummond. Ousted at Revolution for continuing to pray for King James and keeping converse with the rebels. Committed to prison. Died 6th February, 1695.

1697-1717—William Hepburne, A.M., died 12th April. Retired to Stirling "with the ministers about" on the approach of Mar's army in 1715.

1718-1720—Alex. Turcan, A.M., died 18th April.

1721-1730—William Simson, tr. to Dunblane.

1732-1767—Alex. Murray, died 27th December.

1768-1816—John Murray, died 10th August.

1817-1851—Alex. Maxtone, died 21st June.

1852-????—Thomas Hardy.

GASK, OR FINDO-GASK

1572-1574—William Melross, tr. to Fowlis.

1592-1633—Alex. Gall or Gaw.

1624-1635—John Fyff, A.M., tr. to Fowlis.

1635-1649—Wm. Bannatyne, died.

1648-1688—Robert Freebairn, A.M., died.

1676-1680—David Freebairn, A.M., tr. to Auchterarder. Son of previous minister. Assistant and successor to father.

1680-1693—Laurence Mercer. Deprived 10th February by Privy Council. His father and grandfather were ministers of Fossoway. Died 30th January, 1720.

1703-1712—Colin Campbell, A.M., died in December. As a merchant, captured at sea, carried to New Spain, barbarously treated; released by purchase.

1715-1740—William Hunter, died 27th July.

1741-1762—John M'Cleish, 12th March.

1763-1765—Alex. Colvill, tr. to Ormiston.

1766-1798—David Kemp, A.M., died 22nd February.

1798-1802—Patrick M'Isaac, tr. to Comrie.

1803-1815—CHARLES ANDERSON, tr. to Closeburn.

1815-1822—ROBERT JOHN ROBERTSON, tr. to Forteviot. Father of Right Hon. J. P. B. Robertson, Lord President of Court of Session.

1823-1852—THOMAS YOUNG, died 5th September.

1853-????—JAMES MARTIN.

GLENDEVON

1588-1589—ADAM MARSCHELL. Deposed 26th August as "ignorant of the Holy Scriptures and without knowledge of the grounds of religion."

1591-1640—ANDREW KIRK, A.M.

1639-1652—ANDREW KIRK, junr., A.M., died in November. Son of previous minister.

1655-1660—JAMES GRAHAME.

1660-1663—MUNGO WEMYSS, A.M., tr. to Aberdalgie.

1664-1679—WILLIAM SPENCE, A.M., deposed by Bishop and Synod for "disowning the present Government." (See pp. 107-108, 195-207.)

1680-1681—ROBERT STIRLING, A.M. Probably resigned on account of Test.

1682-1688—THOMAS HALL, A.M., tr. to St. Madoes.

1688-1689—ALEX. MELDRUM. Ousted at Revolution.

1690-1691—WM. SPENCE, A.M., tr. to Fossoway. Old minister returned.

1694-1709—GILBERT MELVILLE. Resigned on account of indisposition, and also of the improbability of his having any success by his ministry among that people though he were in health.

1710-1718—ALEX. TURCAN, A.M., tr. to Fowlis-Wester.

1720-1751—DAVID STEVENSON, died 6th February.

1751-1756—JAMES REID, A.M., tr. to Trinity-Gask.

1757-1759—DAVID M'GIBBON, A.M., tr. to Buchanan.

1760-1764—JOHN ANDERSON. Deposed 18th October for brawling, immoderate anger, drunkenness, and indecent behaviour. By one vote of the Assembly, 1765, sentence affirmed as against suspension. Died in Stirling in 1794.

1765-1775—Parish vacant. Patrick Crichton was presented, but Presbytery found there was no call. A new call in 1769 was signed neither by heritor, elder, or head of family. Presbytery were ordered by Assembly to proceed with settlement, but ultimately Mr Crichton gave up the presentation.

1775-1789—ROBERT MATHIE, died 29th March.

1790-1838—JOHN BROWN, died 16th November. Was for many years Clerk of Presbytery, and also Clerk to Synod of Perth and Stirling.

1839-1881—JOHN CUNNINGHAM, died 31st March. In his earlier days Mr Cunningham was celebrated as a tent preacher.

1881-????—EBENEZER BROWN SPEIRS, B.D. Translator of Hegel's "Lectures on the Philosophy of Religion: together with a work on the Proofs of the Existence of God."

MADDERTY

1595-????—ROBERT SINCLAIR, A.M.

1620-1657—JOHN FREEBAIRN, A.M.

1659-1682—JAMES GRAHAME, A.M.

1681-1689—JAMES GRAHAME, jun., A.M. Ousted at Revolution. Son of previous minister. Requested by Kirk-Session in 1707 to give up Communion cups and tokens.

1701-1736—ANDREW BRUGH, A.M., died 14th July.

1736-1741—Parish vacant. Mr George Blaikie was presented, but had his license taken from him by the Synod for "misrepresenting and impugning the principles of the Church anent Patronage." Reponed by Assembly in 1738. Lord Dupplin was asked to waive his right of presentation "for the relief of the church in this strait," but refused. Ultimately Mr Blaikie got an appointment in America, and the difficulty was solved.

1741-1783—ANDREW RAMSAY, died 19th October.

1784-1816—JAMES RAMSAY, died 3rd October. Son of previous minister. Discovered pit of marl in his glebe; was interdicted by the heritors from working it, but received authority to do so from Court of Session. Constructed also a machine for raising sit-fast stones from the ground.

1817-1829—JOHN EDWARD TOUCH, tr. to Kinnoull.

1830-1890—WILLIAM STODDART, D.D., died 2nd December. Lived to the great age of 97: and preached until within a few weeks of his death.

1891-????—JAMES BROWN, M.A.

MONZIE

1593-????—JOHN CLERK, A.M., tr. to Auchterarder.

1595-1601—PATRICK M'QUEINE. Deprived. "Sustained great trouble from certain broken men and evil-disposed persons who burnt and destroyed his house, gave him divers and sundry bloody wounds to the great effusion of his blood, and leaving him for dead, so that he is now altogether unable to use his ordinary calling of the ministry within the kirk."

1599-????—JOHN CLERK, A.M.

1614-????—DAVID DRUMMOND (probably minister of Crieff, having charge also of Monzie.)

1633-????—JOHN MONTEATH, A.M.

1637-1665—James Forsyth, A.M., tr. to Kinross.

1666-1689—James Drummond, A.M. Ousted at Revolution. Said to have been a person of great learning.

1691-1705—William Chalmer, tr. to Dunkeld. Parishioners used to play football on Sabbath morning. Had great difficulty in inducing them to go to church.

1710-1740—Archibald Bowie, died 11th March. Some parishioners joined in Rebellion.

1742-1747—Henry Lundie, tr. to Abercorn.

1749-1761—Donald Munro, A.M., died 26th August.

1762-1785—Robert Walker. Resigned 6th December. Was formerly amanuensis to Ruddiman, the famous grammarian. In 1774, inconsequence of a fama, he left the parish of Monzie under an arrangement with the Presbytery. Parish was served by assistants. Having obtained a living in the Church of England, he resigned. Died 28th February, 1818.

1786-1792—Thomas Barty, tr. to Newtyle.

1792-1794—George Erskine, died 26th April.

1794-1808—Ralph Taylor, died 6th October.

1809-1836—Samuel Cameron, died 16th September. New church opened by him 24th July, 1831.

1836-1843—John Reid Omond. Seceded. Afterwards D.D.; minister of Gilmerton Free Church. Died 4th July, 1892.

1843-1844—George Blair. Resigned 5th November. Afterwards held important educational appointment in Canada.

1845-1846—Geo. Hutchison, tr. to Banchory-Ternan. Afterwards D.D., and Moderator of General Assembly, 1887.

1847-1893—James Taylor, A.M., died 23rd January, "An arrowy and acceptable preacher in the prime of his manhood while his bow abode in strength. Genial critic, shrewd diviner of motive, and sagacious counsellor." —*Pres. tribute.*

1893-????—Hugh M. Jamieson.

MONZIEVAIRD AND STROWAN

(Monzievaird Church dedicated to S. Servanus;
Strowan Church dedicated to S. Ronan. Parishes long united.)

1623-1640—Henry Anderson, A.M.

1642-1646—George Murray, A.M., tr. to Fowlis.

1648-1653—Wm. Wemyss, A.M., tr. to Dron.

1655-1680—James Row, A.M.; formerly of Muthill; got church built at Enoch for united parishes in 1667.

1680-1685—George Mitchell, A.M.

1685-1689—David Young, A.M. Ousted at Revolution.

1692-1720—John Campbell, died 25th March.

1721-1729—Wm. Duncan, died 27th March.

1730-1780—James Porteous, A.M., died 25th Nov.

1776-1778—Wm. Thomson, resigned 1st October. Mr Thomson was assistant and successor to Mr Porteous. When he resigned he had received, he said, "the offer of an office in the republic of letters." He devoted himself to literary pursuits; ultimately became a bookseller's hack, and wrote a great number of works; became LL.D. of Glasgow in 1783; died 16th March, 1817.

1781-1835—Colin Baxter, died 5th January.

1835-1843—John Ferguson. Seceded. Afterwards Free Church minister of Bridge of Allan.

1843-1864—Wm. Robertson, died 9th June. Author of two hymns—"A little child the Saviour came" and "Thee God we praise"—in *Scottish Hymnal*.

1864-1894—John Robert Campbell, died in October.

1895-????—Arthur Gordon, M.A.

MUCKART

1567-1572—James Patoun. Promoted to Bishopric of Dunkeld; accused of treason in 1580.

1583-????—Thomas Swintoun.

1585-1591—James Cokburne. Deposed for non-residence.

1586-????—William Patoun.

1588-1591—Andrew Kirk, A.M., tr. to Glendevon.

1591-1592—Alex. Symsone, A.M., tr. to Alva.

1594-1620—Patrick Davidson, A.M., died.

1622-1640—Alex. Fotheringham, A.M., died in June.

1640-1642—David Drummond, A.M., tr. to Linlithgow.

1644-1656—John Govean, A.M., died in January. Celebrated for his fine penmanship.

1656-1660—James Forsythe, tr. to Airth.

1662-1665—James Forsythe, tr. to Bothkennar. Son of minister of Monzie.

1667-1677—David Moncrieff, A.M., tr. to Aberdalgie.

1677-1697—Robert Sharp, A.M. Deposed for contumacy.

1698-1701—JOHN GIB, A.M., tr. to Cleish.

1703-1717—ANDREW URE, tr. to Fossoway.

1718-1724—DAVID GUTHRIE, died 9th March.

1725-1732—ALEX. WARDROBE, tr. to Whitburn.

1734-1786—ARCHIBALD RENNIE, A.M., died 13th March. A disputed settlement. Ordained by Committee of Commission of Assembly. During his long ministry he preached in church only the first Sunday; never had an elder; never dispensed Lord's Supper; let manse, except dining-room, which he used for service; was tenant of a farm, which he much improved; and bought an estate.

1786-1830—ANDREW GIBSON, died 18th October. Age 90. Gathered again a fair congregation.

1824-1825—ROBERT ALLAN, A.M., tr. to Little Dunkeld.

1831-1832—WILLIAM ROBERTSON, tr. to Logie. Afterwards D.D. and minister of New Greyfriars, Edinburgh.

1832-1843—JAMES THOMSON. Seceded.

1843-????—ALEX. MOORHEAD FERGUSON.

Parish disjoined in 1836 to form part of new Presbytery of Kinross.

MUTHILL

1567-1574—ALEX. GALL, tr. to Strageyth.

1576-1585—ALEX. CHEISHOLME, tr. to Comrie.

1590-1607—JOHN DAVIDSON, A.M., died 7th April. Protested against introduction of Episcopacy in 1606. Named as constant Moderator of Presbytery.

1608-1627—JAMES BURDOUN.

1635-1645—JAMES ROW, A.M., deposed 12th February as a Royalist. Afterwards became minister of Monzievaird.

164?-1649—ARCHIBALD DRUMMOND, A.M., deposed for acceding to a divisive supplication; afterwards became minister of Auchterarder.

1656-1686—JAMES DRUMMOND, A.M. Became D.D. in 1682; Bishop of Buchin in 1684; and resigned Muthill in 1686.

1687-????—JAMES IRVINE, tr., probably to Lonmay.

1689-1693—JAMES INGLIS. Intruded by Earl of Perth, and finally ousted by Privy Council for refusing to pray for William and Mary.

1702-????—WM. CHALMERS, minister of Monzie, was for a short time in Muthill, but afterwards returned to Monzie.

1704-1754—WM. HALY, A.M., died 16th July. Riot at his ordination. Afterwards popular. His curling-stones still exist, and are in possession of Royal Caledonian Club.

1755-1766—James Scott, died 6th July.

1767-1809—John Scott, A.M., died 11th February. Son of previous minister.

1809-1826—John Russell, A.M., died 17th April. Son of Burns' "Black Russell," who had become minister of Stirling. A popular preacher. Present church built for him.

1826-1867—James Walker, A.M., died 21st December.

1868-????—James Rankin, D.D. Formerly minister of Old West Church, Greenock. Author of "Character Studies in the Old Testament," "Handbook of the Church of Scotland," "The Creed in Scotland," "The First Saints," and other works.

TRINITY-GASK AND KINKELL

(Kinkell had Readers, and two Ministers.)

1584-1594—John Hammyl. Deposed.

1637-1639—John Murray, A.M., removed to Trinity-Gask, with which the parish has ever since been united.

MINISTERS OF TRINITY-GASK

1576-1593—Alex. Gall. Formerly at Muthill and Strageyth.

1596-1608—William Oswald.

1639-1662—John Murray, A.M., died in December.

1664-1673—James Bruce, A.M.

1674-1682—Richard Duncan, A.M. Hanged at Crieff on a charge of child murder, a reprieve arriving twenty minutes too late. This is supposed to be the historical fact underlying the well-known popular rhyme, erroneously attributed to Little Dunkeld:—

> "O what a parish, sic a terrible parish,
> O what a parish is that o' Kinkell;
> They hae hangit the minister, drooned the precentor;
> Dang doon the steeple, an' drucken the bell."

The Churches of Trinity-Gask and Kinkell are on opposite sides of the Earn, and the precentor is supposed to have been drowned in crossing between them. The Church of Kinkell is now a ruin, and has no steeple. Its bell was recently discovered in the possession of a church in East Lothian.

1683-1698—James Roy, A.M., died in that year. He and the minister of Muckart were the only members of Presbytery who continued in their charges after the Revolution.

1700-1718—John Murray, A.M., died 22nd November.

1720-1755—Patrick Provand, died 29th November. The parish is popularly known as Tarnty. "Mr Provand, minister of Tarnty," was once ushered into the presence of Lord Kinnoull by an English footman as "Mr Providence, the minister of Eternity."

1756-1769—JAMES REID, A.M., died 24th August.

1770-1776—JOHN KEMP, tr. to New Greyfriars, Edinburgh. Afterwards D.D.; colleague in Tolbooth Church with Dr. Webster, and Secretary to the Society for Propagating Christian Knowledge, in which capacity he visited most of the Hebrides, founding schools. A man of conciliatory and engaging manners. (See pp. 114-115.)

1777-1793—JOHN WRIGHT, tr. to Scone.

1794-1834—JAMES BRUGH, D.D., died 23rd July. Changed spelling of his name to Burgh.

1836-1866—ALEX. HILL GRAY, died 15th May. Had a narrow escape of being vetoed, but, there being some irregularity in the making up of the roll of heads of families, his appointment was sustained.

1866-????—GEORGE WRIGHT KEMP.

Note.—The Information in above lists is largely derived from Dr. Hew Scott's *Fasti Ecclesiae Scoticana.* It has, however, been supplemented and brought down to date.   G. D. M'N.

PRESBYTERY CLERKS

????-1657—LAURENCE MERCER, A.M., minister of Fossoway.

????-1677—WILLIAM WHYT. "On May 8th, 1677, David Whyt, son to umql. William Whyt, supplicated the Presbytery anent ye reste of ye fialls of his deceast father as Clerk to ye Presbyterie, is heard, and those who are deficient are ordered to bring payment against ye next day."

1677-1685—DAVID YOUNG, schoolmaster at Gask and Auchterarder, and afterwards minister of Monzievaird.

1685-1693—LAURENCE MERCER, minister of Gask. Writes a fantastic hand very difficult to read. Mr Mercer was ousted in 1693. His last minute is dated 7th September, 1687. Probably for some years no records were kept.

1703-1707—ANDREW URE, minister of Muckart. Resigns 4th November, 1707.

1707-1711—JOHN DRUMMOND, minister of Crieff. Intimates resignation 14th November 1710.

1711-1729—ARCHD. BOWIE, minister of Monzie, appointed 16th January, 1711, by plurality of votes as against Mr Ure, Muckart, and Mr Haly, Muthill. Held office till 24th April, 1729, when Mr Will. Simson was chosen in his place, who, declining to do duty, Mr John M'Leish was appointed to do it.

1729-1741—JOHN M'CLEISH. Mr M'Cleish was a licentiate residing within the bounds. He seems to have resigned Clerkship on his appointment to parish of Gask.

1741-1747—LACHLAN TAYLOR.

1747-1757—JAMES REID, A.M. At time of his appointment a divinity student; was afterwards minister of Glendevon; resigned Clerkship soon after his translation to Trinity-Gask.

1757-1759—DAVID M'GIBBON, minister of Glendevon. Appointed unanimously 24th April, 1757. Resigned 27th September on his translation to Buchanan.

1759-1768—ALEX. SMYTH, minister of Dunning, appointed unanimously 6th November, 1759; died 20th February, 1768. "The salary and occasional perquisites were continued during the Presbytery's pleasure with the sisters of the deceast, and Mr Robert Walker, minister of Monzie, accepted the office on these terms."

1768-1775—ROBERT WALKER, minister of Monzie, appointed 5th April, 1768. Getting into trouble (see p. 22 (xxii), App.) he had to leave the parish of Monzie, and on 23rd November, 1773, resigned the Clerkship. On 1st February, 1774, he requested to be continued, and stated that "one of your number, whose capacity is unquestionable, has generously consented to take charge of your papers and records." The request was granted, and the person referred to, Mr John Kemp, Trinity-Gask, acted as Clerk till 12th September, 1775, when he was thanked for the care and attention with which he had discharged the duties of that office.

1775-1776—DAVID DAVIDSON, assistant at Monzie, appointed 12th September, 1775, "during the pleasure of the Presbytery and his own good behaviour." One of Mr Walker's assistants. Resigned 7th May, 1776, on being admitted as minister of Kippen.

1776-1784—ALEX. COLDSTREAM, schoolmaster of Crieff, appointed unanimously 7th May, 1776. He never seems to have recorded a single minute of Presbytery in the register, but to have left them all in scroll. On 7th August, 1784, a motion was made by a member of Presbytery that, considering the many proofs of indolence and incapacity which their Clerk has given in the above business of Mr Lawson, and other matters belonging to his office, that he be no longer continued therein. Consideration of this motion was delayed till next meeting (2nd Nov., 1784), when it was unanimously agreed to.

1784-1792—ANDREW DUNCAN, minister of Auchterarder, appointed 2nd November, 1784. On 3rd July, 1792, he intimated to the Presbytery that, having now completed the register of the Presbytery, which had been ten years behind the minute-book, and brought it up to the present date, the doing of which was one object of his undertaking the Clerkship, he now begged to resign that office.

1792-1819—JOHN BROWN, minister of Glendevon, appointed 3rd July, 1792. Held office for long period of twenty-seven years. Was also for many years Clerk of Synod. Resigned (8th June, 1819) the Presbytery Clerkship, thanking them for "the support and assistance they had always given him in the execution of his duty as their Clerk." At same time he nominated as his successor, Mr Robert John Robertson, minister of Gask, "a gentleman whose candour, fidelity, and talents much recommend him to the notice of all that know him, and qualify him particularly to the office of Clerk of the Presbytery."

1819-1822—ROBERT JOHN ROBERTSON, minister of Gask, appointed unanimously on 8th June, 1819; resigned 2nd July, 1822, on his translation to Forteviot.

1822-1829—JOHN EDWARD TOUCH, minister of Madderty, appointed unanimously 2nd July, 1822; resigned 1st September, 1829, on his translation to Kinnoull, and was thanked for his "attention, fidelity, diligence, and accuracy."

1829-1833—JOHN MACFARLANE, minister of Ardoch Chapel, appointed by a majority on 1st September, 1829, as against Mr Maxtone, minister of Fowlis. Resigned 5th March, 1833, on his appointment to Collessie.

1833-1843—JAMES THOMSON, minister of Muckart, appointed unanimously 5th March, 1833; resigned 4th April, 1843, when interdict was served on Presbytery prohibiting *quoad sacra* ministers and elders from voting, "whereupon Mr Thomson, the Clerk, resigned his Clerkship, to which resolution he adhered, notwithstanding the earnest remonstrances of several brethren. Mr Stevenson, assistant and successor in the parish of Crieff, was then appointed interim Clerk, and to him Mr Thomson delivered such papers as he was then possessed of, consisting of scroll and rough copy of minutes and a small parcel of documents."

1843—R. HORNE STEVENSON, assistant and successor in the parish of Crieff, appointed in above circumstances; resigned 26th Sep., 1843, on his translation to St. George's, Edinburgh.

1843-1864—WILLIAM ROBERTSON, minister of Monzievaird, appointed unanimously 26th Sept., 1843. Died 9th June, 1864. "He discharged the duties of Presbytery Clerk for a period of upwards of twenty years. For these duties he was peculiarly well qualified by his extensive acquaintance with the laws and constitution of the Church, by his masterly habits of business, and by the urbanity and kindness of his disposition. And these duties he discharged with a zeal and an ability which entitle his memory to the lasting gratitude of the Presbytery."—*Pres. tribute.*

Note.—Mr Robertson, the Presbytery Clerk, being personally concerned in a case, Mr A. G. Reid, solicitor, Auchterarder, was appointed to act from 16th October, 1850, to 4th November, 1851, as interim Clerk of Presbytery.

1864-1878—JOHN WILSON, D.D., minister of Dunning, appointed unanimously 5th July, 1864. Was also Clerk of Synod. Died 1st March. "His appointment as Clerk of Presbytery fourteen years ago brought him into closer connection with its members, and by his uniform courtesy, his friendliness, his tact in managing business, and his accurate and extensive knowledge of the forms of procedure in ecclesiastical courts, he rendered most valuable service to the Church." — *Pres. tribute.*

1878-????—GEO. D. MACNAUGHTAN, B.D., minister of Ardoch, appointed unanimously (2nd April, 1878), on motion of Dr Cunningham, minister of Crieff, seconded by Mr Bonallo, minister of Blackford.

Lector House believes that a society develops through a two-fold approach of continuous learning and adaptation, which is derived from the study of classic literary works spread across the historic timeline of literature records. Therefore, we aim at reviving, repairing and redeveloping all those inaccessible or damaged but historically as well as culturally important literature across subjects so that the future generations may have an opportunity to study and learn from past works to embark upon a journey of creating a better future.

This book is a result of an effort made by Lector House towards making a contribution to the preservation and repair of original ancient works which might hold historical significance to the approach of continuous learning across subjects.

HAPPY READING & LEARNING!

LECTOR HOUSE LLP
E-MAIL: lectorpublishing@gmail.com

www.ingramcontent.com/pod-product-compliance
Lightning Source LLC
LaVergne TN
LVHW091523170726
843492LV00004B/1031